The Basis of
Morality

The Basis of Morality

Arthur Schopenhauer

Translated with an
Introduction and Notes by
Arthur Brodrick Bullock

Second Edition

DOVER PUBLICATIONS, INC.
Mineola, New York

DOVER PHILOSOPHICAL CLASSICS

Bibliographical Note

This Dover edition, first published in 2005, is an unabridged republication of the Second Edition (1915) of the work originally published in 1903 by George Allen & Unwin Ltd., London.

Library of Congress Cataloging-in-Publication Data

Schopenhauer, Arthur, 1788–1860.
    [Über das Fundament der Moral. English]
    The basis of morality / Arthur Schopenhauer ; translated with an introduction and notes by Arthur Brodrick Bullock.
        p. cm. — (Dover philosophical classics)
    Originally published: 2nd ed. London : G. Allen & Unwin, 1915.
    ISBN 0-486-44653-0 (pbk.)
    1. Ethics. 2. Kant, Immanuel, 1724–1804—Ethics. I. Bullock, Arthur Brodrick, b. 1860. II. Title. III. Series.

B3144.U252E5 2005
170—dc22

2005045547

Manufactured in the United States by Courier Corporation
44653004
www.doverpublications.com

PRIZE ESSAY

on

THE BASIS OF MORALITY

NOT APPROVED

by

THE DANISH ROYAL SOCIETY OF SCIENCES

COPENHAGEN, 30 *January,* 1840.

———————————

'To preach Morality is easy, to found it difficult.'—
(SCHOPENHAUER: *Ueber den Willen in der Natur;* p. 128)

MATRI CARISSIMAE.

Contents

Part III. The Founding of Ethics

Part IV. On the Metaphysical Explanation of the Primal Ethical Phaenomenon

Translator's Preface
to the Second Edition

A PERIOD of twenty years (1840–1860) elapsed between the first and second edition of the original of this work. At that time there were fewer people who cared to investigate the subject; the traditional ethical basis in one or other of its different forms was mostly taken for granted; all attacks on the philosophical orthodoxy of the day were viewed with aversion; and, lastly, the book was only accessible in German. For these reasons the number of readers was very limited.

Since then much has changed. The world's ethical systems, as well as the religions on which they rest, have been subjected to exact investigation, and there has sprung up a large and increasing class of serious persons, who follow with interest the results obtained.

This translation was published in 1903, and the fact that after twelve years a second edition is called for, may, it is hoped, be a sign that the belief then expressed in the preface was not unfounded.

It would be difficult to overrate the importance at the present time of the question: What is the Basis of Morality?

The Will, the character, is primary; the intellect secondary. The Will is in its essence egoistic; hence, despite all the progressive achievements of the intellect, humanity is none the happier, and history remains "little more than the register of the crimes, follies and misfortunes of mankind." Nor can it be said that the old theological basis of ethics, with its **other-worldly** standpoint, has been successful in establishing, or even in promoting, peace and good-will on earth. For many a century this basis has been tried with negative result, and now it is slowly but surely passing away. We may show that the **external** anthropomorphic artificer of the past is but the mythical presentment of the **internal** inscrutable Power, of which man and the phaenomenal universe are the objectivation in terms of his intellect; we may show that in human thought the former view is but the natural and necessary precursor of the latter; but it is difficult to see how the new position is likely to provide a more efficient motive than the old for inducing men to walk in the paths of justice and loving-kindness. Left to itself, Egoism will certainly continue to spread, like some foul and poisonous growth, eating away the healthy tissues of human society, changing well-being into misery, order into chaos, men into fiends.

In this treatise, Compassion, excluding, as it does, every egoistic motive, whether direct or indirect, is presented as the sole remedy, as the one fount of all true virtue, as the only force capable of lightening the world's suffering.

It should be explained that the word translated Compassion is in the original *Mitleid,* which is used in a far wider sense than that usually attaching to its English synonym, a term that was chosen for want of a better. By Compassion is meant that which Wordsworth felt when he said:

> "To me the meanest flower that blows can give
> Thoughts that do often lie too deep for tears."

It is the offspring of that intuitive perception which breaks through the Mâyâ—the veil of delusion, the *principium individuationis,* and reveals the identity of the **ego** with the **non-ego**; so that a man is thereby irresistibly impelled to feel for everything that lives just as he feels for himself,—to be happy with its happiness, and to suffer with its suffering—because he is conscious that it is in fact his very self in another **appearance-form**.

It will be seen that this motive of Compassion, which is the only conceivable basis of non-egoistic, that is, of true morality, rests on no destructible foundation. It is the corollary of the great principle of the Unity of Life, which, discerned at all times by a few gifted natures, has now been lifted out of the region of doubt by modern science, and accepted as an axiom.

Meanwhile new generations are pressing into existence, and growing up without any guide as to conduct except the promptings of their own egoism, which seeks to assert itself in this world all the more fiercely in proportion as belief in another is given up; and already the desolating effects of this disintegrating process of the whole fabric of society are becoming manifest.

It would be of incalculable value to the human race, if all the governments of the world, recognising the immense importance of the question, were to render obligatory in all schools the study of ethics viewed from the standpoint of this treatise,—a standpoint, which in its simplest aspect is well within the grasp of quite young children. The subject, so treated, would form no piece of sterile academic drill, but would become a living force, if entrusted to teachers filled with single-hearted devotion to it, and able to open the minds of the young by the magnetism of their personality.

Hitherto man has failed to perceive that his deadliest foe is his own egoism, which, to gratify itself, has always distorted and obscured the teaching offered by a truer insight. Is it vain to hope that he may at last grow weary of the misery, which in his blindness he inflicts on himself, and seek the way of deliverance?

"Sors de l'enfance, ami, réveille-toi!"

ROME: *August,* 1915.

Translator's Preface
to the First Edition

THIS translation was undertaken in the belief that there are many English-speaking people who feel more than a merely superficial interest in ethical research, but who may not read German with sufficient ease to make them care to take up the original. The present Essay is one of the most important contributions to Ethics since the time of Kant, and, as such, is indispensable to a thorough knowledge of the subject. Moreover, from whatever point of view it be regarded,—whether the reader find, when he closes the book, that his conviction harmonises with the conclusion reached, or not; it would be difficult to find any treatise on Moral Science more calculated to stimulate thought, and lift it out of infantile imitation of some prescribed pattern. The believer in the Kantian, or any other, basis of Ethics, could hardly measure the strength or the weakness of his own position more surely than by comparing it with the Schopenhauerian; while he who is yet in search of a foundation will find much in the following pages to claim his attention.

Those acquainted with the luminous imagery, the subtle irony, the brusque and penetrating vigour of the German, will doubtless admit that it is no easy task to reduce Schopenhauer to adequate English prose; and if this has been attempted by the present writer, no one can be more conscious than he of the manifold shortcomings discoverable. But such as it is, the work is heartily offered to all who still follow the true student's rule, "Gladly wolde he lerne and gladly teche," with the single hope that it may help, however slightly, to widen their knowledge, and ripen their judgment.

My friend, R. E. Candy, Esq., I.C.S., has kindly given me information concerning several Indian names.

ROME: *June,* 1902.

Translator's Introduction

'Ὃν δὲ θεοὶ τιμῶσιν, ὁ καὶ μωμεύμενος αἰνεῖ.
—Theognis: 169.

In 1837 the Danish Royal Society of Sciences propounded, as subject for a prize competition, the question with which this treatise opens; and Schopenhauer, who was glad to seize the opportunity of becoming better known, prepared, and sent to Copenhagen, the earliest form of "The Basis of Morality." In January, 1840, the work was pronounced unsuccessful, though there was no other candidate. In September of the same year it was published by the author, with only a few unimportant additions, but preceded by a long introduction, which, cast in the form of an exceedingly caustic philippic, is, in its way, a masterpiece. In 1860, (only a month before Schopenhauer's death,) the second edition was printed with many enlargements and insertions, the short preface, dated August being one of the last things he wrote.[1]

The reason why the prize was withheld is not far to seek, and need not detain us. At that time the philosophical atmosphere was saturated with Hegel, and, to a certain extent, with Fichte; hence it is easy to imagine with what ruffled, not to say, scandalised feelings the Academy must have risen from its perusal of the work. Moreover, putting Hegel and Fichte out of the question, the position advanced was in 1840 so new, indeed so paradoxical (as Schopenhauer himself admits); there is at times such an aggressiveness in the style; the whole essay is so much more calculated to startle than to conciliate; that we cannot feel much surprise at the official decision.

In the Judgment published by the Society three reasons are given for its unfavourable attitude. The second is declared to be not only dissatisfaction with the mode of discussion (*ipsa disserendi forma*), but also inability to see that Schopenhauer proves his case. As the third is alleged the "unseemly" language employed in connection with certain "*summi*

---

[1] He died September 21st.

philosophi" (Hegel and Fichte). These two objections are of course in themselves perfectly legitimate, and how far the Academy was right or wrong may be left for the reader to determine.

But the first reason stated is of a different kind, and affords as neat an instance of self-stultification proceeding *ex cathedra* as can well be found. It is true that the question is worded vaguely enough, but if it means anything, it asks where the "*philosophiae moralis fons et fundamentum*"—the foundation of moral science—is to be sought for, *i.e.,* where it is to be found. Turning to the Judgment we read: "He" (Schopenhauer) "has omitted to deal with the essential part of the question, **apparently thinking** that he was required to establish some fundamental principle of Ethics": which he **was** required to do, unless the Society's Latin is borrowed from Νεφαλοκοκκυγία. And then it goes on to declare that he treated as secondary, indeed as an *opus supererogationis,* the very thing which the Academy intended should occupy the first place, namely, the connection between Metaphysics and Ethics.[2] But the "*metaphysicae et ethicae nexus,*" so far from being formulated in the question as the chief point to be considered, is not even mentioned! The Society thus denies having asked what it actually did ask, while the discussion, which it asserts was specially indicated, is not suggested by a single word. Its embarrassment is sufficiently shown by this unworthy shifting, to enlarge upon which would here be out of place.[3]

It is not intended to offer any criticism either on Schopenhauer's main position in this essay, or on the various side-issues involved. The reader is supposed to be accurately acquainted with the fundamentals of his philosophy, as contained in *Die Welt als Wille und Vorstellung,* and is invited to be the critic himself. But perhaps a few remarks on the structure and general trend of the work may not be amiss.

After preliminary considerations, partly to show the difficulty of the subject, partly to clear the ground (Part I.), the treatise opens with a searching critique of Kant's Ethical Basis, of the Leading Principle of his system, and of its derived forms. (Part II., Chapters I.-VI.)[4] Schopenhauer's conclusion is that the Categorical Imperative is a very cleverly woven web, yet in reality nothing but the old theological basis in disguise, the latter being the indispensable, if invisible, clothes' peg for the

---

[2]It should be noticed that this "essential part of the question," a few lines before, is said to have been passed over altogether (*omisso enim eo, quod potissimum postulabatur*).

[3]Any one who cares to see how this Judgment, the Danish Royal Society of Sciences, Hegel, Fichte, and "Professors of Philosophy" in general, are all pulverised together under our sage's withering wrath and trenchant irony, should read his Introduction to each Edition.

[4]Incidentally (Chapter III.), duties towards ourselves, properly so called, are shown to be non-existent from the Schopenhauerian standpoint. Cf. the definition of Duty in Part III., Chapter VI.

former; and that Kant's *tour de main* of deducing his Moral Theology from Ethics is like inverting a pyramid. The theory of Conscience is next discussed (Chapter VII.). The half-supernatural element which Kant introduced under the highly dramatic form of a court of justice holding secret session in the breast, is examined, and eliminated; and Conscience is defined as the knowledge that we have of ourselves through our acts.

But if, so far, the result obtained is distinctly unfavourable to Kant, Schopenhauer is glad to agree with him on one point, namely, the theory of Freedom, to a brief notice of which he now passes (Chapter VIII.). He points out that the solution of this question is found in the doctrine of the coexistence of Liberty and Necessity: according to which the basis of our nature, the so-called Intelligible Character, that lies outside the forms attaching to phaenomena, namely, Time, Space, and Causality, is transcendentally free; while the Empirical Character, together with the whole person, being, as a phaenomenon, the transient objectivation of the Intelligible Character, under the laws of the *principium individuationis,* is strictly determined.[5] Part II. closes with a sufficiently amusing examination of Fichte (Chapter IX.). His proper function is shown to be that of a magnifying glass for Kant. By means of this powerful human lens we can see the monstrous shapes into which the Kantian pet creations are capable of developing. Thus we find the Categorical Imperative become a Despotic Imperative, the "Absolute Ought" grown into a fathomless inscrutable Εἱμαρμένη, etc.

With Part III. we reach the positive part of the work. Schopenhauer begins (Chapter I.) by emphasising the necessity of finding a basis for Ethics that appeals, not to the intellect, but to the intuitive perception. Such (he says) can never be any artificial formula, which surely crumbles to powder beneath the rough touch of real life; rather must it be something springing out of the heart of things, and therefore lying at the root of man's nature. But is there, he asks (Chapter II.), after all, such a thing as natural morality? Is anything good ever done absolutely without an egoistic motive? The conclusion arrived at is that, although much may be, and has been, at all times, said in favour of the Sceptical View, and although this view is in fact true as regards the greater number of apparently unselfish acts, yet there can be no doubt that truly moral conduct **does** occur, that deeds of justice and loving-kindness **are** occasionally performed without the smallest hope of reward, or fear of punishment involved in their omission. The last paragraph of this chapter is important because it puts in the clearest light what, according to Schopenhauer, is the end of Ethics. Its aim, he says, is **not** to treat of that which people

---

[5]Schopenhauer treated this subject exhaustively in his Essay on "The Freedom of the Will," which, written immediately before, and more fortunate than, the present treatise, was awarded the prize by the Royal Norwegian Society of Sciences in January, 1839.

ought to do (for "ought" has no place except in theological Morals, whether explicit, or implicit); but "to point out all the varied moral lines of human conduct; to explain them; and to trace them to their ultimate source." This definition, which assigns no educative function to Ethics, strictly agrees with the doctrine of the unchangeableness of character. (*V.* Chapter IX. of this Part.)

Our philosopher then proceeds to show (Chapter III.) that there are two fundamental "antimoral" incentives in man's nature: Egoism and Malice. Be it, however, here remarked that a still simpler classification would reduce these two to one. Malice may well be regarded as nothing but Egoism carried to its extreme, developed to gigantic proportions. It is a distinct source of gratification to certain natures to witness the suffering of another; because a diminution of the latter's capacity for action, whether effected by itself, or not, is regarded by an ego of this kind as an increase of its own power to do as it likes,—as an enhancement of its own glorification.

In Chapter IV. the ultimate test of truly moral conduct is explained to be the absence of all egoistic motivation; and in Chapters V.–VII., by a process of careful reasoning, every human act is traced to one of three original springs, namely, (1) Egoism, (2) Malice, and (3) Compassion; or to a combination of (1) and (3), or (1) and (2).[6] Of these the third is shown to be the only counter-motive to the first and second, and in fact the sole source of the two cardinal virtues, justice and loving-kindness, which are explained as the manifestation of Compassion in a lower, and a higher, degree, respectively. In the course of the demonstration the question as to how far a lie is legitimate comes incidentally under discussion; as also the theory of Duty; duties being defined as "actions, the simple omission of which constitutes a wrong." (Cf. Part II., Chapter III.)

The position now reached, namely, that Compassion is the one and only fount of true morality, because it is the sole non-egoistic source of action, is (says Schopenhauer) a strange paradox; hence the testimony of experience and of universal human sentiment is appealed to, in confirmation of it, under nine different considerations (Chapter VIII.). They are as follows:—

(1) An imaginary case.

---

[6]If, as above suggested, Malice be taken as a form of Egoism, we may simplify as follows:—

Egoism.

(*a*) Lower power: seen in selfishness, covetousness, etc.

(*b*) Higher power: seen in malice, cruelty, etc.

Compassion.

(*a*) Lower power: seen in justice.

(*b*) Higher power: seen in loving-kindness.

Egoism (not in its higher power) may be simultaneously operative with Compassion in every possible proportion.

(2) Cruelty, which means the maximum deficiency in Compassion, is the mark of the deepest moral depravity. Therefore the real moral incentive must be Compassion.

(3) Compassion is the only thoroughly effective spring of moral conduct.

(4) Limitless Compassion for all living things is the surest and most certain token of a really good man.

(5) The evidence of separate matters of detail.

(6) Compassion is more easily discerned in its higher power; it is more obviously the root of loving-kindness than of justice.

(7) Compassion does not stop short with men; it includes all living beings.

(8) Considered simply from the empirical point of view, Compassion is the best possible antidote to Egoism, no less than the most soothing balsam for the world's inevitable suffering.

(9) Rousseau's testimony is quoted, as well as passages from the Pañċa-tantra, Pausanias, Lucian, Stobaeus, and Lessing; and reference is made to Chinese Ethics and Hindu customs.

Part III. closes (Chapter IX.) with an inquiry into the Ethical Difference of Character. The theory that this difference is innate and immutable is supported by numerous extracts from various writers of all periods, and illustrated in many ways. But all the evidence accumulated hardly amounts to more than so many hints and indications, and the matter (says Schopenhauer) was only satisfactorily explained by Kant's doctrine of the Intelligible and Empirical Character. (Cf. Part II., Chapter VIII.) According to this, the ethical difference between man and man is an original and ultimate datum, caused by the transcendentally free act of the Intelligible Character, that is, the Will, as Thing in itself, outside phaenomena; the Empirical Character being, so to say, the reflection of the Intelligible, mirrored through the functions of our perceptive faculty, namely, Time, Space, and Causality. Hence the former, while manifested in plurality and difference of acts, yet necessarily always wears the same unchangeable features, inasmuch as it is but the appearance-form of the unity behind. If the reader asks **why** "the essential constitution of the Thing in itself underlying the phaenomenon" is so enormously different in different individuals, it can only be said that our intellect, conditioned, as it is, by the laws of Causality, Space, and Time, has no power to deal with **noumena**, its range being limited to **phaenomena**; and that therefore this question is one of those which have no conceivable answer. (Cf. *Die Welt als Wille und Vorstellung,* vol. ii., chap. 50., Epiphilosophie.)[7]

---

[7] *V.* Also the *Neue Paralipomena,* chap. vii.; *Zur Ethik,* §248, where Schopenhauer calls this "the hardest of all problems." On the one hand, we have the metaphysical unity of the Will, as Thing in itself, which, as the Intelligible Character, is present, whole and

The discussion now terminated points to the conclusion that nine-tenths, or perhaps nineteen-twentieths, of what we do is, more or less, due to Egoism, conscious or unconscious; while acts of real morality, that is, of unselfish justice and pure loving-kindness (admitting that they occur) are to be attributed to Compassion, that is, the sense of **suffering with** another. Nor is the principle of Altruism new. It is as old as man himself. All the rare and sensitive natures in the world have given utterance to it, each in his own way. Like a golden thread it runs from the earliest Indian literature to George Eliot, to Tolstoï; and every day, for unnumbered ages, "for youth to eld, from sire to son," in lowly dwellings and in princes' palaces, it has been unawares translated into action.

And if we may forecast the future from the past, it would appear that in all the stormy seas yet to be traversed by the human race, before its little day is spent, Compassion will ever be the surest guide to better things; and that the light of knowledge illuminating the path, whereby the world may become relatively happier, will always vary directly as man's susceptibility to its promptings: for **"Durch Mitleid wissend"** is not truer of Parsifal than of all other saviours.

In the fourth Part of the treatise Schopenhauer attempts the metaphysical explanation of Compassion, which for those, who still think that Metaphysics is something more than a pseudo-science of the past—like Alchemy or Astrology—will have special interest.

It should be observed (as is pointed out in our author's Preface to the first edition) that the line of thought followed does not belong to any particular metaphysical school, but to many; being in fact a principle at the root of the oldest systems in the world, and traceable in one form or another down to Kant. As in the dawn of history it was our own Aryan forefathers, who divined with subtle intuition the ideality of Time and Space; so in the fulness of the ages it was reserved for another Aryan of Scotch descent to formulate the same in exact language. Now, by the vast majority of men the ideality of the *principium individuationis* is undoubtedly either not consciously realised at all, or else but dimly perceived under the form of allegories and mythologies. Yet, if this theory be true, if individuation be only a phaenomenon depending on the subjectivity of Time and Space, then Compassion, and its external expression, the ἀγάπη that is greater than Faith and Hope, receive their final explanation. And every εὐθανασία; every word that vibrates in harmony with

---

undivided, in all phaenomena, in every individual; on the other hand, we find, as a fact of experience, the widest possible difference in the Empirical Character, no less of animals than of men. That is to say, "*difference*" must be predicated of the Thing in itself! It is obvious that we here touch a contradiction, which, for the rest, lies at the root of the Schopenhauerian doctrine of the Will.

the inspired rhapsody of 1 Corinthians xiii.; every act of genuine justice, or of true loving-kindness, done by man to man, as well as the uplifting emotion which stirs our hearts at the sight of such conduct:—all these things become fraught with a new and luminous significance: the secret writing is interpreted, its deepest meaning disclosed.

Moreover, the "thou shalt," and the "thou shalt not," no less of the various theologies than of the Categorical Imperative, may from this point of view be accounted for, on the ground of the **identity** of man, so far as he is **noumenal**, with the transcendental Reality behind phaenomena. The crude threats of punishment and promises of reward, the stern Moral Law, poised in mid air,—these hypotheses, and all their varieties (whose function is in reality nothing else but to check Egoism), are seen to be due to the intellect's imperfect comprehension of, or rather, its vague groping after, the transcendental unity of life, however individualised and differentiated as a phaenomenon in Time and Space.[8] It thus becomes apparent that the position developed by Schopenhauer in the third and fourth parts of the Essay is not so much destructive, as explanatory, of the usual theories, which, if once the former be fully grasped, lose themselves in it as stars and moon in the light of day. They are at once interpreted, and shown to be no longer of importance. Similarly, all the religions of the world, "which are the Metaphysics of the people," find their *raison d'être* in the same doctrine. The theory of an **external** δημιουργὸς takes its place as the natural mode of denoting, in children's language, the **internal** metaphysical Entity, whose appearance-form, in terms of our consciousness, is called the Universe. The circle is completed; the discords vanish, and an ultimate harmony is reached.

And so over the thrice-tangled skein of phaenomenal existence a simplifying and integrating light is shed, showing that the πᾶν is but the reflection of the ἕν, under the forms of our faculty of perception, namely, Time, Space, and Causality—forms, which necessarily imply plurality and change, on which, again, in the last resort the *Welt-Schmerz* depends.

"The One remains, the many change and pass;

· · · · · · ·

Life, like a dome of many-coloured glass,
Stains the white radiance of Eternity,
Until Death tramples it to fragments."

---

[8] The reader will remember the fine poetic presentment of this view of things, which Goethe with intuitive perception gives in the *Faust*, Part I., where the Erdgeist says:

"*So schaff' ich am sausenden* WEBSTUHL DER ZEIT,
Und wirke DER GOTTHEIT LEBENDIGES KLEID."

"What an unspeakable gain," says Richard Wagner,[9] "we should bring to those who are terrified by the threats of the Church, and, on the other hand, to those who are reduced to despair by our physicists, if we could quicken the noble edifice of 'Love, Faith, and Hope,' with a clear consciousness of the ideality of the world, conditioned by the laws of Space and Time, which form the sole basis of our perceptive capacity! In that case all anxious inquiries as to a 'Where' and 'When' of the 'other world' would be understood to be only answerable by a blissful smile. For, if there is a solution to these questions, which seem of such boundless importance, our philosopher has given it with incomparable precision and beauty in the following sentence, which, to a certain extent, is only a corollary to the definition of the ideality of Time and Space: 'Peace, Rest, and Bliss dwell only there where there is **no where, and no when**.'" (*V*. Schopenhauer: *Parerga and Paralipomena*, vol. ii., chap. 3, §30 bis.)

---

[9]V. *Gesammelte Schriften und Dichtungen* von Richard Wagner. Zweite Auflage, vol. x. "Was nützt diese Erkenntnis?" p. 361:—*Welchen unsäglichen Gewinn würden wir aber den einerseits von den Drohungen der Kirche Erschreckten, andererseits den durch unsere Physiker zur Verzweiflung Gebrachten zuführen, wenn wir dem erhabenen Gebäude von "Liebe, Glaube und Hoffnung" eine deutliche Erkenntniss der, durch die unserer Wahrnehmung einzig zu Grunde liegenden Gesetze des Raumes und der Zeit bedingten, Idealität der Welt einfügen könnten, durch welche dann alle die Fragen des beängstigten Gemüthes nach einem "Wo" und "Wann" der "anderen Welt" als nur durch ein seliges Lächeln beantwortbar erkannt werden müssten? Denn, giebt es auf diese, so grenzenlos wichtig dünkenden Fragen eine Antwort, so hat sie unser Philosoph, mit unübertrefflicher Präzision und Schönheit, mit diesem, gewissermaassen nur der Definition der Idealität von Zeit und Raum beigegebenen Ausspruche ertheilt: "Friede, Ruhe, und Glückseligkeit wohnt allein da, wo es* KEIN WO UND KEIN WANN *giebt."*

THE QUESTION

THE question advanced by the Royal Society, together with the considerations leading up to it, is as follows:—

Quum primitiva moralitatis idea, sive de summa lege morali principalis notio, sua quadam propria eaque minime logica necessitate, tum in ea disciplina appareat, cui propositum est cognitionem τοῦ ἠθικοῦ explicare, tum in vita, partim in conscientiae judicio de nostris actionibus, partim in censura morali de actionibus aliorum hominum; quumque complures, quae ab illa ider inseparabiles sunt, eamque tanquam originem respiciunt, notiones principales ad τὸ ἠθικόυ spectantes, velut officii notio et imputationis, eadem necessitate eodemque ambitu vim suam exserant,—et tamen inter eos cursus viasque, quas nostrae aetatis meditatio philosophica persequitur, magni momenti esse videatur, hoc argumentum ad disputationem revocare,—cupit Societas, ut accurate haec quaestio perpendatur et pertractetur:

Philosophiae moralis fons et fundamentum *utrum in idea moralitatis, quae immediate conscientia contineatur, et ceteris notionibus fundamentalibus, quae ex illa prodeant, explicandis* **quaerenda sunt,** *an in alio cognoscendi principio?*

(The original idea of morality, or the leading conception of the supreme moral law, occurs by a necessity which seems peculiar to the subject, but which is by no means a logical one, both in that science, whose object it is to set forth the knowledge of what is moral, and also in real life, where it shows itself partly in the judgment passed by conscience on our own actions, partly in our moral estimation of the actions of others; moreover, most of the chief conceptions in Ethics, springing as they do out of that idea, and inseparable from it (as, for instance, the conception of duty, and the ascription of praise or blame) assert themselves with the same necessity, and under the same conditions. In view of these facts and because it appears highly desirable, considering the trend of philosophic investigation in our time, to submit this matter to further scrutiny; the Society desires that the following question be carefully considered and discussed:—

1

Is the fountain and basis of Morals to be sought for in an idea of morality which lies directly in the consciousness (or conscience), and in the analysis of the other leading ethical conceptions which arise from it? or is it to be found in some other source of knowledge?)

PART I.

INTRODUCTION

Chapter I.—The Problem

"WHY do philosophers differ so widely as to the first principles of Morals, but agree respecting the conclusions and duties which they deduce from those principles?"

This is the question which was set as subject for a prize essay by the Royal Society of Holland at Harlem, 1810, and solved by J. C. F. Meister; and in comparison with the task before us, the inquiry presented no extraordinary difficulty. For:—

(1) The present question of the Royal Society has to do with nothing less important than the objectively true basis of morals, and consequently of morality. It is an Academy, be it observed, which invites this inquiry; and hence, from its position, it has no practical purpose in view; it asks for no discourse inculcating the exercise of uprightness and virtue, with arguments based on evidence, of which the plausibility is dwelt on, and the sophistry evaded, as is done in popular manuals. Rather, as its aim is not practical, but only theoretical, it desires nothing but the purely philosophical, that is, the objective, undisguised, and naked exposition of the ultimate basis of all good moral conduct, independent of every positive law, of every unproved assumption, and hence free from all groundwork, whether metaphysical or mythical. This, however, is a problem whose bristling difficulties are attested by the circumstance that all philosophers in every age and land have blunted their wits on it, and still more by the fact that all gods, oriental and occidental, actually derive their existence therefrom. Should therefore this opportunity serve to solve it, assuredly the Royal Society will not have expended its money amiss.

(2) Apart from this, a peculiar disadvantage will be found to attach to any theoretical examination of the basis of morals, because such an investigation is suspiciously like an attempt to undermine, and occasion the collapse of, the structure itself. The fact is, that in this matter we are apt to so closely associate practical aims with theory, that the well-meant zeal of the former is with difficulty restrained from ill-timed intervention. Nor is it within the power of every one to clearly dissociate the purely theoretical search for objective truth, purged of all interest, even of that of morality as practised, from a shameless attack on the heart's sacred

convictions. Therefore he, who here puts his hand to the plough, must, for his encouragement, ever bear in mind that from the doings and affairs of the populace, from the turmoil and bustle of the market-place, nothing is further removed than the quiet retreat and sanctuary of the Academy, where no noise of the world may enter, and where the only god raised on a pedestal is Truth, in solitary, naked sublimity.

The conclusion from these two premises is that I must be allowed complete freedom of speech, as well as the right of questioning everything; and furthermore, that if I succeed in really contributing something, however small, to this subject, then that contribution will be of no little importance.

But there are still other difficulties obstructing my path. The Royal Society asks for a short monograph setting forth the basis of Ethics entirely by itself; which means to say, independent of its connection with the general system, *i.e.,* the actual metaphysics of any philosophy. Such a demand must not only render the accomplishment of the task more difficult, but necessarily make it imperfect. Long ago Christian Wolf, in his *Philosophia Practica* (P. II., §28) observed: "*Tenebrae in philosophia practica non dispelluntur, nisi luce metaphysica effulgente,*" (Darkness in practical philosophy is only dispersed, when the light of metaphysics shines on it;) and Kant in the Preface to his *Grundlegung zur Metaphysik der Sitten* remarks: "Metaphysics must precede, and is in every case indispensable to, moral philosophy." For, just as every religion on earth, so far as it prescribes morality, does not leave the latter to rest on itself, but backs it by a body of dogmas (the chief end of which is precisely to be the prop of the moral sense); so with philosophy, the ethical basis, whatever it be, must itself attach to, and find its support in, one system of metaphysics or another, that is to say, in a presupposed explanation of the world, and of existence in general. This is so, because the ultimate and true conclusion concerning the essential nature of the Universe must necessarily be closely connected with that touching the ethical significance of human action; and because, in any case, that which is presented as the foundation of morality, if it is not to be merely an abstract formula, floating in the clouds, and out of contact with the real world, **must** be some fact or other discoverable either in the objective kosmos, or else in man's consciousness; but, as such, it can itself be only a phaenomenon; and consequently, like all other phaenomena, it requires a further explanation; and this explanation is supplied by Metaphysics. Philosophy indeed is such a connected whole that it is impossible to exhaustively discuss any one part without all the others being involved. Thus Plato says quite correctly: Ψυχῆς οὖν φύσιν ἀξίως λόγου κατανοῆσαι οἴει δυνατὸν εἶναι, ἄνευ τῆς τοῦ ὅλου φύσεως; (Phaedr., p. 371, Ed. Bip.) (Do you think then it is possible to understand at all adequately the nature of the soul, without at the same time understanding the nature of the Whole, *i.e.,* the totality of things?) The metaphysics of nature, the metaphysics of morals, and the metaphysics of the beautiful mutually presuppose each other, and only when taken as connected together do they complete the explanation of things as they really are, and of existence in general. So that whoever should exactly trace one of these three to its ultimate origin, would be found to have necessarily brought the others into his solution of the problem; just as an absolutely clear and exhaustive understanding of any single thing in the world would imply a perfect comprehension of everything else.

Now if we were to start from a given system of metaphysics, which is assumed to be true, we should reach synthetically a basis of morals, and this basis, being, so to say, built up from below, would provide the resulting ethical structure with a sure foundation. But in the present case, since the terms of the question enforce the separation of ethics from all metaphysics, there remains nothing but the analytic method, which proceeds from facts either of external experience, or of consciousness. It is true that thus the ultimate origin of the latter may be traced back to the human spirit, a source which then, however, must be taken as a fundamental fact, a primary phaenomenon, underivable from anything else, with the result that the whole explanation remains simply a psychological one. At best its connection with any general metaphysical standpoint can only be described as accessory. On the other hand, the fundamental datum, the primary phaenomenon of Ethics, so found in man's nature, could itself in its turn be accounted for and explained, if we might first treat of metaphysics, and then by the synthetic method deduce Ethics from it. This would mean, however, nothing less than the construction of a complete system of philosophy, whereby the limits of the given question would be far exceeded. I am, therefore, compelled to answer it within the lines which its own isolated narrowness has laid down.

And lastly, there is the following consideration. The basis on which it is here intended to place Ethics will prove to be a very small one; and the consequence is that of the many lawful, approvable, and praiseworthy actions of mankind, only the minority will be found to spring from purely moral motives, while the majority will have to be attributed to other sources. This gives less satisfaction, has not such a specious glitter as, let us say, a Categorical Imperative, which always stands ready for commands, only that itself in its turn may command what ought to be done, and what ought to be left undone;[1] not to mention other foundations that are entirely material.

---

[1] That is, the Categorical Imperative appears at first as your "obedient humble servant," ready to perform any useful service, *e.g.,* the solving of ethical riddles; while it ends by gaining the upper hand, and commanding.—(*Translator.*)

I can only, therefore, remind the reader of the saying in Ecclesiastes (iv. 6): "Better is an handful with quietness, than both the hands full with travail and vexation of spirit." In all knowledge the genuine, proof-resisting, indestructible coefficient is never large; just as in the earth's metallic strata a hundredweight of stone hides but a few ounces of gold. But whether others will prefer—as I do—the assured to the bulky possession, the small quantity of gold which remains in the crucible to the big lump of matter that was brought along with it; or whether I shall rather be charged with having removed from Ethics its basis, instead of providing one, in so far as I prove that the lawful and commendable actions of mankind often do not contain a particle of pure moral worth, and in most cases only a very little, resting, as they do, otherwise on motives, the sufficiency of which must ultimately be referred to the egoism of the doer; all this I must leave undecided; and I do so, not without anxiety, nay, rather with resignation, because I have long since been of the same mind as Johann Georg von Zimmermann, when he said: "Rest assured until your dying day, that nothing in the world is so rare as a good judge." (*Ueber die Einsamkeit;* Pt. I., Ch. iii., p. 93.)

For all true and voluntary righteousness, for all loving-kindness, for all nobleness, wherever these qualities may be found, my theory can only point to a very small foundation; whereas my opponents confidently construct broad bases for Morals, which are made strong enough for every possible burden, and are at the same time thrust upon every doubter's conscience, accompanied with a threatening side-glance at his own morality. As contrasted with these, my own position is indeed in sore and sorry plight. It is like that of Cordelia before King Lear, with her weakly worded assurance of dutiful affection, compared with the effusive protestations of her more eloquent sisters. So that there seems to be need of a cordial that may be furnished by some maxim taken from intellectual hunting grounds, such as, *Magna est vis veritatis, et praevalebit.* (Great is the strength of truth, and it will prevail.) But to a man who has lived and laboured even this fails to give much encouragement. Meanwhile, I will for once make the venture with truth on my side; and what opposes me will at the same time oppose truth.

Chapter II.—General Retrospect

FOR the people morality comes through, and is founded on, theology, as the express will of God. On the other hand, we see philosophers, with few exceptions, taking special pains to entirely exclude this kind of foundation; indeed, so they may but avoid it, they prefer even to find a refuge in sophistry. Whence comes this antithesis? Assuredly no more efficient basis for Ethics can be imagined than the theological; for who would be so bold as to oppose the will of the Almighty and the Omniscient? Unquestionably, no one; if only this will were proclaimed in an authentic, official manner (if one may say so), whereby no possible room for doubt could be left. This, however, is precisely the condition which does not admit of being realised. It is rather the inverse process which is attempted. The law declared to be the will of God men try to accredit as such, by demonstrating its agreement with our own independent, and hence, natural moral views, and an appeal is consequently made to these as being more direct and certain. But this is not all. We perceive that an action performed solely through threat of punishment and promise of reward would be moral much more in appearance than in reality; since, after all, it would have its root in Egoism, and in the last resort the scale would be turned by the greater or less amount of credulity evinced in each case. Now it was none other than Kant who destroyed the foundations of Speculative Theology, which up to his time were accounted unshakable. Speculative Theology had hitherto sustained Ethics, and in order to procure for the former an existence of some sort, if only an imaginary one, his wish was to proceed inversely, and make Ethics sustain Speculative Theology. So that it is now more than ever impossible to think of basing Ethics on Theology; for no one knows any longer which of the two is to be the supporter, and which the supported, and the consequence is a *circulus vitiosus*.

It is precisely through the influence of Kant's philosophy; through the contemporaneous effect of the unparalleled progress made in all the natural sciences, with regard to which every past age in comparison with our own appears childish; and lastly, through the knowledge of Sanskrit literature, and of those most ancient and widest spread faiths, Brahmanism and Buddhism, which, as far as time and space go, are the most important religious systems of mankind, and, as a matter of fact, are the original native religions of our own race, now well known to be of Asiatic descent—our race, to which in its new strange home they once more send a message across the centuries;—it is because of all this, I say, that the fundamental philosophical convictions of learned Europe have in the course of the last fifty years undergone a revolution, which perhaps many only reluctantly admit, but which cannot be denied. The result of this change is that the old supports of Ethics have been shown to be rotten, while the assurance remains that Ethics itself can never collapse; whence the conviction arises that for it there must exist a groundwork different from any hitherto provided, and adaptable to the advanced views of the age. The need of such is making itself felt more and more, and in it we undoubtedly find the reason that has induced the Royal Society to make the present important question the subject of a prize essay.

In every age much good morality has been preached; but the explanation of its *raison d'être* has always been encompassed with difficulties. On the whole we discern an endeavour to get at some objective truth, from which the ethical injunctions could be logically deduced; and it has been sought for both in the nature of things, and in the nature of man; but in vain. The result was always the same. The will of each human unit was found to gravitate solely towards its own individual welfare, the idea of which in its entirety is designated by the term "blissfulness" (*Glückseligkeit*); and this striving after self-satisfaction leads mankind by a path very different to the one morality would fain point out. The endeavour was next made now to identify "blissfulness" with virtue, now to represent it as virtue's consequence and effect. Both attempts have always failed; and this for no want of sophistry. Then recourse was had to artificial formulas, purely objective and abstract, as well *a posteriori* as *a priori,* from which correct ethical conduct undoubtedly admitted of being deduced. But there was nothing found in man's nature to afford these a footing, whereby they might have availed to guide the strivings of his volition, in face of its egoistic tendency. It appears to me superfluous to verify all this by describing and criticising every hitherto existing foundation of morality; not only because I share Augustine's opinion, *non est pro magno habendum quid homines senserint, sed quae sit rei veritas* (It is the truth about a thing, not men's opinions thereon, that is of importance); but also because it would be like γλαύκας εἰς ᾿Αθήνας κομίζειν (*i.e.,* carrying coals to Newcastle); for previous attempts to give a foundation to Ethics are sufficiently well-known to the Royal Society, and the very question proposed shows that it is also convinced of their inadequateness. Any reader less well-informed will find a careful, if not complete, presentment of the attempts hitherto made, in Garve's *Uebersicht der vornehmsten Principien der Sittenlehre,* and again, in Stäudlin's *Geschichte der Moralphilosophie.* It is of course very disheartening to reflect that Ethics, which so directly concerns life, has met with the same unhappy fate as the abstruse science of Metaphysics, and that its first principle, though perpetually sought for ever since the time of Socrates, has still to be found. Moreover, we must remember that in Ethics, much more than in any other science, what is essential is contained in its fundamental propositions; the deductions are so simple that they come of themselves. For all are capable of drawing a conclusion, but few of **judging**. And this is exactly the reason why lengthy text-books and dissertations on Morals are as superfluous as they are tedious. Meantime, if I may postulate an acquaintance with all the former foundations of Ethics, my task will be lightened. Whoever observes how ancient as well as modern philosophers (the Church creed sufficed for the middle ages) have had recourse to the most diverse and extraordinary arguments, in order to provide for the generally recognised requirements of morality a basis capable of proof, and how notwithstanding they admittedly failed; he will be able to measure the difficulty of the problem, and estimate my contribution accordingly. And he who has learned to know that none of the roads hitherto struck on lead to the goal, will be the more willing to tread with me a very different path from these—a path which up to now either has not been noticed, or else has been passed over with contempt; perhaps because it was the most natural one.[2] As a matter of fact my solution of the question will remind many of Columbus' egg.

It is solely to the latest attempt at giving a basis to Ethics—I mean the Kantian—that a critical examination will be devoted. I shall make it all the more exhaustive, partly because the great ethical reform of Kant gave to this science a foundation having a real superiority to previous ones; and partly because it still remains the last important pronouncement in this domain; for which reason it has obtained general acceptance up to the present day, and is universally taught, although differently garnished by certain changes in the demonstration and in the terminology. It is the ethical system of the last sixty years, which must be removed ere we enter on another path. Furthermore, my criticism of the Kantian basis will give me occasion to examine and discuss most of the fundamental conceptions of Ethics, and the outcome of this investigation I shall later on be able to postulate. Besides, inasmuch as opposites illustrate each other, it is exactly this course which will be the best preparation and guide, indeed the direct way, to my own position, which in its essential points is diametrically opposed to Kant's. It would therefore be a very perverse beginning to skip the following criticism, and turn at once to the positive part of my exposition, which then would remain only half intelligible.

In any case the time has assuredly arrived for once to cite Ethics before the bar of a searching scrutiny. During more than half a century it has been lying comfortably on the restful cushion which Kant arranged for it—the cushion of the Categorical Imperative of Practical Reason. In our day this Imperative is mostly introduced to us under a name which, being smoother and less ostentatious, has obtained more currency. It is

---

[2]Io dir non vi saprei per qual sventura,
　　O piuttosto per qual fatalità,
Da noi credito ottien più l' impostura,
　　Che la semplice e nuda verità.

CASTI.

[I cannot tell what mischief sly,
　　Or rather what fatality,
Leads man to credit more the lie
　　Than truth in naked purity.]

(Translator.)

called "the Moral Law"; and thus entitled, with a passing bow to reason and experience, it slips through unobserved into the house. Once inside, there is no end to its orders and commands; nor can it ever afterwards be brought to account. It was proper, indeed inevitable, that Kant, as the inventor of the thing, should remain satisfied with his creation, particularly as he shelved by its means errors still more glaring. But to be obliged to look on and see asses disporting themselves on the comfortable cushion which he prepared, and which since his time has been more and more trampled on and flattened out—this truly is hard. I allude to the daily hackney compilers, who, with the ready confidence born of stupidity, imagine that they have given a foundation to Ethics, if they do but appeal to that "Moral Law" which is alleged to be inherent in our **reason**; and then they complacently weave upon this such a confused and wide-reaching tissue of phrases that they succeed in rendering unintelligible the clearest and simplest relations of life: and all this, without ever once seriously asking themselves whether in point of fact there really does exist such a "Moral Law," as a convenient code of morality, graven in our heads or hearts.

Hence I admit the especial pleasure I feel in proceeding to remove from Ethics its broad cushion of repose, and I unreservedly declare my intention of proving that Kant's Practical Reason and Categorical Imperative are completely unwarrantable, baseless, and fabricated assumptions; and I shall further show that Kant's whole system, like those of his predecessors, is in want of a solid foundation. Consequently Ethics will again be consigned to its former entirely helpless condition, there to remain, until I come to demonstrate the true moral principle of human nature—a principle which is incontestably efficient, and has its root in our very being. The latter, however, has no such broad basis to offer as the above-mentioned cushion; so that, doubtless, those who are accustomed to take things easily, will not abandon their comfortable old seat, before they are thoroughly aware how deeply the ground on which it stands is undermined.

PART II.

CRITIQUE OF KANT'S BASIS OF ETHICS

Chapter I.—Preliminary Remarks

IT IS Kant's great service to moral science that he purified it of all Eudaemonism. With the ancients, Ethics was a doctrine of Eudaemonism; with the moderns for the most part it has been a doctrine of salvation. The former wished to prove that virtue and happiness are identical; but this was like having two figures which never coincide with each other, no matter how they may be placed. The latter have endeavoured to connect the two, not by the principle of identity, but by that of causation, thus making happiness the result of virtue; but to do this, they were obliged to have recourse to sophisms, or else to assume the existence of a world beyond any possible perception of the senses.

Among the ancients Plato alone forms an exception: his system is not eudaemonistic; it is mystic, instead. Even the Ethics of the Cynics and Stoics is nothing but a special form of Eudaemonism, to prove which, there is no lack of evidence and testimony, but the nature of my present task forbids the space.[1]

The ancients, then, equally with the moderns, Plato being the single exception, agree in making virtue only a means to an end. Indeed, strictly speaking, even Kant banished Eudaemonism from Ethics more in appearance than in reality, for between virtue and happiness he still leaves a certain mysterious connection;—there is an obscure and difficult passage in his doctrine of the Highest Good, where they occur together; while it is a patent fact that the course of virtue runs entirely counter to that of happiness. But, passing over this, we may say that with Kant the ethical principle appears as something quite independent of experience and its teaching; it is transcendental, or metaphysical. He recognises that human conduct possesses a significance that oversteps all possibility of experience, and is therefore actually the bridge leading to that which he

---

[1]For a complete demonstration v. *Die Welt als Wille und Vorstellung,* Vol. I., §16, p. 103, sqq., and Vol. II., Chap. 16, p. 166, sqq. of the third edition. [*Die Welt als Wille und Vorstellung,* that is, *The World as Will and Idea;* "Idea" being used much as εἴδωλον sometimes is (cf. Xen. *Sym.,* 4, 21), in the sense of "an image in the mind," "a mental picture."— (*Translator.*)]

calls the "intelligible"[2] world, the *mundus noumenôn,* the world of Things in themselves.

The fame, which the Kantian Ethics has won, is due not only to this higher level, which it reached, but also to the moral purity and loftiness of its conclusions. It is by the latter that most people have been attracted, without paying much attention to the foundation, which is propounded in a very complex, abstract and artificial form; and Kant himself required all his powers of acumen and synthesis to give it an appearance of solidity. Fortunately, he separated his Ethics from the exposition of its basis, devoting to the latter a special work entitled the *Grundlegung zur Metaphysik der Sitten,* the theme of which will be found to be precisely the same as that of our prize essay. For on page xiii of the preface he says: "The present treatise is nothing else but an attempt to find out and establish the supreme principle of morality. This is an investigation, whose scope is complete in itself, and which should be kept apart from all other moral researches." It is in this book that we find the basis, that is to say, the essentials of his Ethics set forth with an acute penetration and systematic conciseness, as in no other of his writings. It has, moreover, the great advantage of being the first of Kant's moral works, appearing,[3] as it did, only four years later than the *Kritik der Reinen Vernunft,* and consequently it dates from the period when, although he was sixty-one, the detrimental effect of old age on his intellect was not yet perceptible. On the other hand, this is distinctly traceable in the *Kritik der Praktischen Vernunft,* which was published in 1788, or one year later than the unhappy remodelling of the *Kritik der Reinen Vernunft* in the second edition, whereby the latter, his immortal master-piece, was obviously marred. An analysis of this question is to be found in the preface to the new edition by Rosenkranz,[4] from which my own investigation makes it impossible for me to dissent. The *Kritik der Praktischen Vernunft* contains in its essentials the same material as the above-mentioned *Grundlegung;* only the latter has a more concise and rigorous form, while in the former the subject is handled with greater prolixity, interspersed with digressions, and even padded with some pieces of moral rhetoric, to heighten the impression. When Kant wrote it, he had at last, and late in life, become

---

[2]It seems better to keep this technical word than to attempt a cumbrous periphrasis. The meaning is perfectly clear. The *sensibilia* (*phaenomena*) are opposed to the *intelligibilia* (*noumena*), which compose the transcendental world. So the individual, in so far as he is a phaenomenon, has an empirical character; in so far as he is a noumenon, his character is intelligible (*intelligibilis*). The *mundus intelligibilis,* or *mundus noumenôn* is the κόσμος νοητὸς of New Platonism.—(*Translator.*)

[3]It was published in 1785: *The Kritik der Reinen Vernunft,* first edition, in 1781.—(*Translator.*)

[4]His analysis is really derived from myself, but in this place I am speaking incognito.

deservedly famous; hence, being certain of boundless attention, he allowed greater play to the garrulity of old age.

But the *Kritik der Praktischen Vernunft* contains two sections which are peculiar to itself. First: the exposition of the relation between Freedom and Necessity (pp. 169–179 of the fourth edition, and pp. 223–231 in Rosenkranz). This passage is above all praise, and undoubtedly was framed earlier in his life, as it is entirely in harmony with his treatment of the same subject in the *Kritik der Reinen Vernunft* (pp. 560–586; Rosenkranz, p. 438, sqq.). And secondly: the *Moraltheologie,* which will more and more come to be recognised as the real object Kant had in view. In his *Metaphysische Anfangsgründe der Tugendlehre* this *pendant* to the deplorable *Rechtslehre,* written in 1797, the debility of old age is at length fully preponderant. For all these reasons the present criticism will mainly deal with the treatise first mentioned, *viz.,* the *Grundlegung zur Metaphysik der Sitten,* and the reader will please understand that all the page numbers given by themselves refer to it. Both the other works will only be considered as accessory and secondary. For a proper comprehension of the present criticism, which, in probing the Kantian Ethics to its depths, bears directly and principally on this *Grundlegung,* it is very desirable that the latter be carefully read through again, so that the mind may have a perfectly clear and fresh presentment of what it contains. It is but a matter of 128 and xiv pages (in Rosenkranz only 100 pages altogether). I shall quote from the third edition of 1792, adding the page number of the new complete publication by Rosenkranz, with an R. prefixed.

Chapter II.—On the Imperative Form of the Kantian Ethics

KANT'S πρῶτον ψεῦδος (first false step) lies in his conception of Ethics itself, and this is found very clearly expressed on page 62 (R., p. 54): "In a system of practical philosophy we are not concerned with adducing reasons for that which takes place, but with formulating laws regarding that which **ought to take place, even if it never does take place**." This is at once a distinct *petitio principii.* Who tells you that there are laws to which our conduct *ought* to be subject? Who tells you that that **ought to take place, which in fact never does take place**? What justification have you for making this assumption at the outset, and consequently for forcing upon us, as the only possible one, a system of Ethics couched in the imperative terms of legislation? I say, in contradistinction to Kant, that the student of Ethics, and no less the philosopher in general, must content himself with explaining and interpreting that which is given, in other words, that which really is, or takes place, so as to obtain an **un-**

derstanding of it, and I maintain furthermore that there is plenty to do in this direction, much more than has hitherto been done, after the lapse of thousands of years. Following the above *petitio principii,* Kant straightway, without any previous investigation, assumes in the preface (which is entirely devoted to the subject), that purely moral laws exist; and this assumption remains thenceforth undisturbed, and forms the very foundation of his whole system. We, however, prefer first of all to examine the conception denoted by the word "law." The true and original meaning of the term is limited to law as between citizens; it is the *lex,* νόμος, of the Romans and Greeks, a human institution, and depending on human volition. It has a secondary, derived, figurative, metaphorical meaning, when applied to Nature, whose operations, partly known *a priori,* partly learnt by experience, and which are always constant, we call natural laws. Only a very small portion of these natural laws can be discerned *a priori,* and with admirable acuteness, Kant set them apart, and classed them under the name "Metaphysics of Nature." There is also undoubtedly a law for the human will, in so far as man belongs to Nature; and this law is strictly provable, admits of no exception, is inviolable, and immovable as the mountains, and does not, like the Categorical Imperative, imply a **quasi**-necessity, but rather a complete and absolute one. It is the law of **motivation,** a form of the law of causation; in other words, it is the causation which is brought about by the medium of the understanding. It is the sole demonstrable law to which the human will **as such** is subject. It means that every action can only take place in consequence of a sufficient motive. Like causality in general, it is a natural law. On the other hand, **moral** laws, apart from human institution, state ordinance, or religious doctrine, cannot rightly be assumed as existing without proof. Kant, therefore, by taking such laws for granted, is guilty of a *petitio principii,* which is all the bolder, in that he at once adds (page vi of the preface) that a moral law ought to imply "**absolute necessity**." But "absolute necessity" is everywhere characterised by an inevitable chain of consequence; how, then, can such a conception be attached to these alleged moral laws (as an instance of which he adduces "thou shalt not lie"[5])? Every one knows, and he himself admits, that no such consecution for the most part takes place; the reverse, indeed, is the rule.

In scientific Ethics before we admit as controlling the will other laws besides that of motivation—laws which are original and independent of all human ordinance—we must first prove and deduce their existence; that is, provided in things ethical we are concerned not merely with recommending honesty, but with practising it. Until that proof be furnished, I shall recognise only one source to which is traceable the importation

---

[5]Du sollt (*sic*) nicht lügen.

into Ethics of the conception **Law, Precept, Obligation**. It is one which is foreign to philosophy. I mean the Mosaic Decalogue. Indeed the spelling "**du sollt**"[6] in the above instance of a moral law, the first put forward by Kant, naïvely betrays this origin. A conception, however, which can point to no other source than this, has no right, without undergoing further scrutiny, thus to force its way into philosophical Ethics. It will be rejected, until introduced by duly accredited proof. Thus on the threshold of the subject Kant makes his first *petitio principii,* and that no small one.

Our philosopher, then, by begging the question in his preface, simply assumes the conception of **Moral Law** as given and existing beyond all doubt; and he treats the closely related conception of Duty (page 8, R., p. 16) exactly in the same way. Without subjecting it to any further test, he admits it forthwith as a proper appurtenance of Ethics. But here, again, I am compelled to enter a protest. This conception, equally with the kindred notions of **Law, Command, Obligation**, etc., taken thus unconditionally, has its source in theological morals, and it will remain a stranger to philosophical morals, so long as it fails to furnish sufficient credentials drawn either from man's nature, or from the objective world. Till then, I can only recognise the Decalogue as the origin of all these connected conceptions. Since the rise of Christianity there is no doubt that philosophical has been unconsciously moulded by theological ethics. And since the latter is essentially dictatorial, the former appears in the shape of precepts and inculcation of Duty, in all innocence, and without any suspicion that first an ulterior sanction is needful for this *rôle*; rather does she suppose it to be her proper and natural form. It is true that all peoples, ages, and creeds, and indeed all philosophers (with the exception of the materialists proper) have undeniably recognised that the ethical significance of human conduct is a metaphysical one, in other words, that it stretches out beyond this phaenomenal existence and reaches to eternity; but it is equally true that the presentment of this fact in terms of Command and Obedience, of Law and Duty, is no part of its essence. Furthermore, separated from the theological hypotheses whence they have sprung, these conceptions lose in reality all meaning, and to attempt a substitute for the former by talking with Kant of **absolute** obligation and of **unconditioned** duty, is to feed the reader with empty words, nay more, is to give him a *contradictio in adjecto*[7] to digest.

Every obligation derives all sense and meaning simply and solely from its relation to threatened punishment or promised reward. Hence, long before Kant was thought of, Locke says: "For since it would be utterly in

---

[6]Sollt is the old form for "*sollst.*" Cf. Eng., *shalt*: Icel. *skalt.*—(*Translator.*)

[7]A contradiction in the adjective. This occurs when the epithet applied to a noun contradicts its essential meaning.—(*Translator.*)

vain, to suppose a rule set to the free actions of man, without annexing to it some enforcement of good and evil to determine his will; we must, wherever we suppose a law, suppose also some reward or punishment annexed to that law" (*Essay on the Human Understanding,* Bk. II., ch. 33, §6). What **ought** to be done is therefore necessarily conditioned by punishment or reward; consequently, to use Kant's language, it is essentially and inevitably **hypothetical**, and never, as he maintains, **categorical**. If we think away these conditions, the conception of obligation becomes void of sense; hence **absolute obligation** is most certainly a *contradictio in adjecto.* A commanding voice, whether it come from within, or from without, cannot possibly be imagined except as threatening or promising. Consequently obedience to it, which may be wise or foolish according to circumstances, is yet always actuated by selfishness, and therefore morally worthless.

The complete unthinkableness and nonsense of this conception of an **unconditioned obligation**, which lies at the root of the Kantian Ethics, appears later in the system itself, namely in the *Kritik der Praktischen Vernunft*: just as some concealed poison in an organism cannot remain hid, but sooner or later must come out and show itself. For this **obligation**, said to be so **unconditioned**, nevertheless postulates more than one condition in the background; it assumes a rewarder, a reward, and the immortality of the person to be rewarded.

This is of course unavoidable, if one really makes Duty and Obligation the fundamental conception of Ethics; for these ideas are essentially relative, and depend for their significance on the threatened penalty or the promised reward. The guerdon which is assumed to be in store for virtue shows clearly enough that only in appearance she works for nothing. It is, however, put forward modestly veiled, under the name of the **Highest Good**, which is the union of Virtue and Happiness. But this is at bottom nothing else but a morality that derives its origin from Happiness, which means, a morality resting on selfishness. In other words, it is Eudaemonism, which Kant had solemnly thrust out of the front door of his system as an intruder, only to let it creep in again by the postern under the name of the **Highest Good**. This is how the assumption of **unconditioned absolute obligation**, concealing as it does a contradiction, avenges itself. **Conditioned** obligation, on the other hand, cannot of course be any first principle for Ethics, since everything done out of regard for reward or punishment is necessarily an egoistic transaction, and as such is without any real moral value. All this makes it clear that a nobler and wider view of Ethics is needed, if we are in earnest about our endeavour to truly account for the significance of human conduct—a significance which extends beyond phaenomena and is eternal.

As all obligation is entirely dependent on a condition, so also is all duty. Both conceptions are very closely related, indeed almost identical. The only difference between them might be said to be that obligation in general may rest on mere force, whereas duty involves the sense of obligation deliberately undertaken, such as we see between master and servant, principal and subordinate, rulers and the ruled. And since no one undertakes a duty *gratis,* every duty implies also a right. The slave has no duties, because he has no rights; but he is subject to an obligation which rests on sheer force. In the following Part I shall explain the only meaning which the conception "**Duty**" has in Ethics.

If we put Ethics in an **imperative** form, making it a Doctrine of Duties, and regard the moral worth or worthlessness of human conduct as the fulfilment or violation of duties, we must remember that this view of Duty, and of Obligation in general, is undeniably derived solely from theological Morals, and primarily from the Decalogue, and consequently that it rests essentially and inseparably on the assumption of man's dependence on another will which gives him commands and announces reward or punishment. But the more the assumption of such a will is in Theology positive and precise, the less should it be quietly and unsuspectingly introduced into philosophical Morals. Hence we have no right to assume beforehand that for the latter the **imperative Form**, the ordaining of commands, laws, and duties is an essential and a matter of course; and it is a very poor shift to substitute the word "absolute" or "categorical" for the external condition which is indissolubly attached to such conceptions by their very nature: for this gives rise, as explained above, to a *contradictio in adjecto.*

Kant, then, without more ado or any close examination, borrowed this **imperative Form** of Ethics from theological Morals. The hypotheses of the latter (in other words, Theology) really lie at the root of his system, and as these alone in point of fact lend it any meaning or sense, so they cannot be separated from, indeed are implicitly contained in, it. After this, when he had expounded his position the task of developing in turn a Theology out of his Morals—the famous *Moraltheologie*—was easy enough. For the conceptions which are implicitly involved in his Imperative, and which lie hidden at the base of his Morals, only required to be brought forward and expressed explicitly as postulates of Practical Reason. And so it was that, to the world's great edification, a Theology appeared depending simply on Ethics, indeed actually derived therefrom. But this came about because the ethical system itself rests on concealed theological hypotheses. I mean no derisive comparison, but in its form the process is analogous to that whereby a conjurer prepares a surprise for us, when he lets us find something where he had previously employed his art to place it. Described in the abstract, Kant's procedure is this: what ought to have been his first principle, or hypothesis (*viz.,* Theology) he

made the conclusion, and what ought to have been deduced as the conclusion (*viz.,* the Categorical Command) he took as his hypothesis.[8] But
after he had thus turned the thing upside down, nobody, not even he
himself, recognised it as being what it really was, namely the old well-
known system of theological Morals. How this trick was accomplished
we shall consider in the sixth and seventh chapters of the present Part.

Ethics was of course frequently put in the imperative form, and treated
as a doctrine of duties also in pre-Kantian philosophy; but it was always
then based upon the will of a God whose existence had been otherwise
proved, and so there was no inconsequence. As soon, however, as the attempt was made, as Kant attempted, to give a foundation to Ethics independent of this will, and establish it without metaphysical hypotheses,
there was no longer any justification for taking as its basis the words
"thou shalt," and "it is thy duty" (that is, the imperative form), without
first deducing the truth thereof from some other source.

Chapter III.—On the Assumption of Duties Towards Ourselves in Particular

THIS form of the doctrine of duties was very acceptable to Kant, and in
working out his position he left it untouched; for, like his predecessors,
along with the duties towards others he ranged also duties towards ourselves. I, however, entirely reject this assumption, and, as there will be no
better opportunity, I shall here incidentally explain my view.

Duties towards ourselves must, just as all others, be based either on
right or on love. Duties towards ourselves based on right are impossible,
because of the self-evident fundamental principle *volenti non fit injuria*
(where the will assents, no injury is done). For what I do is always what
I will; consequently also what I do to myself is never anything but what
I will, therefore it cannot be unjust. Next, as regards duties towards ourselves based on love. Ethics here finds her work already done, and comes
too late. The impossibility of violating the duty of self-love is at once assumed by the first law of Christian Morals: "Love thy neighbour as thyself." According to this, the love which each man cherishes for himself
is postulated as the *maximum,* and as the condition of all other love; while
the converse, "Love thyself as thy neighbour" is never added; for every
one would feel that the latter does not claim enough. Moreover, self-love
would be the sole duty regularly involving an *opus supererogationis.* Kant
himself says in the *Metaphysische Anfangsgründe zur Tugendlehre,* p. 13 (R.,

---

[8]Like the converse of a geometrical proposition, this Kantian inversion is not necessarily
true; its validity, in fact, depends on the conclusion being implicitly contained in the hypothesis.—(*Translator.*)

p. 230): "That which each man inevitably wills of himself, does not belong to the conception of Duty." This idea of duties towards ourselves is nevertheless still held in repute, indeed it enjoys for the most part special favour; nor need we feel surprise. But it has an amusing effect in cases where people begin to show anxiety about their persons, and talk quite earnestly of the duty of self-preservation; the while it is sufficiently clear that fear will lend them legs soon enough, and that they have no need of any law of duty to help them along.

First among the duties towards ourselves is generally placed that of not committing suicide, the line of argument taken being extremely prejudiced and resting on the shallowest basis. Unlike animals, man is not only a prey to **bodily** pain limited to the passing moment, but also to those incomparably greater **mental** sufferings, which, reaching forwards and backwards, draw upon the future and the past; and nature, by way of compensation, has granted to man alone the privilege of being able to end his life at his own pleasure, before she herself sets a term to it; thus, while animals necessarily live so long as they **can**, man need only live so long as he **will**.

Whether he ought on ethical grounds to forego this privilege is a difficult question, which in any case cannot be decided by the usual superficial reasoning. The arguments against suicide which Kant does not deem unworthy of adducing (p. 53, R., p. 48 and p. 67, R., p. 57), I cannot conscientiously describe as other than pitiable, and quite undeserving of an answer. It is laughable indeed to suppose that reflections of such a kind could have wrested the dagger from the hands of Cato, of Cleopatra, of Cocceius Nerva (Tac., *Ann.*, vi. 26) or of Arria the wife of Paetus (Plin., *Ep.*, iii. 16). If real moral motives for not committing suicide actually exist, it is certain that they lie very deep, and cannot be reached by the plummet of ordinary Ethics. They belong to a higher view of things than is adaptable even to the standpoint of the present treatise.[9]

That which generally comes next on the rubric of duties towards ourselves may be divided partly into rules of worldly wisdom, partly into hygienic prescriptions; but neither class belongs to Morals in the proper sense. Last on the catalogue comes the prohibition of unnatural lust—onanism, *paederastia,* and bestiality. On these onanism is mainly a vice of childhood, and must be fought against much more with the weapon of dietetics than with that of ethics; hence we find that the authors of books directed against it are physicians (*e.g.*, Tissot and others) rather than moralists. After dietetics and hygiene have done their work, and struck it

---

[9]There are ascetic reasons, which may be found in the Fourth Book, Vol. I., §69, of my chief work (*Die Welt als Wille und Vorstellung*).

down by irrefutable reasoning, if Ethics desires to take up the matter, she finds little left for her to do. Bestiality, again, is of very rare occurrence; it is thoroughly abnormal and exceptional, and, moreover, so loathsome and foreign to human nature, that itself, better than all arguments of reason, passes judgment on itself, and deters by sheer disgust. For the rest, as being a degradation of human nature, it is in reality an offence against the species as such, and in the abstract; not against human units. Of the three sexual perversions of which we are speaking it is consequently only with *paederastia* that Ethics has to do, and in treating of Justice this vice finds its proper place. For Justice is infringed by it, in face of which fact, the dictum *volenti non fit injuria* is unavailing. The injustice consists in the seduction of the younger and inexperienced person, who is thereby ruined physically and morally.

Chapter IV.—On the Basis of the Kantian Ethics

WITH the imperative Form of Ethics, which in Chapter II. we proved to be a *petitio principii,* is directly connected a favourite idea of Kant's, that may be excused, but cannot be adopted. Sometimes we see a physician, after having employed a certain remedy with conspicuous success, henceforth prescribing it for almost all diseases; to such a one Kant may be likened. By separating the *a priori* from the *a posteriori* in human knowledge he made the most brilliant and pregnant discovery that Metaphysics can boast of. What wonder then that thereafter he should try to apply this method, this sundering of the two forms, everywhere, and should consequently make Ethics also consist of two parts, a pure, *i.e.,* an *a priori* knowable part, and an empirical? The latter of these he rejects as unreliable for the purpose of founding Ethics. To trace out the former and exhibit it by itself is his purpose in the *Grundlegung der Metaphysik der Sitten,* which he accordingly represents as a science purely *a priori,* exactly in the same way as he sets forth the *Metaphysische Anfangsgründe der Naturwissenschaft.* He asserts in fact that the **Moral Law**, which without warrant, without deduction, or proof of any sort, he postulates as existing, is furthermore a Law knowable *a priori* and independent of all **internal** or **external experience**; it "**rests**" (he says) "**solely on conceptions of pure Reason; and is to be taken as a synthetic proposition a priori**" (*Kritik der Praktischen Vernunft*: p. 56 of fourth Edition; R., p. 142). But from this definition the implication immediately follows that such a Law can only be formal, like everything else known *a priori,* and consequently has only to do with the **Form** of actions, not with their **Essence**. Let it be thought what this means! He emphatically adds (p. vi of the preface to the *Grundlegung*; R., p. 5) that it is "useless to look for it either subjectively in man's nature, or objectively in the accidents of the external world," and (preface of the same, page vii; R., p. 6) that "nothing whatever connected with it can be borrowed from knowledge relating to man, *i.e.,* from anthropology." On page 59 (R., p. 52) he repeats, "That one ought on no account to fall into the mistake of trying to derive one's principle of morality from the special constitution of human nature"; and again, on page 60 (R., p. 52), he says that, "Everything derived from any natural disposition peculiar to man, or from certain feelings and propensities, or indeed from any special trend attaching solely to human nature, and not necessarily to be taken as the Will of **every rational being**," is incapable of affording a foundation for the moral law. This shows beyond all possibility of contradiction that Kant does not represent the alleged moral law **as a fact of consciousness**, capable of empirical proof—which is how the later would-be philosophers, both individually and collectively, wish to pass it off. In discarding every empirical basis for Morals, he rejects all internal, and still more decidedly all external, experience. Accordingly he founds—and I call special attention to this—his moral principle not on any provable **fact of consciousness**, such as an inner natural disposition, nor yet upon any objective relation of things in the external world. No! That would be an empirical foundation. Instead of this, **pure conceptions a priori**, *i.e.,* conceptions, which so far contain nothing derived from internal or external experience, and thus are simply shells without kernels—these are to be made the basis of Morals. Let us consider the full meaning of such a position. Human consciousness as well as the whole external world, together with all the experience and all the facts they comprise, are swept from under our feet. We have nothing to stand upon. And what have we to hold to? Nothing but a few entirely abstract, entirely unsubstantial conceptions, floating in the air equally with ourselves. It is from these, or, more correctly, from the mere form of their connection with judgments made, that **a Law** is declared to proceed, which by so-called **absolute necessity** is supposed to be valid, and to be strong enough to lay bit and bridle on the surging throng of human desires, on the storm of passion, on the giant might of **egoism**. We shall see if such be the case.

With this preconceived notion that the basis of Morals must be necessarily and strictly **a priori**, and entirely free from everything empirical, another of Kant's favourite ideas is closely connected. The moral principle that he seeks to establish is, he says, **a synthetic proposition a priori, of merely formal contents**, and hence exclusively a matter of **Pure Reason**; and accordingly, as such, to be regarded as valid not **only for men**, but for **all possible rational beings**; indeed he declares it to hold good for man "on this account alone," *i.e.,* because *per accidens* man comes under the category of rational beings. Here lies the cause of his basing the Moral principle not on any feeling, but on **pure Reason** (which knows nothing but itself and the statement of its antithesis). So that this **pure Reason** is taken, not as it really and exclusively is—an intellectual faculty of man—but **as a self-existent hypostatic essence**, yet without the smallest authority; the pernicious effects of such example and precedent being sufficiently shown in the pitiful philosophy of the present day. Indeed, this view of Morals as existing not for men, as men, but for all rational beings, as such, is with Kant a principle so firmly established, an idea so favourite, that he is never tired of repeating it at every opportunity.

I, on the contrary, maintain that we are never entitled to raise into a *genus* that which we only know of in a single species. For we could bring nothing into our idea of the *genus* but what we had abstracted from this one species; so that what we should predicate of the *genus* could after all only be understood of the single species. While, if we should attempt to think away (without any warrant) the particular attributes of the species, in order to form our *genus,* we should perhaps remove the exact condition whereby the remaining attributes, hypostatised as a *genus,* are made possible. Just as we recognise **intelligence in general** to be an attribute of animal beings alone, and are therefore never justified in thinking of it as existing outside, and independent, of animal nature; so we recognise **Reason** as the exclusive attribute of the human race, and have not the smallest right to suppose that Reason exists externally to it, and then proceed to set up a *genus* called "Rational Beings," differing from its single known species "Man"; still less are we warranted in laying down laws for such imaginary **rational beings in the abstract**. To talk of rational beings external to men is like talking of **heavy beings** external to bodies. One cannot help suspecting that Kant was thinking a little of the dear cherubim, or at any rate counted on their presence in the conviction of the reader. In any case this doctrine contains a tacit assumption of an *anima rationalis,* which as being entirely different from the *anima sensitiva,* and the *anima vegetativa,* is supposed to persist after death, and then to be indeed nothing else but *rationalis.* But in the *Kritik der Reinen Vernunft* Kant himself has expressly and elaborately made an end of this most transcendent hypostasis. Nevertheless, in his ethics generally, and in the *Kritik der Praktischen Vernunft* especially, there seems always to hover in the background the thought that the inner and eternal essence of man consists of **Reason**. In this connection, where the matter only occurs incidentally, I must content myself with simply asserting the contrary. Reason, as indeed the intellectual faculty as a whole, is secondary, is an attribute of phaenomena, being in point of fact conditioned by the organism; whereas it is the **Will** in man which is his very self, the only part of him which is metaphysical, and therefore indestructible.

The success with which Kant had applied his method to the theoretical side of philosophy led him on to extend it to the practical. Here also he endeavoured to separate pure *a priori* from empirical *a posteriori* knowledge. For this purpose he assumed that just as we know *a priori* the laws of Space, of Time, and of Causality, so in like manner, or at any rate analogously, we have the moral plumb-line for our conduct given us prior to all experience, and revealed in a Categorical Imperative, an absolute "Ought." But how wide is the difference between this alleged moral law *a priori,* and our theoretical knowledge *a priori* of Space, Time, and Causality! The latter are nothing but the expression of the forms, *i.e.,* the functions of our intellect, whereby alone we are capable of grasping an objective world, and wherein alone it can be mirrored; so that the world (as we know it) is absolutely conditioned by these forms, and all experience **must** invariably and exactly correspond to them—just as everything that I see through a blue glass must appear blue. While the former, the so-called moral law, is something that experience pours ridicule on at every step; indeed, as Kant himself says, it is doubtful whether in practice it has ever really been followed on any single occasion. How completely unlike are the things which are here classed together under the conception of **apriority**! Moreover, Kant overlooked the fact that, according to his own teaching, in theoretical philosophy, it is exactly the **Apriority** of our knowledge of Time, Space, and Causality—independent as this is of experience—that limits it strictly to phaenomena, *i.e.,* to the picture of the world as reflected in our consciousness, and makes it entirely invalid as regards the real nature of things, *i.e.,* as regards whatever exists independently of our capacity to grasp it.

Similarly, when we turn to practical philosophy, his alleged moral law, if it have an *a priori* origin in ourselves, must also be only phaenomenal, and leave entirely untouched the essential nature of things. Only this conclusion would stand in the sharpest contradiction as much to the facts themselves, as to Kant's view of them. For it is precisely the moral principle in us that he everywhere (*e.g., Kritik der Praktischen Vernunft,* p. 175; R., p. 228) represents as being in the closest connection with the real essence of things, indeed, as directly in contact with it; and in all passages in the *Kritik der Reinen Vernunft,* where the mysterious Thing in itself comes forward a little more clearly, it shows itself as the **moral principle** in us, as **Will**. But of this he failed to take account.

In Chapter II. of this Part, I explained how Kant took over bodily from theological Morals the **imperative form** of Ethics, *i.e.,* the conception of obligation, of law, and of duty; and how at the same time he was constrained to leave behind that which in the realm of theology alone lends force and significance to these ideas. But he felt the need of some basis for them, and accordingly went so far as to require that the **conception of duty** itself should be also the **ground of its fulfilment**; in other words, that it should itself be its own enforcement. An action, he says (p. 11; R., p. 18), has no genuine moral worth, unless it be done simply as a matter of duty, and for duty's sake, without any liking for it being felt; and the character only begins to have value, if a man, who has no sympathy in his heart, and is cold and indifferent to others' sufferings, and who is **not by nature a lover of his kind**, is nevertheless a doer of good actions, solely out of a pitiful sense of duty. This assertion, which is revolting to true moral sentiment; this apotheosis of lovelessness, the exact opposite, as it is, of the Christian doctrine of Morals, which places love before everything else, and teaches that without it nothing profiteth (1 Cor. xiii. 3); this stupid moral pedantry has been ridiculed by Schiller in two apposite epigrams, entitled *Gewissensskrupel* (Scruples of Conscience) and *Entscheidung* (Decision).[10]

It appears that some passages in the *Kritik der Praktischen Vernunft,* which exactly suit this connection, were the immediate occasion of the verses. Thus, for instance, on p. 150 (R., p. 211) we find: "Obedience to the moral law, which a man feels incumbent on him, is based not on voluntary inclination, nor on endeavour willingly put forth, without any authoritative command, but on a sense of duty." Yes, it must be **commanded**! What slavish morality! And again on p. 213 (R., p. 257): "Feelings of compassion, and of tender-hearted sympathy would be actually troublesome to persons who think aright, because through such emotions their well weighed maxims would become confused, and so the desire would grow up to be rid of them, and to be subject solely to the lawgiver—Reason." Now I maintain without hesitation that what opens the hand of the above-described (p. 11; R., p. 18) loveless doer of good, who is indifferent to the sufferings of other people, cannot (provided he have no secondary motives) be anything else than a slavish δεισιδαιμονία (fear of the gods), equally whether he calls his fetich "Categorical Imperative" or Fitzlipuzli.[11] For what but fear can move a hard heart?

Furthermore, on p. 13 (R., p. 19), in accordance with the above view, we find that the moral worth of an action is supposed to lie, by no means in the **intention** which led to it, but in the maxim which was followed. Whereas I, on the contrary, ask the reader to reflect that it is the **intention alone** which decides as to the moral worth, or worthlessness, of an

---

[10]These epigrams form the close of Schiller's poem "Die Philosophen," which is worth reading in this connection.—(*Translator.*)

[11]More correctly, Huitzilopochtli: a Mexican deity.

action, so that the same act may deserve condemnation or praise according to the intention which determined it. Hence it is that, whenever men discuss a proceeding to which some moral importance is attached, the **intention** is always investigated, and by this standard alone the matter is judged; as, likewise, it is in the **intention** alone that every one seeks justification, if he see his conduct misinterpreted, or excuse, if its consequence be mischievous.

On p. 14 (R., p. 20) we at last reach the definition of Duty, which is the fundamental conception of Kant's entire ethical system. It is: "The necessity of an action out of respect for the law." But what is **necessary** takes place with absolute certainty; while conduct based on pure duty generally does not come off at all. And not only this; Kant himself admits (p. 25; R., p. 28) that there are **no certain instances** on record of conduct determined solely by pure duty; and on p. 26 (R., p. 29) he says: "It is utterly impossible to know with certainty from experience whether there has ever really been one single case in which an action, however true to duty, has rested simply on its idea." And similarly on p. 28 (R., p. 30) and p. 49 (R., p. 50). In what sense then can **necessity** be attributed to such an action? As it is only fair always to put the most favourable interpretation on an author's words, we will suppose him to mean that an act true to duty is **objectively** necessary, but **subjectively** accidental. Only it is precisely this that is more easily said than thought; for where is the **Object** of this **objective** necessity, the consequence of which for the most part, perhaps indeed always, fails to be realised in objective reality? With every wish to be unbiassed, I cannot but think that the expression—**necessity of an action**—is nothing but an artificially concealed, very forced paraphrase of the word "ought."[12] This will become clearer if we notice that in the same definition the word *Achtung* (respect) is employed, where *Gehorsam* (obedience) is meant. Similarly in the note on p. 16 (R., p. 20) we read: "*Achtung* signifies simply the subordination of my will to a law. The direct determination of the will by a law, and the consciousness that it is so determined—this is what is denoted by *Achtung*." In what language? In German the proper term is *Gehorsam*. But the word *Achtung,* so unsuitable as it is, cannot without a reason have been put in place of the word *Gehorsam*. It must serve some purpose; and this is obviously none other than to veil the derivation of the imperative form, and of the conception of duty, from theological Morals; just as we saw above that the expression "necessity of an action," which is such a forced and awkward substitute for the word "shall," was only chosen because "shall" is the exact language of the Decalogue. The above definition: "Duty is the necessity of an action out of respect for the law," would therefore read in

---

[12]Or "shall," as in the "thou shalt" of the Decalogue.—(*Translator.*)

natural, undisguised, plain language: "Duty signifies an action which **ought** to be done out of obedience to a law." This is "the real form of the poodle."[13]

But now as to the Law, which is the real foundation stone of the Kantian Ethics. **What does it contain? And where is it inscribed?** This is the chief point of inquiry. In the first place, be it observed that we have two questions to deal with: the one has to do with the **Principle**, the other with the **Basis** of Ethics—two entirely different things, although they are frequently, and sometimes indeed intentionally, confused.

The **principle** or main proposition of an ethical system is the shortest and most concise definition of the line of conduct which it prescribes, or, if it have no imperative form, of the line of conduct to which it attaches real moral worth. It thus contains, in the general terms of a single enunciation, the direction for following the path of virtue, which is derived from that system: in other words, it is the ὅ,τι[14] of virtue. Whereas the **Basis** of any theory of Ethics is the διότι[15] of virtue, the **reason** of the obligation enjoined, of the exhortation or praise given, whether it be sought in human nature, or in the external conditions of the world, or in anything else. As in all sciences, so also in Ethics the ὅ,τι must be clearly distinguished from the διότι. But most teachers of Morals wilfully confound this difference: probably because the ὅ,τι is so easy, the διότι so exceedingly difficult, to give. They are therefore glad to try to make up for the poverty on the one hand, by the riches on the other, and to bring about a happy marriage between Πενία (poverty) and Πόρος (plenty), by putting them together in **one** proposition.[16] This is generally done by taking the familiar ὅ,τι out of the simple form in which it can be expressed, and forcing it into an artificial formula, from which it is only to be deduced as the conclusion of given premises; and the reader is led by this performance to feel as if he had grasped not only the thing, but its cause as well. We may easily convince ourselves of this by recalling all the most familiar principles of Morals. As, however, in what follows I have no intention of imitating acrobatic tricks of this sort, but purpose proceeding with all honesty and straightforwardness, I cannot make the principle of Ethics equivalent to its basis, but must keep the two quite

---

[13]"*Des Pudels Kern*"; *V.* Goethe's *Faust,* Part I. *Studirzimmer.* Schopenhauer means that his analysis has forced the real meaning out of Kant's language, just as Faust by his exorcism compels Mephistopheles, who was in the form of a poodle, to resume his true form.— (*Translator.*)

[14]ὅ,τι: *i.e.,* the "what" a thing is; its principle, or essence.—(*Translator.*)

[15]διότι: *i.e.,* the "wherefore" of a thing; its *raison d'être,* its underlying cause.—(*Translator.*)

[16]Schopenhauer was doubtless thinking of the famous myth in Plato's *Symposium* Chap. 23 (Teubner's edition, Leipzig, 1875), where Eros is represented as the offspring of Πόρος and Πενία, who on the birthday of Aphrodite were united in the garden of Zeus.— (*Translator.*)

separate. Accordingly, this ὅ,τι—*i.e.,* the principle, the fundamental proposition—as to which in its essence all teachers of Morals are really at one, however much they may clothe it in different costumes, I shall at once express in the form which I take to be the simplest and purest possible, *viz.*: *Neminem laede, immo omnes, quantum potes, juva.* (Do harm to no one; but rather help all people, as far as lies in your power.) This is in truth the proposition which all ethical writers expend their energies in endeavouring to account for. It is the common result of their manifold and widely differing deductions; it is the ὅ,τι for which the διότι is still sought after; the consequence, the cause of which is wanting. Hence it is itself nothing but the *Datum* (the thing given), in relation to which the *Quaesitum* (the thing required) is the problem of every ethical system, as also of the present prize essay. The solution of this riddle will disclose the real foundation of Ethics, which, like the philosopher's stone, has been searched for from time immemorial. That the *Datum*, the ὅ,τι, the principle is most purely expressed by the enunciation I have given, can be seen from the fact that it stands to every other precept of Morals as a conclusion to given premises, and therefore constitutes the real goal it is desired to attain; so that all other ethical commandments can only be regarded as paraphrases, as indirect or disguised statements, of the above simple proposition. This is true, for instance, even of that trite and apparently elementary maxim: *Quod tibi fieri non vis, alteri ne feceris.*[17] (Do not to another what you are unwilling should be done to yourself.) The defect here is that the wording only touches the duties imposed by law, not those required by virtue;—a thing which can be easily remedied by the omission of *non* and *ne*. Thus changed, it really means nothing else than: *Neminem laede, immo omnes, quantum potes, juva.* But as this sense is only reached by a periphrasis, the formula gains the appearance of having also revealed its own ultimate foundation, its διότι; which, however, is not the case, because it does not in the least follow that, if I am unwilling that something be done to myself, I ought not to do it to others. The same is true of every other principle of leading proposition of Ethics that has hitherto been put forward.

If we now return to the above question:—how does the law read, in obeying which, according to Kant, duty consists? and on what is it based?—we shall find that our philosopher, like most others, has in an extremely artificial manner closely connected the principle of Morals with its basis. I again call attention to what I have already examined at the outset—I mean, the Kantian claim that the principle of Ethics must be purely *a priori* and purely formal, indeed an *a priori* synthetical proposition, which consequently may not contain anything material, nor rest

---

[17]Hugo Grotius attributes it to the Emperor Severus.

upon anything empirical, whether objectively in the external world, or subjectively in consciousness, such as any feeling, inclination, impulse, and the like. Kant was perfectly aware of the difficulty of this position; for on p. 60 (R., p. 53) he says: "It will be seen that philosophy has here indeed reached a precarious standpoint, which yet is to be immovable, notwithstanding that it is neither dependent on, nor supported by, anything in heaven or on earth." We shall therefore with all the greater interest and curiosity await the solution of the problem he has set himself, namely, how something is to arise out of nothing, that is, how out of purely *a priori* conceptions, which contain nothing empirical or material, the laws of material human action are to grow up. This is a process which we may find symbolised in chemistry, where out of three invisible gases (Azote, Hydrogen, and Chlorine[18]), and thus in apparently empty space, solid sal-ammoniac is evolved before our eyes.

I will, however, explain, more clearly than Kant either would or could, the method whereby he accomplishes this difficult task. The demonstration is all the more necessary because what he did appears to be seldom properly understood. Almost all Kant's disciples have fallen into the mistake of supposing that he presents his Categorical Imperative directly as a fact of consciousness. But in that case its origin would be anthropological, and, as resting on experience, although internal, it would have an empirical basis: a position which runs directly counter to the Kantian view, and which he repeatedly rejects. Thus on p. 48 (R., p. 44) he says: "It cannot be empirically determined whether any such Categorical Imperative exists everywhere"; and again, on p. 49 (R., p. 45): "The possibility of the Categorical Imperative must be investigated entirely on *a priori* grounds, because here we are not helped by any testimony of experience as to its reality." Even Reinhold, his first pupil, missed this point; for in his *Beiträge zur Uebersicht der Philosophie am Anfange des* 19. *Jahrhunderts,* No. 2, p. 21, we find him saying: "Kant assumes the moral law to be a direct and certain reality, an original fact of the moral consciousness." But if Kant had wished to make the Categorical Imperative a fact of consciousness, and thus give it an empirical foundation, he certainly would not have failed at least to put it forward as such. And this is precisely what he never does. As far as I know, the Categorical Imperative appears for the first time in the *Kritik der Reinen Vernunft* (p. 802 of the first, and p. 830 of the fifth, edition), entirely **ex nunc** (unexpectedly), without any preamble, and merely connected with the preceding sentence by an altogether unjustifiable "therefore." It is only in the *Grundlage zur Metaphysik der Sitten*—a book to which we here devote

---

[18]Azote=Nitrogen. The formula for Ammonium Chloride or Sal-ammoniac is NH_4Cl.— (*Translator*).

especial attention—that it is first introduced expressly and formally, as a deduction from certain concepts. Whereas in Reinhold's *Formula concordiae des Kriticismus*,[19] we actually read on p. 122 the following sentence: "We distinguish moral self-consciousness from the **experience** with which it, as an original fact transcending all knowledge, is bound up in the human consciousness; and we understand by such self-consciousness the **direct consciousness of duty**, that is, of the **necessity** we are under of admitting the legitimacy—whether pleasurable or the reverse—of the will, as the stimulus and as the measure of its own operations."

This would of course be "a charming *thesis,* with a very pretty *hypothesis* to boot."[20] But seriously: into what an outrageous *petitio principii* do we find Kant's moral law here developed! If **that** were true, Ethics would indubitably have a basis of incomparable solidity, and there would be no need of any questions being set for prize essays, to encourage inquiry in this direction. But the greatest marvel would be, that men had been so slow in discovering such a fact of consciousness, considering that for the space of thousands of years a basis for Morals has been sought after with zealous patient toil. How Kant himself is responsible for this deplorable mistake, I shall explain further on; nevertheless, one cannot but wonder at the undisputed predominance of such a radical error among his disciples. Have they never, whilst writing all their numberless books on the Kantian philosophy, noticed the disfigurement which the *Kritik der Reinen Vernunft* underwent in the second edition, and which made it an incoherent, self-contradictory work? It seems that this has only now come to light; and, in my opinion, the fact has been quite correctly analysed in Rosenkranz's preface to the second volume of his complete edition of Kant's works. We must, however, remember that many scholars, being unceasingly occupied as teachers and authors, find very little time left for private and exact research. It is certain that *docendo disco* (I learn by teaching) is not unconditionally true; sometimes indeed one is tempted to parody it by saying: *semper docendo nihil disco* (by always teaching I learn nothing); and even what Diderot puts into the mouth of Rameau's nephew is not altogether without reason: "'And as for these teachers, do you suppose they understand the sciences they give instruction in? Not a bit of it, my dear sir, not a bit of it. If they possessed sufficient knowledge to be able to teach them, they would not do so.' 'Why?' 'Because they would have devoted their lives to the study of them.'"—(Goethe's translation, p. 104.) Lichtenberg too says: "I have rather observed that professional people are often exactly those who do

---

[19]To be found in the fifth number of the *Beiträge zur Uebersicht der Philosophie am Anfange des 19. Jahrhunderts*—a journal of the greatest importance for critical philosophy.
[20]"*Einen erklecklichen* SATZ, *ja, und der auch was* SETZT.*"*—SCHILLER.

not know best." But to return to the Kantian Ethics: most persons, provided only the conclusion reached agrees with their moral feelings, immediately assume that there is no flaw to be found in its derivation; and if the process of deduction looks difficult, they do not trouble themselves much about it, but are content to trust the faculty.

Thus the foundation which Kant gave to his moral law by no means consists in its being proved empirically to be a fact of consciousness; neither does he base it on an appeal to moral feeling, nor yet on a *petitio principii,* under its fine modern name of an "absolute Postulate." It is formed rather of a very subtle process of thought, which he twice advances, on p. 17 and p. 51 (R., p. 22, and p. 46), and which I shall now proceed to make clear.

Kant, be it observed, ridiculed all empirical stimuli of the will, and began by removing everything, whether subjective or objective, on which a law determining the will's action could be empirically based. The consequence is, that he has nothing left for the substance of his law but simply its **Form**. Now this can only be the abstract conception of **lawfulness**. But the conception of lawfulness is built up out of what is valid for all persons equally. Therefore the substance of the law consists of the conception of what is universally valid, and its contents are of course nothing else than its **universal validity**. Hence the formula will read as follows: "Act only in accordance with that precept which you can also wish should be a general law for all rational beings." This, then, is the real foundation—for the most part so greatly misunderstood—which Kant constructed for his principle of Morals, and therefore for his whole ethical system. Compare also the *Kritik der Praktischen Vernunft,* p. 61 (R., p. 147); the end of Note 1.

I pay Kant a tribute of sincere admiration for the great acumen he displayed in carrying out this dexterous feat, but I continue in all seriousness my examination of his position according to the standard of truth. I will only observe—and this point I shall take up again later on—that here **reason**, because, and in so far as, it works out the above explained special ratiocination, receives the name of **practical reason**. Now the Categorical Imperative of Practical Reason is the law which results from this process of thought. Consequently Practical Reason is not in the least what most people, including even Fichte, have regarded it—a special faculty that cannot be traced to its source, a *qualitas occulta,* a sort of moral instinct, like Hutcheson's "moral sense"; but it is (as Kant himself in his preface, p. xii. [R., p. 8], and elsewhere, often enough declares) one and the same with **theoretical reason**—is, in fact, **theoretical reason** itself, in so far as the latter works out the ratiocinative process I have described. It is noticeable that Fichte calls the Categorical Imperative of Kant an **absolute Postulate** (*Grundlage der gesammten Wissenschaftslehre,* Tübingen, 1802, p. 240, Note). This is the modern, more showy, expression for *petitio principii,* and thus we see that he, too, regularly accepted the Categorical Imperative, and consequently must be included among those who have fallen into the mistake above criticised.

The objection, to which this Kantian basis of Morals is at once and directly exposed, lies in the fact that such an origin of a moral law in us is impossible, because of its assumption that man would quite of his own accord hit on the idea of looking about for, and inquiring after, a law to which his will should be subject, and which should shape its actions. This procedure, however, cannot possibly occur to him of itself; at best it could only be after another moral stimulus had supplied the first impulse and motive thereto; and such a stimulus would have to be positively operative, and real; and show itself to be such, as well as spontaneously influence, indeed force its presence upon, the mind. But anything of this sort would run counter to Kant's assumption, which, according to the chain of reasoning above described, is to be regarded as **itself** the origin of all moral conceptions—in fact, the *punctum saliens* of Morality. Consequently, as long as there is no such antecedent incentive (because, *ex hypothesi,* there exists no other moral stimulus but the process of thought already explained), so long Egoism alone must remain as the plumb-line of human conduct, as the guiding thread of the law of motivation; so long the entirely empirical and egoistic motives of the moment, alone and unchecked, must determine, in each separate case, the conduct of a man; since, on this assumption, there is no voice to arrest him, neither does any reason whatever exist, why he should be minded to inquire after, to say nothing of anxiously searching for, a law which should limit and govern his will. And yet it is only possible on this supposition that he should think out the above remarkable piece of mental legerdemain. It matters not how far we may care to put a strict and exact interpretation on this Kantian process, or whether we choose to tone it down to some dim, obscurely felt operation of thought. No modification of it can attack the primary truths that out of nothing, nothing comes, and that an effect requires a cause. The moral stimulus, like every motive that effects the will, must in all cases make itself felt spontaneously, and therefore have a positive working, and consequently be real. And because for men the only thing which has reality is the empirical, or else that which is supposed to have a possibly empirical existence, therefore it follows that the moral stimulus cannot but be empirical, and show itself as such of its own accord; and without waiting for us to begin our search, it must come and press itself upon us, and this with such force that it may, at least possibly, overcome the opposing egoistic motives in all their giant strength. For Ethics has to do with actual human conduct, and not with the *a priori* building of card houses—a performance which yields results that no man would ever turn to in the stern stress and battle of life, and which, in face of the storm of our passions, would be about as serviceable as a syringe in a great fire.

I have already noticed above how Kant considered it a special merit of his moral law that it is founded solely on abstract, pure *a priori* conceptions, consequently on **pure reason**; whereby its validity obtains (he says) not only for men, but for all rational beings as such. All the more must we regret that pure, abstract conceptions *a priori,* without real contents, and without any kind of empirical basis can never move, at any rate, men; of other rational beings I am of course incapable of speaking. The second defect, then, in Kant's ethical basis is its lack of real substance. So far this has escaped notice, because the real nature of his foundation has in all probability been thoroughly understood only by an exceedingly small number of those who were its enthusiastic propagandists. The second fault, I repeat, is entire want of reality, and hence of possible efficacy. The structure floats in the air, like a web of the subtlest conceptions devoid of all contents; it is based on nothing, and can therefore support nothing, and move nothing. And yet Kant loaded it with a burden of enormous weight, namely, the hypothesis of the Freedom of the Will. In spite of his oft declared conviction that freedom in human action has absolutely no place; that theoretically not even its possibility is thinkable (*Kritik der Praktischen Vernunft,* p. 168; R., p. 223); that, if the character of a man, and all the motives which work on him were exactly known, his conduct could be calculated as certainly and as precisely as an eclipse of the moon (*ibidem,* p. 177; R., p. 230): he nevertheless makes an assumption of freedom (although only *idealiter,* and as a postulate) by his celebrated conclusion: "You can, because you ought"; and this on the strength of his precious ethical basis, which, as we see, floats in the air incorporeal. But if it has once been clearly recognised that a thing **is not**, and **cannot be**, what is the use of all the postulates in the world? It would be much more to the purpose to cast away that on which the postulate is based, because it is an impossible supposition; and this course would be justified by the rule *a non posse ad non esse valet consequentia;*[21] and by a *reductio ad absurdum,* which would at the same time be fatal to the Categorical Imperative. Instead of which one false doctrine is built up on the other.

The inadmissibility of a basis for Morals consisting of a few entirely abstract and empty conceptions must have been apparent to Kant himself in secret. For in the *Kritik der Praktischen Vernunft,* where (as I have al-

---

[21]To argue from impossibility to non-existence is valid—*i.e.,* the impossibility of a thing makes its non-existence a safe conclusion.—(*Translator.*)

ready said) he is not so strict and methodical in his work, and where we find him becoming bolder on account of the fame he had gained, it is remarkable how the ethical basis gradually changes its nature, and almost forgets that it is a mere web of abstract ideas; in fact, it seems distinctly desirous of becoming more substantial. Thus, for instance, on p. 81 (R., p. 163) of the above work are the words: "The Moral Law **in some sort a fact of Pure Reason**." What is one to think of this extraordinary expression? In every other place that which is fact is opposed to what is knowable by pure reason. Similarly on p. 83 (R., p. 164) we read of "a Reason which directly determines the Will"; and so on.

Now let us remember that in laying his foundation Kant expressly and repeatedly rejects every anthropological basis, everything that could prove the Categorical Imperative to be a fact of consciousness, because such a proof would be empirical. Nevertheless, his successors were so emboldened by incidental utterances like the above that they went to much greater lengths. Fichte in his work, *System der Sittenlehre*, p. 49, warns us expressly "not to allow ourselves to be misled into trying to explain, and derive from external sources, the consciousness that we have duties, because this would be detrimental to the dignity and absoluteness of the law." A very nice excuse! Again on p. 66 he says: "The principle of Morality is a thought which is based on the **intellectual intuition** of the absolute activity of the intelligence, and which is directly conceived by the pure intelligence of its own accord." What a fine flourish to conceal the helplessness of this clap-trap! Whoever may like to convince himself how Kant's disciples, little by little, totally forgot and ignored the real nature of the foundation and derivation which their master originally gave to the moral law, should read a very interesting essay in Reinhold's *Beiträge zur Uebersicht der Philosophie im Anfange des* 19. *Jahrhunderts,* No. 2, 1801. In it, on pp. 105 and 106, it is maintained "that in the Kantian philosophy Autonomy (which is the same thing as the Categorical Imperative) is a fact of consciousness, and cannot be traced further back, inasmuch as it declares itself by means of a direct consciousness."

But in this case, it would have an anthropological, and consequently empirical, foundation—a position which is diametrically opposed to Kant's explicit and repeated utterances. Again, on p. 108 we find: "Both in the practical philosophy of criticism, and in the whole of the purified or higher transcendental philosophy, Autonomy is that which is founded, and which founds, by itself alone; and which is neither capable of, nor requires, any other foundation; it is that which is absolutely original, true and certain *per se*; the primal truth; the *prius* κατ' ἐξοχήν (*par excellence*); the absolute principle. Whoever, therefore, imagines, requires, or seeks any basis for this Autonomy external to itself, can only be regarded by the Kantian School as wanting in moral consciousness;[22] or else as failing to interpret this consciousness correctly, through the employment of false first principles in his speculations. The School of Fichte and Schelling declares him to be afflicted with a dulness of intellect that renders him incapable of being a philosopher, and forms the characteristic of the unholy *canaille,* and the sluggish brute, or (to use Schelling's more veiled expression) of the "*profanum vulgus* and the *ignavum pecus*." Every one will understand how much truth there can be in a doctrine which it is sought to uphold by such defiant and dogmatic rhetoric. Meanwhile, we must doubtless explain by the respect that this language inspired, the really childish credulity with which Kant's followers accepted the Categorical Imperative, and at once treated it as a matter beyond dispute. The truth is that in this case any objections raised to a theoretical assertion might easily be confounded with moral obliquity; so that every one, although he had no very clear idea in his own mind of the Categorical Imperative, yet preferred to be silent, believing, as he did, in secret, that others were probably better off, and had succeeded in evolving a clearer and more definite mental picture of it. For no one likes to turn his conscience inside out.

Thus in the Kantian School Practical Reason with its Categorical Imperative appears more and more as a hyperphysical fact, as a Delphian temple in the human soul, out of whose dark recesses proceed oracles that infallibly declare not, alas! what **will**, but what **ought** to, happen. This doctrine of Practical Reason, as a direct and immediate fact, once it had been adopted, or rather introduced by artifice combined with defiance, was unhappily later on extended also to Theoretical Reason; and not unnaturally: for Kant himself had often said that both are but one and the same Reason (*e.g.,* Preface, p. xii; R., p. 8). After it had been once admitted that in the domain of the Practical there is a Reason which dictates *ex tripode,*[23] it was an easy step to concede the same privilege to Theoretical Reason also, closely related as the latter is to the former—indeed, consubstantial with it. The one was thus pronounced to be just as immediate as the other, the advantage of this being no less immense than obvious.

Then it was that all philosophasters and fancymongers, with J. H. Jacobi—the denouncer of atheists—at their head, came crowding to this postern which was so unexpectedly opened to them. They wanted to

---

[22]*Dacht' ich's doch! Wissen sie nichts Vernünftiges mehr zu erwidern,*
    Schieben sie's Einem geschwind in das Gewissen hinein.
                        —SCHILLER, *Die Philosophen.*

    Just as I thought! Can they give no more any answer of reason,
      Quickly the ground is changed: Conscience, they say, is at fault.
                        —(*Translator.*)
[23]As from the Pythian tripod: *i.e.,* with official authority, *ex cathedrâ.*

bring their small wares to market, or at least to save what they most val-ued of the old heirlooms which Kant's teaching threatened to pulverise. As in the life of the individual a single youthful mistake often ruins the whole career; so when Kant made that one false assumption of a Practical Reason furnished with credentials exclusively transcendent, and (like the supreme courts of appeal) with powers of decision "without grounds," the result was that out of the austere gravity of the Critical Philosophy was evolved a teaching utterly heterogeneous to it. We hear of a Reason at first only dimly "surmising," then clearly "comprehending" the "Supersensuous," and at last endowed with a perfect "intellectual intu-ition" of it. Every dreamer could now promulgate his mental freaks as the "absolute," *i.e.,* officially issued, deliverances, and revelations of this Reason. Nor need we be surprised if the new privilege was fully taken advantage of.

Here, then, is the origin of that philosophical method which appeared immediately after Kant, and which is made up of clap-trap, of mystifica-tion, of imposture, of deception, and of throwing dust in the eyes. This era will be known one day in the History of Philosophy as "The Period of Dishonesty." For it was signalised by the disappearance of the charac-teristic of honesty, of searching after truth in common with the reader, which was well marked in the writings of all previous philosophers. The philosophaster's object was not to instruct, but to befool his hearers, as every page attests. At first Fichte and Schelling shine as the heroes of this epoch; to be followed by the man who is quite unworthy even of them, and greatly their inferior in point of talent—I mean the stupid and clumsy charlatan Hegel. The Chorus is composed of a mixed company of professors of philosophy, who in solemn fashion discourse to their public about the Endless, the Absolute, and many other matters of which they can know absolutely nothing.

As a stepping-stone to raise Reason to her prophetic throne a wretched *jeu d'esprit* was actually dragged in, and made to serve. It was asserted that, as the word *Vernunft* (Reason) comes from *vernehmen* (to comprehend), therefore *Vernunft* means a capacity to **comprehend** the so-called "Supersensuous," i.e., Νεφελοκοκκυγία,[24] or Cloud-cuckoo-town. This pretty notion met with boundless approval, and for the space of thirty years was constantly repeated in Germany with immense satis-faction; indeed, it was made the foundation of philosophic manuals. And yet it is as clear as noonday that of course *Vernunft* (Reason) comes from *vernehmen* (to comprehend), but only because Reason makes man supe-rior to animals, so that he not only hears, but also **comprehends** (*ver-nimmt*)—by no means, what is going on in Cloud-cuckoo-town—but

---

[24] *V.* Aristoph., *Aves,* 819 *et alibi.*—(*Translator.*)

what is said, as by one reasonable person to another, the words spoken being **comprehended** (*vernommen*) by the listener; and this capacity is called **Reason** (*Vernunft*).

Such is the interpretation that all peoples, ages, and languages have put on the word Reason. It has always been understood to mean the possession of general, abstract, non-intuitive ideas, named **concepts**, which are denoted and fixed by means of words. This faculty alone it is which in reality gives to men their advantage over animals. For these abstract ideas, or concepts, that is, mental impressions formed of the sum of many separate things, are the condition of **language** and through it of actual **thought**; through which again they determine the consciousness not only of the present (which animals also have), but of the past and the future as such; whence it results that they are the *modulus,* so to say, of clear recollection, of circumspection, of foresight, and of intention; the constant factor in the evolution of systematic co-operation, of the state, of trades, arts, sciences, religions, and philosophies, in short, of everything that so sharply distinguishes human from animal life. Beasts have only **intuitive** ideas, and therefore also only intuitive motives; consequently the dependence of their volition on motives is manifest. With man this dependence is no less a fact; he, too (with due allowance for individual character), is affected by motives under the strictest law of necessity. Only these are for the most part not **intuitive** but **abstract** ideas, that is, conceptions, or thoughts, which nevertheless are the result of previous intuitions hence of external influences. This, however, gives him a **relative** freedom—relative, that is, as compared with an animal. For his action is not determined (as it is in all other creatures) by the surroundings of the moment as intuitively perceived, but by the thoughts he has derived from experience, or gained by instruction. Consequently the motive, by which he, too, is necessarily swayed, is not always at once obvious to the looker-on simultaneously with the act; it lies concealed in the brain. It is this that lends to all his movements, as well as to his conduct and work as a whole, a character manifestly different from that observable in the habits of beasts. He seems as though guided by finer, invisible threads; whence all his acts bear the stamp of deliberation and premeditation, thus gaining an appearance of independence, which sufficiently distinguishes them from those of animals. All these great differences, however, spring solely out of the capacity for **abstract ideas, concepts**. This capacity is therefore the essential part of **Reason**, that is, of the faculty peculiar to man, and it is called τὸ λόγιμον,[25] τὸ λογιστικόν, **ratio, la ragione, il discorso, raison, reason, discourse of reason**. If I were asked what the distinction is

---

[25]λόγιμος means "remarkable," being never used in the sense of "rational." Τὸ λογικὸν is perhaps a possible expression; the right word is λόγος.—(*Translator.*)

between it and **Verstand, νοῦς, intellectus, entendement, understanding**; I should reply thus: The latter is that capacity for knowledge which animals also possess in varying degrees, and which is seen in us at its highest development; in other words, it is the direct consciousness of the law of **Causality**—a consciousness which precedes all experience, being constituted by the very form of the understanding, whose essential nature is, in fact, therein contained. On it depends in the first place the intuitive perception of the external world; for the senses by themselves are only capable of **impression**, a thing which is very far from being **intuitive perception**; indeed, the former is nothing but the material of the latter: νοῦς ὁρᾷ καὶ νοῦς ἀκούει, τ'ἄλλα κωφὰ καὶ τυφλά. (The mind sees, the mind hears; everything else is deaf and blind.) **Intuitive perception** is the result of our directly referring the impressions of the sense-organs to their cause, which, exactly because of this act of the intelligence, presents itself as an **external object** under the mode of intuition proper to us, *i.e.,* in **space**. This is a proof that the Law of Causality is known to us *a priori,* and does not arise from experience, since experience itself, inasmuch as it presupposes intuitive perception, is only possible through the same law. All the higher qualities of the intellect, all cleverness, sagacity, penetration, acumen are directly proportional to the exactness and fulness with which the workings of Causality in all its relations are grasped; for all knowledge of the **connection** of things, in the widest sense of the word, is based on the comprehension of this law, and the clearness and accuracy with which it is understood is the measure of one man's superiority to another in **understanding**, shrewdness, cunning. On the other hand, the epithet **reasonable** has at all times been applied to the man who does not allow himself to be guided by **intuitive** impressions, but by **thoughts** and **conceptions**, and who therefore always sets to work logically after due reflection and forethought. Conduct of this sort is everywhere known as **reasonable**. Not that this by any means implies uprightness and love for one's fellows. On the contrary, it is quite possible to act in the most reasonable way, that is, according to conclusions scientifically deduced, and weighed with the nicest exactitude; and yet to follow the most selfish, unjust, and even iniquitous maxims. So that never before Kant did it occur to any one to identify just, virtuous, and noble conduct with **reasonable**; the two lines of behaviour have always been completely separated, and kept apart. The one depends on the **kind of motivation**; the other on the difference in fundamental principles. Only after Kant (because he taught that virtue has its source in Pure Reason) did the virtuous and the reasonable become one and the same thing, despite the usage of these words which all languages have adopted—a usage which is not fortuitous, but the work of universal, and therefore uniform, human judgment. "Reasonable" and "vicious" are terms that go very well together; indeed great, far-reaching crimes are only possible from their union. Similarly, "unreasonable" and "noble-minded" are often found associated; *e.g.,* if I give to-day to the needy man what I shall myself require to-morrow more urgently than he; or, if I am so far affected as to hand over to one in distress the sum which my creditor is waiting for; and such cases could be multiplied indefinitely.

We have seen that this exaltation of Reason to be the source of all virtue rests on two assertions. First, as **Practical Reason**, it is said to issue, like an oracle, peremptory Imperatives purely *a priori*. Secondly, taken in connection with the false explanation of **Theoretical Reason**, as given in the *Kritik der Reinen Vernunft,* it is presented as a certain faculty essentially concerned with the **Unconditioned**, as manifested in three alleged Ideas[26] (the impossibility of which the intellect at the same time recognises *a priori*). And we found that this position, as an *exemplar vitiis imitabile,*[27] led our muddy-headed philosophers, Jacobi at their head, from bad to worse. They talked of **Reason** (*Vernunft*) as directly comprehending (*vernehmend*) the "**Supersensuous**," and absurdly declared that it is a certain mental property which has to do essentially with things transcending all experience, *i.e.,* with metaphysics; and that it perceives directly and intuitively the ultimate causes of all things, and of all Being, the Supersensuous, the Absolute, the Divine, etc. Now, had it been wished to use Reason, instead of deifying it, such assertions as these must long ago have been met by the simple remark that, if man, by virtue of a special organ, furnished by his Reason, for solving the riddle of the world, possessed an innate metaphysics that only required development; in that case there would have to be just as complete agreement on metaphysical matters as on the truths of arithmetic and geometry; and this would make it totally impossible that there should exist on the earth a large number of radically different religions, and a still larger number of radically different systems of philosophy. Indeed, we may rather suppose that, if any one were found to differ from the rest in his religious or philosophical views, he would be at once regarded as a subject for mental pathology. Nor would the following plain reflection have failed to present itself. If we discovered a species of apes which intentionally prepared instruments for fighting, or building, or for any other purpose; we should immediately admit that it was endowed with Reason. On the other hand, if we meet with savages destitute of all metaphysics, or of all religion (and there are such); it does not occur to us to deny them Reason on that account. The Reason that **proves** its pretended super-

[26]The three Ideas are: (1) The Psychological; (2) The Cosmological; (3) The Theological. *V.* The Paralogisms of Pure Reasons, in the Dialectics: *Kritik der Reinen Vernunft,* Part I.—(*Translator.*)

[27]An example easy to be imitated in its faults. *V.* Horace, *Ep.* Lib. I., xix. 17.—(*Translator.*)

sensuous knowledge was duly brought back to bounds by Kant's critique; but Jacobi's wonderful Reason, that directly **comprehends** the supersensuous, he must indeed have thought **beneath** all criticism. Meanwhile, a certain imperious and oracular Reason of the same kind is still, at the Universities, fastened on the shoulders of our innocent youth.

NOTE

If we wish to reach the real origin of this hypothesis of Practical Reason, we must trace its descent a little further back. We shall find that it is derived from a doctrine, which Kant totally confuted, but which nevertheless, in this connection, lies secretly (indeed he himself is not aware of it) at the root of his assumption of a Practical Reason with its Imperatives and its Autonomy—a reminiscence of a former mode of thought. I mean the so-called Rational Psychology, according to which man is composed of two entirely heterogeneous substances—the material body, and the immaterial soul. Plato was the first to formulate this dogma, and he endeavoured to prove it as an objective truth. But it was Descartes who, by working it out with scientific exactness, perfectly developed and completed it. And this is just what brought its fallacy to light, as demonstrated by Spinoza, Locke, and Kant successively. It was demonstrated by Spinoza; because his philosophy consists chiefly in the refutation of his master's twofold dualism, and because he entirely and expressly denied the two Substances of Descartes, and took as his main principle the following proposition: "*Substantia cogitans et substantia extensa una eademque est substantia, quae jam sub hoc, jam sub illo attributo comprehenditur.*"[28] It was demonstrated by Locke; for he combated the theory of innate ideas, derived all knowledge from the sensuous, and taught that it is not impossible that Matter should think. And lastly, it was demonstrated by Kant, in his *Kritik der Rationalen Psychologie,* as given in the first edition. Leibnitz and Wolf were the champions on the bad side; and this brought Leibnitz the undeserved honour of being compared to the great Plato, who was really so unlike him.

But to enter into details here would be out of place. According to this Rational Psychology, the soul was originally and in its essence a **perceiving** substance, and only as a consequence thereof did it become possessed of volition. According as it carried on these two modes of its activity, Perception and Volition, conjoined with the body, or incorporeal, and entirely *per se,* so it was endowed with a lower or higher faculty of perception, and of volition in like kind. In its higher faculty the immaterial soul was active solely by itself, and without co-operation of the

---

[28]The thinking substance, and substance in extension are one and the self-same substance, which is contained now under the latter attribute (*i.e.,* extension), now under the former (*i.e.,* the attribute of thinking).—*Ethica,* Part II., Prop. 7. Corollary.

body. In this case it was *intellectus purus,* being composed of concepts, belonging exclusively to itself, and of the corresponding acts of will, both
of which were absolutely spiritual, and had nothing sensuous about
them—the sensuous being derived from the body.[29] So that it perceived
nothing else but pure Abstracts, Universals, innate conceptions, *aeternae
veritates,* etc.; wherefore also its volition was entirely controlled by purely
spiritual ideas like these. On the other hand, the soul's **lower** faculty of
Perception and Volition was the result of its working in concert and
close union with the various organs of the body, whereby a prejudicial
effect was produced on its unmixed spiritual activity. Here, *i.e.,* to this
lower faculty, was supposed to belong every **intuitive** perception, which
consequently would have to be obscure and confused, while the **abstract**, formed by separating from objects their qualities, would be clear!
The will, which was determined by perceptions thus sensuously conditioned, formed the lower Volition, and it was for the most part bad; for
its acts were guided by the impulse of the senses; while the other will (the
higher) was untrammelled, was guided by Pure Reason, and appertained
only to the immaterial soul. This doctrine of the Cartesians has been best
expounded by De la Forge, in his *Tractatus de Mente Humana,* where in
chap. 23 we read:[30] *Non nisi eadem voluntas est, quae appellatur appetitus sen-
sitivus, quando excitatur per judicia, quae formantur consequenter ad perceptiones
sensuum; et quae appetitus rationalis nominatur, cum mens judicia format de pro-
priis suis ideis, independenter a cogitationibus sensuum confusis, quae inclina-
tionum ejus sunt causae. . . . Id, quod occasionem dedit, ut duae istae diversae
voluntatis propensiones pro duobus diversis appetitibus sumerentur, est, quod
saepissime unus alteri opponatur, quia propositum, quod mens superaedificat pro-
priis suis perceptionibus, non semper consentit cum cogitationibus, quae menti a
corporis dispositione suggeruntur, per quam saepe obligatur ad aliquid volendum,
dum ratio ejus eam aliud optare facit.*

   Out of the dim reminiscence of such views there finally arose Kant's
doctrine of the Autonomy of the Will, which, as the mouthpiece of

---

[29]*Intellectio pura est intellectio, quae circa nullas imagines corporeas versatur.* (Pure intelligence is
   intelligence that has nothing to do with any bodily forms.)—Cart., *Medit.,* p. 188.

[30]It is nothing but one and the same will, which at one time is called sensuous desire, when
   it is stimulated by acts of judgment, formed in consequence of perceptions of the senses;
   and which at another time is called rational desire (*i.e.* desire of the reason), when the
   mind forms acts of judgment about its own proper ideas, independently of the thoughts
   belonging to, and mixed up with, the senses; which thoughts are the causes of the mind's
   tendencies. . . . That these two diverse propensities of the will should be regarded as two
   distinct desires is occasioned by the fact that very often the one is opposed to the other,
   because the intention, which is built up by the mind on the foundation of its own proper
   perceptions, does not always agree with the thoughts which are suggested to the mind
   by the body's disposition; whereby it (the mind) is often constrained to will something,
   while its reason makes it choose something different.—(*Translator.*)

Pure, Practical Reason, lays down the law for all rational beings as such, and recognises nothing but **formal** motives, as opposed to **material**; the latter determining only the lower faculty of desires, to which the higher is hostile. For the rest, this whole theory, which was not really systematically set forth till the time of Descartes, is nevertheless to be found as far back as Aristotle. In his *De Anima* I. 1, it is sufficiently clearly stated; while Plato in the *Phaedo* (pp. 188 and 189, edit. Bipont.) had already paved the way, with no uncertain hints. After being elaborated to great perfection by the Cartesian doctrine, we find it a hundred years later waxed bold and strong, and occupying the foremost place; but precisely for this reason forced to reveal its true nature. An excellent *résumé* of the view which then prevailed is presented in Muratori's *Della Forza della Fantasia,* chaps. 1–4 and 13. In this work the imagination is regarded as a purely material, corporeal organ of the brain (the lower faculty of perception), its function being to intuitively apprehend the external world on the data of the senses; and nought remains for the immaterial soul but thinking, reflecting, and determining. It must have been felt how obviously this position involves the whole subject in doubt. For if Matter is capable of the intuitive apprehension of the world in all its complexity, it is inconceivable that it should not also be capable of abstracting this intuition; wherefrom everything else would follow. Abstraction is of course nothing else than an elimination of the qualities attaching to things which are not necessary for general purposes, in other words, the individual and special differences. For instance, if I disregard, or abstract, that which is peculiar to the sheep, ox, stag, camel, etc., I reach the conception of ruminants. By this operation the ideas lose their intuitiveness, and as merely abstract, non-intuitive notions or concepts, they require words to fix them in the consciousness, and allow of their being adequately handled. All this shows that Kant was still under the influence of the after-effect of that old-time doctrine, when he propounded his Practical Reason with its Imperatives.

Chapter V.—On the Leading Principle of the Kantian Ethics

AFTER having tested in the preceding chapter the actual basis of Kant's Ethics, I now turn to that which rests on it—his **leading principle** of Morals. The latter is very closely connected with the former; indeed, in a certain sense, they both grew up together. We have seen that the formula expressing the principle reads as follows: "Act only in accordance with that precept which you can also wish should be a general law for all rational beings." It is a strange proceeding for a man, who *ex hypothesi* is seeking a law to determine what he should do, and what he should leave undone, to be instructed first to search for one fit to regulate the conduct of all possible rational beings; but we will pass over that. It is sufficient only to notice the fact that in the above guiding rule, as put forth by Kant, we have obviously not reached the moral law itself, but only a fingerpost, or indication where it is to be looked for. The money, so to say, is not yet paid down, but we hold a safe draft for it. And who, then, is the cashier? To say the truth at once: a paymaster in this connection surely very unexpected, being neither more nor less than **Egoism**, as I shall now demonstrate.

The precept, it is said, which **I can wish** were the guide of all men's conduct, is itself the real moral principle. That which **I can wish** is the hinge on which the given direction turns. But what **can** I truly wish, and what not? Clearly, in order to determine what I can wish in the matter under discussion, I require yet another criterion; for without such I could never find the key to the instruction which comes to me like a sealed order. Where, then, is this criterion to be discovered? Certainly nowhere else but in my Egoism, which is the nearest, ever ready, original, and living standard of all volition, and which has at any rate the _jus primi occupantis_ before every moral principle. The direction for finding the real moral law, which is contained in the Kantian rule, rests, as a matter of fact, on the tacit assumption that I can only wish for **that** which is most to my advantage. Now because, in framing a precept to be generally followed, I cannot regard myself as always active, but must contemplate my playing a **passive** part _eventualiter_ and at times; therefore from this point of view my **egoism** decides for justice and loving-kindness; not from any wish to **practise** these virtues, but because it desires to **experience** them. We are reminded of the miser, who, after listening to a sermon on beneficence, exclaims:

> "Wie gründlich ausgeführt, wie schön!—
> Fast möcht' ich betteln gehn."
> (How well thought out, how excellent!—
> Almost I'd like to beg.)

This is the indispensable key to the direction in which Kant's leading principle of Ethics is embedded; nor can he help supplying it himself. Only he refrains from doing so at the moment of propounding his precept, lest we should feel shocked. It is found further on in the text, at a decent distance, so as to prevent the fact at once leaping to light, that here, after all, in spite of his grand _a priori_ edifice, **Egoism** is sitting on the judge's seat, scales in hand. Moreover, it does not occur, till after he has decided, from the point of view of the _eventualiter_ passive side, that this position holds good for the active _rôle_ as well. Thus, on p. 19 (R., p. 24) we read: "That I could not **wish** for a general law to establish lying, because people would no longer believe me, or else pay me back in the **same coin**." Again on p. 55 (R., p. 49): "The universality of a law to the effect that every one could promise what he likes, without any intention of keeping his word, would make the promise itself, together with the object in view, whatever that might be, impossible; for **no one** would **believe** it." On p. 56 (R., p. 50), in connection with the maxim of **hardheartedness**, we find the following: "A will, which should determine this, would contradict itself; for cases can occur, in which a man needs the love and sympathy of others, and in which he, by virtue of such a natural law, evolved from his own will, would deprive himself of all hope of the help, which he desires." Similarly in the *Kritik der Praktischen Vernunft* (Part I., vol. i., chap. 2, p. 123; R., p. 192): "If every one were to regard others' distress with total indifference, and you were to belong to such an order of things; would you be there with the concurrence of your will?" *Quam temere in nosmet legem sancimus iniquam!*[31] one could reply. These passages sufficiently show in what sense the phrase, "to be able to wish," in Kant's formula is to be understood. But it is in the *Metaphysische Anfangsgründe der Tugendlehre*, that this real nature of his ethical principle is most clearly stated. In §30 we read: "For every one wishes to be helped. If, however, a man were to give utterance to his rule of unwillingness to help others, all people would be justified in refusing him assistance. Thus this rule of selfishness contradicts itself." **Would be justified**, he says, **would be justified**! Here, then, it is declared, as explicitly as anything can be, that moral obligation rests solely and entirely on presupposed **reciprocity**; consequently it is utterly selfish, and only admits of being interpreted by egoism, which, under the condition of **reciprocity**, knows how to make a compromise cleverly enough. Such a course would be quite in place if it were a question of laying down the fundamentals of state-organisation, but not, when we come to construct those of ethics. In the *Grundlegung*, p. 81 (R., p. 67), the following sentence occurs: "The principle of always acting in accordance with that precept which you can also wish were universally established as law—this is the only condition under which a man's will can never be in antagonism with itself." From what has been said above, it will be apparent that the true meaning of the word "antagonism" may be thus explained: if a man should sanction the precept of injustice and hard-heartedness, he would subsequently, in the event of his playing a **passive** part, recall it, and so his will would **contradict** itself.

From this analysis it is abundantly clear that Kant's famous leading principle is not—as he maintains with tireless repetition—a **categorical**,

---

[31]How rashly do we sanction an unjust law, which will come home to ourselves!—(Hor., *Sat.*, Lib. I., iii. 67.)

but in reality a **hypothetical** Imperative; because it tacitly presupposes the **condition** that the law to be established for what I do—inasmuch as I make it universal—shall also be a law for what is done to me; and because I, under this condition, as the *eventualiter* non-active party, **cannot** possibly **wish** for injustice and hard-heartedness. But if I strike out this proviso, and, trusting perhaps to my surpassing strength of mind and body, think of myself as always **active**, and never **passive**; then, in choosing the precept which is to be universally valid, if there exists no basis for ethics other than Kant's, I can perfectly well wish that injustice and hard-heartedness should be the general rule, and consequently order the world

> Upon the simple plan,
> That they should take, who have the power,
> And they should keep, who can.
> —(WORDSWORTH.)

In the foregoing chapter we showed that the Kantian leading principle of Ethics is devoid of all real foundation. It is now clear that to this singular defect must be added, notwithstanding Kant's express assertion to the contrary, its concealed **hypothetical** nature, whereby its basis turns out to be nothing else than Egoism, the latter being the secret interpreter of the direction which it contains. Furthermore, regarding it solely as a formula, we find that it is only a periphrasis, an obscure and disguised mode of expressing the well-known rule: *Quod tibi fieri non vis, alteri ne feceris* (do not to another what you are unwilling should be done to yourself); if, that is, by omitting the *non* and *ne,* we remove the limitation, and include the duties taught by love as well as those prescribed by law. For it is obvious that this is the only precept which I can wish should regulate the conduct of all men (speaking, of course, from the point of view of the possibly **passive** part I may play, where my **Egoism** is touched). This rule, *Quod tibi fieri, etc.,* is, however, in its turn, merely a circumlocution for, or, if it be preferred, a premise of, the proposition which I have laid down as the simplest and purest definition of the conduct required by the common consent of all ethical systems; namely, *Neminem laede, immo omnes, quantum potes, juva* (do harm to no one; but rather help all people, as far as lies in your power). The true and real substance of Morals is this, and never can be anything else. But on what is it based? What is it that lends force to this command? This is the old and difficult problem with which man is still to-day confronted. For, on the other side, we hear Egoism crying with a loud voice: *Neminem juva, immo omnes, si forte conducit, laede* (help nobody, but rather injure all people, if it brings you any advantage); nay more, Malice gives us the variant: *Immo omnes, quantum potes, laede* (but rather injure all people as far as you can). To bring into the lists a combatant equal, or rather superior to Egoism and Malice combined—this is the task of all Ethics. *Heic Rhodus, heic salta!*[32]

The division of human duty into two classes has long been recognised, and no doubt owes its origin to the nature of morality itself. We have (1) the duties ordained by law (otherwise called the perfect, obligatory, narrower duties), and (2) those prescribed by virtue (otherwise called imperfect, wider, meritorious, or, preferably, the duties taught by love). On p. 57 (R., p. 60) we find Kant desiring to give a further confirmation to the moral principle, which he propounded, by undertaking to derive this classification from it. But the attempt turns out to be so forced, and so obviously bad, that it only testifies in the strongest way against the soundness of his position. For, according to him, the duties laid down by statutes rest on a precept, the contrary of which, taken as a general natural law, is declared to be quite **unthinkable** without contradiction; while the duties inculcated by virtue are made to depend on a maxim, the opposite of which can (he says) be conceived as a general natural law, but cannot possibly be wished for. I beg the reader to reflect that the rule of injustice, the reign of might instead of right, which in the Kantian view is not even thinkable as a natural law, is in reality, and in point of fact, the dominant order of things not only in the animal kingdom, but among men as well. It is true that an attempt has been made among civilised peoples to obviate its injurious effects by means of all the machinery of state government; but as soon as this, wherever, or of whatever kind, it be, is suspended or eluded, the natural law immediately resumes its sway. Indeed between nation and nation it never ceases to prevail; the customary jargon about justice is well known to be nothing but diplomacy's official style; the real arbiter is brute force. On the other hand, genuine, *i.e.,* voluntary, acts of justice, do occur beyond all doubt, but always only as exceptions to the rule. Furthermore: wishing to give instances by way of introducing the above-mentioned classification, Kant establishes the duties prescribed by law first (p. 53; R., p. 48) through the so-called duty towards oneself,—the duty of not ending one's life voluntarily, if the pain outweigh the pleasure. Accordingly, the rule of suicide is held to be not even **thinkable** as a general natural law. I, on the

---

[32]"Here is Rhodes, here make your leap!" *I.e.,* "Here is the place of trial, here let us see what you can do!" This Latin proverb is derived from one of Æsop's fables. A braggart boasts of having once accomplished a wonderful jump in Rhodes, and appeals to the evidence of the eye-witnesses. The bystanders then exclaim: "Friend, if this be true, you have no need of witnesses; for this is Rhodes, and your leap you can make here." The words are: ἀλλ᾽, ὦ φίλε, εἰ τοῦτο ἀληθές ἐστιν, οὐδὲν δεῖ σοι μαρτύρων· αὕτη γὰρ ῾Ρόδος καὶ πήδημα. *V. Fabulae Aesopicae Collectae.* Edit. Halm, Leipzig: Teubner. 1875. Nr. 203*b*, p. 102. The other version of the fable (Nr. 203, p. 101) gives: ὦ οὗτος, εἰ ἀληθές τοῦτ᾽ ἐστιν, οὐδὲν δεῖ σοι μαρτύρων· ἰδοὺ ἡ ῾Ρόδος, ἰδοὺ καὶ τὸ πήδημα.—(*Translator.*)

contrary, maintain that, since here there can be no intervention of state control, it is exactly this rule which is proved to be an actually existing, unchecked natural law. For it is absolutely certain (as daily experience attests) that men in the vast majority of cases turn to self-destruction directly the gigantic strength of the innate instinct of self-preservation is distinctly overpowered by great suffering. To suppose that there is any thought whatever that can have a deferring effect, after the fear of death, which is so strong and so closely bound up with the nature of every living thing, has shown itself powerless; in other words, to suppose that there is a thought still mightier than this fear—is a daring assumption, all the more so, when we see, that it is one which is so difficult to discover that the moralists are not yet able to determine it with precision. In any case, it is certain that arguments against suicide of the sort put forward by Kant in this connection (p. 53; R., p. 48, and p. 67; R., p. 57) have never hitherto restrained any one tired of life even for a moment. Thus a natural law, which incontestably exists, and is operative every day, is declared by Kant to be simply **unthinkable** without contradiction, and all for the sake of making his Moral Principle the basis of the classification of duties! At this point it is, I confess, not without satisfaction that I look forward to the groundwork which I shall give to Ethics in the sequel. From it the division of Duty into what is prescribed by law, and what is taught by love, or, better, into justice and loving-kindness, results quite naturally though a principle of separation which arises from the nature of the subject, and which entirely of itself draws a sharp line of demarcation; so that the foundation of Morals, which I shall present, has in fact ready to hand that confirmation, to which Kant, with a view to support his own position, lays a completely groundless claim.

Chapter VI.—On the Derived Forms of the Leading Principle of the Kantian Ethics

IT is well known that Kant put the leading principle of his Ethics into another quite different shape, in which it is expressed directly; the first being indirect, indeed nothing more than an indication as to how the principle is to be sought for. Beginning at p. 63 (R., p. 55), he prepares the way for his second formula by means of very strange, ambiguous, not to say distorted,[33] definitions of the conceptions **End** and **Means**, which may be much more simply and correctly denoted thus: an **End** is the direct motive of an act of the Will, a **Means** the indirect: *simplex sigillum veri* (sim-

---

[33]To keep the play of words in "*geschrobene,*" "*verschrobene,*" we may perhaps render them: "twisted" . . . "mistwisted."—(*Translator.*)

plicity is the seal of truth). Kant, however, slips through his wonderful enunciations to the statement: "Man, indeed every rational being, exists **as an end in himself**." On this I must remark that "to exist **as an end in oneself**" is an unthinkable expression, a *contradictio in adjecto*.[34] To be an end means to be an object of volition. Every end can only exist in relation to a will, whose end, *i.e.,* (as above stated), whose direct motive it is. Only thus can the idea, "**end**" have any sense, which is lost as soon as such connection is broken. But this relation, which is essential to the thing, necessarily excludes every "in itself." "End in oneself" is exactly like saying: "Friend in oneself;—enemy in oneself;—uncle in oneself;—north or east in itself;—above or below in itself"; and so on. At bottom the "end in itself" is in the same case as the "absolute ought"; the same thought—the theological—secretly, indeed, unconsciously lies at the root of each as its condition. Nor is the "absolute worth," which is supposed to be attached to this alleged, though unthinkable, "end in itself," at all better circumstanced. It also must be characterised, without pity, as a *contradictio in adjecto*. Every "worth" is a valuation by comparison, and its bearing is necessarily twofold. First, it is **relative**, since it exists for some one; and secondly, it is **comparative**, as being compared with something else, and estimated accordingly. Severed from these two conditions, the conception, "worth," loses all sense and meaning, and so obviously, that further demonstration is needless. But more: just as the phrases "end in itself" and "absolute worth" outrage logic, so true morality is outraged by the statement on p. 65 (R., p. 56), that irrational beings (that is, animals) are **things**, and should therefore be treated simply as **means**, which are not at the same time **ends**. In harmony with this, it is expressly declared in the *Metaphysische Anfangsgründe der Tugendlehre,* §16: "A man can have no duties towards any being, except towards his fellowmen"; and then, §17, we read: "To treat animals cruelly runs counter to the duty of man **towards himself**; because it deadens the feeling of sympathy for them in their sufferings, and thus weakens a natural tendency which is very serviceable to morality in relation to **other men**." So one is only to have compassion on animals for the sake of practice, and they are as it were the pathological phantom on which to train one's sympathy with men! In common with the whole of Asia that is not tainted by Islâm (which is tantamount to Judaism), I regard such tenets as odious and revolting. Here, once again, we see withal how entirely this philosophical morality, which is, as explained above, only a theological one in disguise, depends in reality on the biblical Ethics. Thus, because Christian morals leave animals out of consideration (of which more later on); therefore in philosophical morals they

---

[34]A contradiction in that which is added. A term applied to two ideas which cannot be brought into a thinkable relationship.—(*Translator.*)

are of course at once outlawed; they are merely "things," simply **means** to ends of any sort; and so they are good for vivisection, for deer-stalking, bull-fights, horse-races, etc., and they may be whipped to death as they struggle along with heavy quarry carts. Shame on such a morality which is worthy of Pariahs, Chaṇḍālas and Mlechchas[35]; which fails to recognise the Eternal Reality immanent in everything that has life, and shining forth with inscrutable significance from all eyes that see the sun! This is a morality which knows and values only the precious species that gave it birth; whose characteristic—**reason**—it makes the condition under which a being may be an object of moral regard.

By this rough path, then,—indeed, *per fas et nefas* (by fair means and by foul), Kant reaches the second form in which he expresses the fundamental principle of his Ethics: "Act in such a way that you at all times treat mankind, as much in your own person, as in the person of every one else, not only as a Means, but also as an End." Such a statement is a very artificial and roundabout way of saying: "Do not consider yourself alone, but others also"; this in turn is a paraphrase for: *Quod tibi fieri non vis, alteri ne feceris* (do not to another what you are unwilling should be done to yourself); and the latter, as I have said, contains nothing but the premises to the conclusion, which is the true and final goal of all morals and of all moralising; *Neminem laede, immo omnes, quantum potes juva* (do harm to no one; but rather help all people as far as lies in your power). Like all beautiful things, this proposition looks best unveiled. Be it only observed that the alleged duties towards oneself are dragged into this second Kantian edict intentionally and not without difficulty. Some place of course had to be found for them.[36]

Another objection that could be raised against the formula is that the malefactor condemned to be executed is treated merely as an instrument, and not as an end, and this with perfectly good reason; for he is the indispensable means of upholding the terror of the law by its fulfilment, and of thus accomplishing the law's end—the repression of crime.

But if this second definition helps nothing towards laying a foundation for Ethics, if it cannot even pass muster as its leading principle, that is, as an adequate and direct summary of ethical precepts; it has nevertheless the merit of containing a fine *aperçu* of moral psychology, for it marks **egoism** by an exceedingly characteristic token, which is quite worth while being here more closely considered. This **egoism**, then, of which

---

[35]A Chaṇḍāla (or Ćaṇḍāla) means one who is born of a Brahman woman by a Śūdra husband, such a union being an abomination. Hence it is a term applied to a low common person. Mlechcha (or Mleććha) means a foreigner; one who does not speak Sanskrit, and is not subject to Hindu institutions. The transition from "a barbarian" to a bad or wicked man, is easy.—(*Translator.*)

[36]These so-called duties have been discussed in Chapter III. of this Part.

each of us is full, and to conceal which, as our *partie honteuse,* we have invented **politeness**, is perpetually peering through every veil cast over it, and may especially be detected in the fact that our dealings with all those, who come across our path, are directed by the one object of trying to find, before everything else, and as if by instinct, a possible **means** to any of the numerous **ends** with which we are always engrossed. When we make a new acquaintance, our first thought, as a rule, is whether the man can be useful to us in some way. If he can do **nothing** for our benefit, then as soon as we are convinced of this, he himself generally becomes **nothing** to us. To seek in all other people a possible means to our ends, in other words, to make them our instruments, is almost part of the very nature of human eyes; and whether the instrument will have to suffer more or less in the using, is a thought which comes much later, sometimes not at all. That we assume others to be similarly disposed is shown in many ways; *e.g.,* by the fact that, when we ask any one for information or advice, we lose all confidence in his words directly we discover that he may have some **interest** in the matter, however small or remote. For then we immediately take for granted that he will make us a means to his ends, and hence give his advice not in accordance with his **discernment**, but with his **desire**, and this, no matter how exact the former may be, or how little the latter seem involved; since we know only too well that a cubic inch of desire weighs much more than a cubic yard of discernment. Conversely, when we ask in such cases: "What ought I to do?" as a rule, nothing else will occur to our counsellor, but how we should shape our action to suit his own ends; and to this effect he will give his reply immediately, and as it were mechanically, without so much as bestowing a thought on **our** ends; because it is his Will that directly dictates the answer, or ever the question can come before the bar of his real judgment. Hence he tries to mould our conduct to his own benefit, without even being conscious of it, and while he supposes that he is speaking out of the abundance of his discernment, in reality he is nothing but the mouth-piece of his own desire; indeed, such self-deception may lead him so far as to utter lies, without being aware of it. So greatly does the influence of the Will preponderate that of the Intelligence. Consequently, it is not the testimony of our own consciousness, but rather, for the most part, that of our interest, which avails to determine whether our language be in accordance with what we discern, or what we desire. To take another case. Let us suppose that a man pursued by enemies and in danger of life, meets a pedlar and inquires for some by-way of escape; it may happen that the latter will answer him by the question: "Do you need any of my wares?" It is not of course meant that matters are **always** like this. On the contrary, many a man is found to show a direct and real participation in another's weal and woe, or (in

Kant's language) to regard him as an end and not as a means. How far it seems natural, or the reverse, to each one to treat his neighbour for once in the way as an end, instead of (as usual) a means,—this is the criterion of the great ethical difference existing between character and character; and that on which the mental attitude of sympathy rests in the last resort will be the true basis of Ethics, and will form the subject of the third part of this Essay.

Thus, in his second formula, Kant distinguishes Egoism and its opposite by a very characteristic trait; and this point of merit I have all the more gladly brought out into strong light and illustrated, because in other respects there is little in the groundwork of his Ethics that I can admit.

The third and last form in which Kant put forward his Moral Principle is the **Autonomy** of the Will: "The Will of every rational being is universally legislative for all rational beings." This of course follows from the first form. As a consequence of the third, however, we are asked to believe (see p. 71; R., p. 60) that the specific characteristic of the Categorical Imperative lies in the **renunciation of all interest** by the Will when acting from a sense of duty. All previous moral principles had thus (he says) broken down, "because the latter invariably attributed to human actions at bottom a certain **interest**, whether originating in compulsion, or in pleasurable attraction—an interest which might be one's own, or another's" (p. 73; R., p. 62). (**Another's**: let this be particularly noticed.) "Whereas a universally legislative Will must prescribe actions which are **not** based on any **interest** at all, but solely on a feeling of duty." I beg the reader to think what this really means. As a matter of fact, nothing less than volition without motive, in other words, effect without cause. Interest and Motive are interchangeable ideas; what is interest but *quod mea interest,* that which is of importance to me? And is not this, in one word, whatever stirs and sets in motion my Will? Consequently, what is an interest other than the working of a motive upon the Will? Therefore where a motive moves the Will, there the latter has an interest; but where the Will is affected by no motive, there in truth it can be as little active, as a stone is able to leave its place without being pushed or pulled. No educated person will require any demonstration of this. It follows that every action, inasmuch as it necessarily must have a motive, necessarily also presupposes an interest. Kant, however, propounds a second entirely new class of actions which are performed without any interest, *i.e.,* without motive. And these actions are—all deeds of justice and loving-kindness! It will be seen that this monstrous assumption, to be refuted, needed only to be reduced to its real meaning, which was concealed through the word "interest" being trifled with. Meanwhile Kant celebrates (p. 74 sqq.; R., p. 62) the triumph of his Autonomy of the Will by setting up a moral Utopia called the Kingdom of Ends, which is peopled with nothing but **rational**

beings *in abstracto.* These, one and all, are always willing, without willing any actual **thing** (*i.e.,* without interest): the only thing that they will is that they may all perpetually will in accordance with **one** maxim (*i.e.,* Autonomy). *Difficile est satiram non scribere*[37] (it is difficult to refrain from writing a satire).

But there is something else to which Kant is led by his autonomy of the will; and it involves more serious consequences than the little innocent Kingdom of Ends, which is perfectly harmless and may be left in peace. I mean the conception of **human dignity**. Now this "dignity" is made to rest solely on man's autonomy, and to lie in the fact that the law which he ought to obey is his own work, his relation to it thus being the same as that of the subjects of a constitutional government to their statutes. As an ornamental finish to the Kantian system of morals such a theory might after all be passed over. Only this expression "**Human Dignity**," once it was uttered by Kant, became the shibboleth of all perplexed and empty-headed moralists. For behind that imposing formula they concealed their lack, not to say, of a real ethical basis, but of any basis at all which was possessed of an intelligible meaning; supposing cleverly enough that their readers would be so pleased to see themselves invested with such a "dignity" that they would be quite satisfied.[38] Let us, however, look at this conception a little more carefully, and submit it to the test of reality. Kant (p. 79; R., p. 66) defines **dignity** as "an unconditioned, incomparable value." This is an explanation which makes such an effect by its magnificent sound that one does not readily summon up courage to examine it at close quarters; else we should find that it too is nothing but a hollow hyperbole, within which there lurks like a gnawing worm, the *contradictio in adjecto.* Every value is the estimation of one thing compared with another; it is thus a conception of comparison, and consequently relative; and this relativity is precisely that which forms the essence of the idea. According to Diogenes Laertius (Book VII., chap. 106),[39] this was already correctly taught by the Stoics. He says: τὴν δὲ ἀξίαν εἶναι ἀμοιβὴν δοκιμάστου, ἣν ἂν ὁ ἔμπειρος τῶν πραγμάτων τάξῃ· ὅμοιον εἰπεῖν, ἀμείβεσθαι πυροὺς πρὸς τὰς σὺν ἡμιόνῳ κριθάς.[40] An **incomparable, unconditioned, absolute**

---

[37]Juvenal, *Sat.* I. 30.

[38]It appears that G. W. Block in his *Neue Grundlegung der Philosophie der Sitten,* 1802, was the first to make "Human Dignity" expressly and exclusively the foundation-stone of Ethics, which he then built up entirely on it.

[39]V. Diogenes Laertius, *de Clarorum Philosophorum Vitis, etc.,* edit. C. Gabr. Cobet. Paris; Didot, 1862. In this edition the passage quoted is in chap. 105 *ad fin.,* p. 182.—(*Translator.*)

[40]They teach that "worth" is the equivalent value of a thing which has been tested, whatever an expert may fix that value to be; as, for instance, to take wheat in exchange for barley and a mule.—(*Translator.*)

value, such as "dignity" is declared by Kant to be, is thus, like so much else in Philosophy, the statement in words of a thought which is really unthinkable; just as much as "the highest number," or "the greatest space."

> "*Doch eben wo Begriffe fehlen,*
> *Da stellt ein WORT zu rechter Zeit sich ein.*"
> (But where conceptions fail,
> Just there a WORD comes in to fill the blank.)

So it was with this expression, "**Human Dignity**." A most acceptable phrase was brought into currency. Thereon every system of Morals, that was spun out through all classes of duty, and all forms of casuistry, found a broad basis; from which serene elevation it could comfortably go on preaching.

At the end of his exposition (p. 124; R., p. 97), Kant says: "But how it is that **Pure Reason** without other motives, that may have their derivation elsewhere, can by itself be **practical**; that is, how, without there being any object for the Will to take an antecedent interest in, the simple principle of the universal validity of all the precepts of Pure Reason, as laws, can of itself provide a motive and bring about an interest which may be called purely moral; or, in other words, how it is that Pure Reason can be practical;—to explain this problem, all human reason is inadequate, and all trouble and work spent on it are vain." Now it should be remembered that, if any one asserts the existence of a thing which cannot even be conceived as possible, it is incumbent on him to prove that it is an actual reality; whereas the Categorical Imperative of Practical Reason is expressly **not** put forward as a fact of consciousness, nor otherwise founded on experience. Rather are we frequently cautioned not to attempt to explain it by having recourse to empirical anthropology. (Cf. *e.g.,* p. vi. of the preface; R., p. 5; and pp. 59, 60; R., p. 52). Moreover, we are repeatedly (*e.g.,* p. 48; R., p. 44) assured "that no instance can show, and consequently there can be no empirical proof, that an Imperative of this sort exists everywhere." And further, on p. 49 (R., p. 45), we read, "that the reality of the Categorical Imperative is not a fact of experience." Now if we put all this together, we can hardly avoid the suspicion that Kant is jesting at his readers' expense. But although this practice may be allowed by the present philosophical public of Germany, and seem good in their eyes, yet in Kant's time it was not so much in vogue; and besides, Ethics, then, as always, was precisely the subject that least of all could lend itself to jokes. Hence we must continue to hold the conviction that what can neither be conceived as possible, nor proved as actual, is destitute of all credentials to attest its existence. And if, by a strong effort of the imagination, we try to picture to ourselves a man, possessed, as it were, by a *daemon,* in the form of an **absolute Ought**, that speaks only in Categorical Imperatives, and, confronting his wishes and inclinations, claims to be the perpetual controller of his actions; in this figure we see no true portrait of human nature, or of our inner life; what we **do** discern is an artificial substitute for theological Morals, to which it stands in the same relation as a wooden leg to a living one.

Our conclusion, therefore, is, that the Kantian Ethics, like all anterior systems, is devoid of any sure foundation. As I showed at the outset, in my examination of its **imperative Form**, the structure is at bottom nothing but an inversion of theological Morals, cloaked in very abstract formulae of an apparently *a priori* origin. That this disguise was most artificial and unrecognisable is the more certain, from the fact that Kant, in all good faith, was actually himself deceived by it, and really believed that he could establish, independently of all theology, and on the basis of pure intelligence *a priori,* those conceptions of the Law and of the hests of Duty, which obviously have no meaning except in theological Ethics; whereas I have sufficiently proved that with him they are destitute of all real foundation, and float loosely in mid air. However, the mask at length falls away in his own workshop, and **theological Ethics** stands forth unveiled, as witness his doctrine of the Highest Good, the Postulates of Practical Reason; and lastly, his Moral Theology. But this revelation freed neither Kant nor the public from their illusion as to the real state of things; on the contrary, both he and they rejoiced to see all those precepts, which hitherto had been sanctioned by Faith, now ratified and established by Ethics (although only *idealiter,* and for practical purposes). The truth is that they, in all sincerity, put the effect for the cause, and the cause for the effect, inasmuch as they failed to perceive that at the root of this system of Morals there lay, as absolutely necessary assumptions, however tacit and concealed, all the alleged consequences that had been drawn from it.

At the end of this severe investigation, which must also have been tiring to my readers, perhaps I may be allowed, by way of diversion, to make a jesting, indeed frivolous comparison. I would liken Kant, in his self-mystification, to a man who at a ball has been flirting the whole evening with a masked beauty, in hopes of making a conquest; till at last, throwing off her disguise, she reveals herself—as his wife.

Chapter VII.—Kant's Doctrine of Conscience

THE alleged Practical Reason with its Categorical Imperative, is manifestly very closely connected with Conscience, although essentially different from it in two respects. In the first place, the Categorical

Imperative, as commanding, necessarily speaks **before** the act, whereas Conscience does not till afterwards. **Before** the act Conscience can at best only speak indirectly, that is, by means of reflection, which holds up to it the recollection of previous cases, in which similar acts after they were committed received its disapproval. It is on this that the etymology of the word **Gewissen** (Conscience) appears to me to rest, because only what has already taken place is **gewiss**[41] (certain). Undoubtedly, through external inducement and kindled emotion, or by reason of the internal discord of bad humour, impure, base thoughts, and evil desires rise up in all people, even in the best. But for these a man is not morally responsible, and need not load his conscience with them; since they only show what the genus *homo*, not what the **individual**, who thinks them, would be capable of doing. Other motives, if not simultaneously, yet almost immediately, come into his consciousness, and confronting the unworthy inclinations prevent them from ever being crystallised into deeds; thus causing them to resemble the out-voted minority of an acting committee. By deeds alone each person gains an empirical knowledge no less of himself than of others, just as it is deeds alone that burden the conscience. For, unlike thoughts, these are not problematic; on the contrary, they are certain (*gewiss*), they are unchangeable, and are not only thought, but **known** (*gewusst*). The Latin *conscientia*,[42] and the Greek συνείδησις[43] have the same sense. Conscience is thus the **knowledge** that a man has about what he has done.

The second point of difference between the alleged Categorical Imperative and Conscience is, that the latter always draws its material from experience; which the former cannot do, since it is purely *a priori*. Nevertheless, we may reasonably suppose that Kant's Doctrine of Conscience will throw some light on this new conception of an **absolute Ought** which he introduced. His theory is most completely set forth in the *Metaphysische Anfangsgründe zur Tugendlehre*, §13, and in the following criticism I shall assume that the few pages which contain it are lying before the reader.

The Kantian interpretation of Conscience makes an exceedingly imposing effect, before which one used to stand with reverential awe, and all the less confidence was felt in demurring to it, because there lay heavy on the mind the ever-present fear of having theoretical objections construed as practical, and, if the correctness of Kant's view were denied, of being regarded as devoid of conscience. I, however, cannot be led astray in this manner, since the question here is of theory, not of practice; and

---

[41]Both words are, of course, derived from *wissen = scire* = εἰδέναι.—(*Translator.*)

[42]Cf. Horace's *conscire sibi, pallescere culpa: Epist.* I. 1, 61. To be conscious of having done wrong, to turn pale at the thought of the crime.

[43]Συνείδησις = *consciousness* (of right or wrong done.)—(*Translator.*)

I am not concerned with the preaching of Morals, but with the exact investigation of the ultimate ethical basis.

We notice at once that Kant employs exclusively Latin legal terminology, which, however, would seem little adapted to reflect the most secret stirrings of the human heart. Yet this language, this judicial way of treating the subject, he retains from first to last, as though it were essential and proper to the matter. And so we find brought upon the stage of our inner self a complete Court of justice, with indictment, judge, plaintiff, defendant, and sentence;—nothing is wanting. Now if this tribunal, as portrayed by Kant, really existed in our breasts, it would be astonishing if a single person could be found to be, I do not say, **so bad**, but **so stupid**, as to act against his conscience. For such a supernatural assize, of an entirely special kind, set up in our consciousness, such a secret court—like another Fehmgericht[44]—held in the dark recesses of our inmost being, would inspire everybody with a terror and fear of the gods strong enough to really keep him from grasping at short transient advantages, in face of the dreadful threats of superhuman powers, speaking in tones so near and so clear. In real life, on the contrary, we find that the efficiency of conscience is generally considered such a vanishing quantity that all peoples have bethought themselves of helping it out by means of positive religion, or even of entirely replacing it by the latter. Moreover, if Conscience were indeed of this peculiar nature, the Royal Society could never have thought of the question put for the present Prize Essay.

But if we look more closely at Kant's exposition, we shall find that its imposing effect is mainly produced by the fact that he attributes to the moral verdict passed on ourselves, as its peculiar and essential characteristic, a form which in fact is not so at all. This metaphorical bar of judgment is no more applicable to moral self-examination than it is to every other reflection as regards what we have done, and might have done otherwise, where no ethical question is involved. For it is not only true that the same procedure of indictment, defence, and sentence is occasionally assumed by that obviously spurious and artificial conscience which is based on mere superstition; as, for instance, when a Hindu reproaches himself with having been the murderer of a cow, or when a Jew remembers that he has smoked his pipe at home on the Sabbath; but even the self-questioning which springs from no ethical source, being indeed rather unmoral than moral, often appears in a shape of this sort, as the following case may exemplify. Suppose I, good-naturedly, but thought-

---

[44]The celebrated Secret Tribunal of Westphalia, which came into prominence about A.D. 1220. In A.D. 1335 the Archbishop of Cologne was appointed head of all the Fehme benches in Westphalia by the Emperor Charles IV. The reader will remember the description of the trial scene in Scott's *Anne of Geierstein*. Perhaps the Court of Star Chamber comes nearest to it in English History.—(*Translator.*)

lessly, have made myself surety for a friend, and suppose there comes with evening the clear perception of the heavy responsibility I have taken on myself—a responsibility that may easily involve me in serious trouble, as the wise old saying, ἐγγύα· πάρα δ᾽ ἄτα![45] predicts; then at once there rise up within me the Accuser and the Counsel for the defence, ready to confront each other. The latter endeavours to palliate my rashness in giving bail so hastily, by pointing out the stress of circumstance or of obligation, or, it may be, the simple straightforwardness of the transaction; perhaps he even seeks excuse by commending my kind heart. Last of all comes the Judge who inexorably passes the sentence: "A fool's piece of work!" and I am overwhelmed with confusion.

So much for this judicial form of which Kant is so fond; his other modes of expression are, for the most part, open to the same criticism. For instance, that which he attributes to conscience, at the beginning of the paragraph, as its peculiar property, applies equally to all other scruples of an entirely different sort. He says: "It (conscience) follows him like his shadow, try though he may to escape. By pleasures and distractions he may be stupefied and lulled to sleep, but he cannot avoid occasionally waking up and coming to himself; and then he is immediately aware of the terrible voice," etc. Obviously, this may be just as well understood, word for word, of the secret consciousness of some person of private means, who feels that his expenses far exceed his income, and that thus his capital is being affected, and will gradually melt away.

We have seen that Kant represents the use of legal terms as essential to the subject, and that he keeps to them from beginning to end; let it now be noted how he employs the same style for the following finely devised sophism. He says: "That a person accused by his conscience should be identified with the judge is an absurd way of portraying a court of justice; for in that case the accuser would invariably lose." And he adds, by way of elucidating this statement, a very ambiguous and obscure note. His conclusion is that, if we would avoid falling into a contradiction, we must think of the judge (in the judicial conscience-drama that is enacted in our breasts) as different from us, in fact, as another person; nay more, as one that is an omniscient knower of hearts, whose hests are obligatory on all, and who is almighty for every purpose of executive authority.[46] He thus passes by a perfectly smooth path from conscience to superstition, making the latter a necessary consequence of the former; while he

---

[45]If you give a pledge, be sure that Ate (the goddess of mischief) is beside you; *i.e.,* beware of giving pledges.—Thales ap. Plat. *Charm.* 165 A.

[46]Kant leads up to this position with great ingenuity, by having recourse to the theory of the two characters coexistent in man—the *noumenal* (or *intelligible*) and the *empirical*; the one being in time, the other, timeless; the one, fast bound by the law of causality, the other free.—(*Translator.*)

is secretly sure that he will be all the more willingly followed because the reader's earliest training will have certainly rendered him familiar with such ideas, if not have made them his second nature. Here, then, Kant finds an easy task,—a thing he ought rather to have despised; for he should have concerned himself not only with preaching, but also with practising truthfulness. I entirely reject the above quoted sentence, and all the conclusions consequent thereon, and I declare it to be nothing but a shuffling trick. It is **not true** that the accuser must always lose, when the accused is the same person as the judge; at least not in the court of judgment in our hearts. In the instance I gave of one man going surety for another, did the accuser lose? Or must we in this case also, if we wish to avoid a contradiction, really assume a personification after Kant's fashion, and be driven to view objectively as **another person** that voice whose deliverance would have been those terrible words: "A fool's piece of work!"? A sort of Mercury, forsooth, in living flesh? Or perhaps a prosopopoeia of the Μῆτις (cunning) recommended by Homer (*Il.* xxiii. 313 sqq.)?[47] But thus we should only be landed, as before, on the broad path of superstition, aye, and pagan superstition too.

It is in this passage that Kant indicates his Moral Theology, briefly indeed, yet not without all its vital points. The fact that he takes care not to attribute to it any objective validity, but rather to present it merely as a form subjectively unavoidable, does not free him from the arbitrariness with which he constructs it, even though he only claims its necessity for human consciousness. His fabric rests, as we have seen, on a tissue of baseless assumptions.

So much, then, is certain. The entire imagery—that of a judicial drama—whereby Kant depicts conscience is wholly unessential and in no way peculiar to it; although he keeps this figure, as if it were proper to the subject, right through to the end, in order finally to deduce certain conclusions from it. As a matter of fact it is a sufficiently common form, which our thoughts easily take when we consider any circumstance of real life. It is due for the most part to the conflict of opposing motives which usually spring up, and which are successively weighed and tested by our reflecting reason. And no difference is made whether these motives are moral or egoistic in their nature, nor whether our deliberations are concerned with some action in the past, or in the future. Now if we strip from Kant's exposition its dress of legal metaphor, which is only an optional dramatic appendage, the surrounding nimbus with all its imposing effect immediately disappears as well, and there remains nothing but the fact that sometimes, when we think over our actions, we are seized with a certain self-dissatisfaction, which is marked

---

[47] Ἀλλ' ἄγε δὴ σύ, φίλος, μῆτιν ἐμβάλλεο θυμῷ, κ.τ.λ.

by a special characteristic. It is with our conduct *per se* that we are discontented, not with its result, and this feeling does not, as in every other case in which we regret the stupidity of our behaviour, rest on **egoistic** grounds. For on these occasions the cause of our dissatisfaction is precisely because we have been **too** egoistic, because we have taken too much thought for ourselves, and not enough for our neighbour; or perhaps even because, without any resulting advantage, we have made the misery of others an object in itself. That we may be dissatisfied with ourselves, and saddened by reason of sufferings which we have inflicted, not undergone, is a plain fact and impossible to be denied. The connection of this with the only ethical basis that can stand an adequate test we shall examine further on. But Kant, like a clever special pleader, tried by magnifying and embellishing the original *datum* to make all that he possibly could of it, in order to prepare a very broad foundation for his Ethics and Moral Theology.

Chapter VIII.—Kant's Doctrine of the Intelligible[48] and Empirical Character. Theory of Freedom

THE attack I have made, in the cause of truth, on Kant's system of Morals, does not, like those of my predecessors, touch the surface only, but penetrates to its deepest roots. It seems, therefore, only just that, before I leave this part of my subject, I should bring to remembrance the brilliant and conspicuous service which he nevertheless rendered to ethical science. I allude to his doctrine of the co-existence of Freedom and Necessity. We find it first in the *Kritik der Reinen Vernunft* (pp. 533–554 of the first, and pp. 561–582 of the fifth, edition); but it is still more clearly expounded in the *Kritik der Praktischen Vernunft* (fourth edition, pp. 169–179; R., pp. 224–231).

The strict and absolute necessity of the acts of Will, determined by motives as they arise, was first shown by Hobbes, then by Spinoza, and Hume, and also by Dietrich von Holbach in his *Système de la Nature*; and lastly by Priestley it was most completely and precisely demonstrated. This point, indeed, has been so clearly proved, and placed beyond all doubt, that it must be reckoned among the number of perfectly established truths, and only crass ignorance could continue to speak of a freedom, of a *liberum arbitrium indifferentiae* (a free and indifferent choice) in the individual acts of men. Nor did Kant, owing to the irrefutable reasoning of his predecessors, hesitate to consider the Will as fast bound in the chains of Necessity, the matter admitting, as he thought, of no

---

[48] *V.* Note on "intelligible" in Chapter I. of this Part.—(*Translator.*)

further dispute or doubt. This is proved by all the passages in which he speaks of freedom only from the **theoretical** standpoint. Nevertheless, it is true that our actions are attended with a consciousness of independence and original initiative, which makes us recognise them as our own work, and every one with ineradicable certainty feels that he is the real author of his conduct, and morally **responsible** for it. But since responsibility implies the possibility of having acted otherwise, which possibility means freedom in some sort or manner; therefore in the consciousness of responsibility is indirectly involved also the consciousness of freedom. The key to resolve the contradiction, that thus arises out of the nature of the case, was at last found by Kant through the distinction he drew with profound acumen, between phaenomena and the Thing in itself (*das Ding an sich*). This distinction is the very core of his whole philosophy, and its greatest merit.

The individual, with his immutable, innate character, strictly determined in all his modes of expression by the law of Causality, which, as acting through the medium of the intellect, is here called by the name of Motivation,—the individual so constituted is only the **phaenomenon** (*Erscheinung*). The **Thing** in **itself** which underlies this phaenomenon is outside of Time and Space, consequently free from all succession and plurality, one, and changeless. Its constitution in itself is the **intelligible character**, which is equally present in all the acts of the individual, and stamped on every one of them, like the impress of a signet on a thousand seals. The empirical character of the phaenomenon—the character which manifests itself in time, and in succession of acts—is thus determined by the intelligible character; and consequently, the individual, as phaenomenon, in all his modes of expression, which are called forth by motives, must show the invariableness of a natural law. Whence it results that all his actions are governed by strict necessity. Now it used to be commonly maintained that the character of a man may be transformed by moral admonitions and remonstrances appealing to reason; but when the distinction between the intelligible and empirical character had once been drawn, it followed that the unchangeableness, the inflexible rigidity of the empirical character, which thinking people had always observed, was explained and traced to a rational basis, and consequently accepted as an established fact by Philosophy. Thus the latter was so far harmonised with experience, and ceased to stand abashed before popular wisdom, which long before had spoken the words of truth in the Spanish proverb: *Lo que entra con el capillo, sale con la mortaja* (that which comes in with the child's cap, goes out with the winding-sheet); or: *Lo que en la leche se mama, en la mortaja se derrama* (what is imbibed with the milk, is poured out again in the winding-sheet).

This doctrine of the coexistence of Freedom and Necessity I regard as the greatest of all the achievements of human sagacity. With the Transcendental Aesthetics it forms the two great diamonds in the crown of Kant's fame, which will never pass away. In his Treatise on Freedom, Schelling obviously served up the Kantian teaching in a paraphrase, which by reason of its lively colouring and graphic delineation, is for many people more comprehensible. The work would deserve praise if its author had had the honesty to say that he is drawing on Kant's wisdom, not on his own. As it is, a certain part of the philosophic public still credits him with the entire performance.

The theory itself, and the whole question regarding the nature of Freedom, can be better understood if we view them in connection with a general truth, which I think, is most concisely expressed by a formula frequently occurring in the scholastic writings: *Operari sequitur esse.*[49] In other words, everything in the world operates in accordance with what it is, in accordance with its inherent nature, in which, consequently, all its modes of expression are already contained potentially, while actually they are manifested when elicited by external causes; so that external causes are the means whereby the essential constitution of the thing is revealed. And the modes of expression so resulting form the **empirical** character; whereas its hidden, ultimate basis, which is inaccessible to experience, is the **intelligible** character, that is, the real nature *per se* of the particular thing in question. Man forms no exception to the rest of nature; he too has a changeless character, which, however, is strictly individual and different in each case. This character is of course **empirical** as far as we can grasp it, and therefore only **phaenomenal**; while the **intelligible** character is whatever may be the real nature in itself of the person. His actions one and all, being, as regards their external constitution, determined by motives, can never be shaped otherwise than in accordance with the unchangeable individual character. As a man is, so he is bound to act. Hence for a given person in every single case, there is absolutely only one way of acting possible: *Operari sequitur esse.*[50] Freedom belongs only to the intelligible character, not to the empirical. The *operari* (conduct) of a given individual is necessarily determined externally by motives, internally by his character; therefore everything that he does necessarily takes place. But in his *esse* (i.e., in what he is), **there**, we find Freedom. He **might have been** something different; and guilt or merit attaches to that which he **is**. All that he does follows from what he **is**, as a mere corollary. Through Kant's doctrine we are freed from the primary error of connecting Necessity with *esse* (what one is), and Freedom with *operari* (what one does); we become **aware** that this is a

---

[49]*I.e.,* what is done is a consequence of that which is.

[50]*I.e.,* his acts are a consequence of what he is.

misplacement of terms, and that exactly the inverse arrangement is the true one. Hence it is clear that the moral responsibility of a man, while it first of all, and obviously, of course, touches what he does, yet at bottom touches what he **is**; because, what he is being the original **datum**, his conduct, as motives arise, could never take any other course than that which it actually does take. But, however strict be the necessity, whereby, in the individual, acts are elicited by motives, it yet never occurs to anybody—not even to him who is convinced of this necessity—to exonerate himself on that account, and cast the blame on the motives; for he knows well enough that, objectively considered, any given circumstance, and its causes, perfectly admitted quite a different, indeed, a directly opposite course of action; nay, that such a course would actually have taken place, **if only he had been a different person**. That he is precisely such a one as his conduct proclaims him to be, and no other—this it is for which he feels himself responsible; in his *esse* (what he is) lies the vulnerable place, where the sting of conscience penetrates. For Conscience is nothing but acquaintance with one's own self—an acquaintance that arises out of one's actual mode of conduct, and which becomes ever more intimate. So that it is the *esse* (what one is) which in reality is accused by conscience, while the *operari* (what one does) supplies the incriminating evidence. Since we are only conscious of **Freedom** through the sense of **responsibility**; therefore where the latter lies the former must also be; in the *esse* (in one's being). It is the *operari* (what one does) that is subject to necessity. But we can only get to know ourselves, as well as others **empirically**; we have no *a priori* knowledge of our character. Certainly our natural tendency is to cherish a very high opinion of it, because the maxim: *Quisque praesumitur bonus, donec probetur contrarium* (every one is presumed to be good, until the contrary is proved), is perhaps even more true of the inner court of justice than of the world's tribunals.

NOTE

He who is capable of recognising the essential part of a thought, though clothed in a dress very different from what he is familiar with, will see, as I do, that this Kantian doctrine of the intelligible and empirical character is a piece of insight already possessed by Plato. The difference is, that with Kant it is sublimated to an abstract clearness; with Plato it is treated mythically, and connected with metempsychosis, because, as he did not perceive the ideality of Time, he could only represent it under a temporal form. The identity of the one doctrine with the other becomes exceedingly plain, if we read the explanation and illustration of the Platonic myth, which Porphyrius has given with such clear exactitude, that its agreement with the abstract language of Kant comes out unmistakably. In the second book of his Eclogues, chap. 8, §§37–40,[51] Stobaeus has preserved for us *in extenso* that part of one of Porphyrius' lost writings which specially comments on the myth in question, as Plato gives it in the second half of the tenth book of the Republic.[52] The whole section is eminently worth reading. As a specimen I shall quote the short §39, in the hope of inducing any one who cares for these things to study Stobaeus for himself. It will then immediately become apparent that this Platonic myth is nothing less than an allegory of the profound truth which Kant stated in its abstract purity, as the doctrine of the intelligible and empirical character, and consequently that the latter had been reached, in its essentials, by Plato thousands of years ago. Indeed, this view seems to go back much further still, for Porphyrius is of opinion that Plato took it from the Egyptians. Certainly we already find the same theory in the Brahmanical doctrine of metempsychosis, and it is from this Indian source that the Egyptian priests, in all probability, derived their wisdom. §39 is as follows:—

Τὸ γὰρ ὅλον βούλημα τοιοῦτ᾽ ἔοικεν εἶναι τὸ τοῦ
Πλάτωνος· ἔχειν μὲν τὸ αὐτεξούσιον τὰς ψυχάς, πρὶν
εἰς σώματα καὶ βίους διαφόρους ἐμπεσεῖν, εἰς τὸ ἢ τοῦτον
τὸν βίον ἕλεσθαι, ἢ ἄλλον, ὅν, μετὰ ποιᾶς ζωῆς καὶ
σώματος οἰκείου τῇ ζωῇ, ἐκτέλεσειν μέλλει· (καὶ γὰρ
λέοντος βίον ἐπ᾽ αὐτῇ εἶναι ἕλεσθαι, καὶ ἀνδρός).
Κἀκεῖνο μέντοι τὸ αὐτεξούσιον, ἅμα τῇ πρός τινα τῶν
τοιούτων βίων πτώσει, ἐμπεπόδισται. Κατελθοῦσαι
γὰρ εἰς τὰ σώματα, καὶ ἀντὶ ψυχῶν ἀπολυτῶν γεγονυῖαι
ψυχαὶ ζώων, τὸ αὐτεξούσιον φέρουσιν οἰκεῖον τῇ τοῦ
ζώου κατασκευῇ, καὶ ἐφ᾽ ὧν μὲν εἶναι πολύνουν καὶ
πολυκίνητον, ὡς ἐπ᾽ ἀνθρώπου, ἐφ᾽ ὧν δὲ ὀλιγοκίνητον
καὶ μονότροπον, ὡς ἐπὶ τῶν ἄλλων σχεδὸν πάντων ζώων·
Ἠρτῆσθαι δὲ τὸ αὐτεξούσιον τοῦτο ἀπὸ τῆς κατασκετῆς,
κινούμενον μὲν ἐξ αὐτοῦ, φερόμενον δὲ κατὰ τὰς ἐκ τῆς
κατασκευῆς γιγνομένας προθυμίας.[53]

---

[51] *V.* Joannes Stobaeus. *Eclogae Physicae et Ethicae,* edit. Curtius Wachsmuth et Otto Hense; Weidmann, Berlin, 1884. Vol. II., pp. 163–168.—(*Translator.*)

[52] *V.* Plat., *Rep.,* edit. Stallbaum, 614 sqq. It is the ἀπόλογος Ἡρὸς τοῦ Ἀρμενίου.—(*Translator.*)

[53] To sum up. What Plato meant seems to be this. Souls (he said) have free power before passing into bodies and different modes of being, to choose this or that form of life, which they will pass through in a certain kind of existence, and in a body adapted thereto. (For a soul may choose a lion's, equally with a man's, mode of being.) But this free power of choice is removed simultaneously with entrance into one or other of such

Chapter IX.—Fichte's Ethics as a Magnifying Glass for the Errors of the Kantian

JUST as in Anatomy and Zoology, many things are not so obvious to the pupil in preparations and natural products as in engravings where there is some exaggeration; so if there is any one who, after the above criticism, is still not entirely satisfied as to the worthlessness of the Kantian foundation of Ethics, I would recommend him Fichte's *System der Sittenlehre,* as a sure means of freeing him from all doubt.

In the old German Marionnettes a fool always accompanied the emperor, or hero, so that he might afterwards give in his own way a highly coloured version of what had been said or done. In like manner behind the great Kant there stands the author of the *Wissenschaftslehre,*[54] a true *Wissenschaftsleere.*[55] In order to secure his own, and his family's welfare, Fichte formed the idea of creating a sensation by means of subtle mystification. It was a very suitable and reasonable plan, considering the nature of the German philosophic public, and he executed it admirably by **outdoing** Kant in every particular. He appeared as the latter's living superlative, and produced a perfect caricature of his philosophy by magnifying all its salient points. Nor did the Ethics escape similar treatment. In his *System der Sittenlehre,* we find the Categorical Imperative grown into a Despotic Imperative; while the absolute "Ought," the law-giving Reason, and the Hest of Duty have developed into a **moral Fate**, an unfathomable Necessity, requiring mankind to act strictly in accordance with certain maxims. To judge (pp. 308, 309) from the pompous show made, a great deal must depend on these formulae, although one never quite discovers **what**. So much only seems clear. As in bees there is implanted an instinct to build cells and a hive for life in common, so men (it is alleged) are endowed with an impulse leading them to play in common a great, strictly moral, world-embracing Comedy, their part being merely to figure as puppets—nothing else. But there is this important difference between the bees and men. The hive is really brought to completion; while instead of a moral World-Comedy, as a matter of fact, an

---

forms of life. For when once they have descended into bodies, and instead of unfettered souls have become the souls of living things, then they take that measure of free power which belongs in each case to the organism of the living thing. In some forms this power is very intelligent and full of movement, as in man; in some it has but little energy, and is of a simple nature, as in almost all other creatures. Moreover, this free power depends on the organism in such a way that while its capability of action is caused by itself alone, its impulses are determined by the desires which have their origin in the organism.— (*Translator.*)

[54]*I.e.* Scientific Doctrine.

[55]*I.e.* Scientific Blank. Perhaps we might translate:—"Scientific Instruction" and "Scientific Misinstruction."—(*Translator.*)

exceedingly immoral one is enacted. Here, then, we see the imperative form of the Kantian Ethics, the moral Law, and the absolute "Ought" pushed further and further till a system of ethical **Fatalism** is evolved, which, as it is worked out, lapses at times into the comic.[56]

If in Kant's doctrine we trace a certain moral pedantry; with Fichte this pedantry reaches the absurd, and furnishes abundant material for satire. Let the reader notice, for example (pp. 407–409), how he decides the well-known instance of casuistry, where of two human lives one must be lost. We find indeed all the errors of Kant raised to the superlative. Thus, on p. 199, we read: "To act in accordance with the dictates of sympathy, of compassion, and of loving-kindness is distinctly unmoral; indeed this line of conduct, as such, is contrary to morality." Again, on p. 402: "The impulse that makes us ready to serve others must never be an inconsiderate good-nature, but a clearly thought-out purpose; that, namely, of furthering as much as possible the causality of Reason." However, between these sallies of ridiculous pedantry, Fichte's real philosophic crudeness peeps out clearly enough, as we might only expect in the case of a man whose teaching left no time for learning. He seriously puts forward the *liberum arbitrium indifferentiae* (a free and indifferent choice), giving as its foundation the most trivial and frivolous reasons. (Pp. 160, 173, 205, 208, 237, 259, 261.) There can be no doubt that a motive, although working through the medium of the intelligence, is, nevertheless, a cause, and consequently involves the same necessity of effect as all other causes; the corollary being that all human action is a

[56]As evidence of the truth of my words, space prevents me from quoting more than a few passages. P. 196: "The moral instinct is absolute, and its requirements are peremptory, without any object outside itself." P. 232: "In consequence of the Moral Law, the empirical Being in Time must be an exact copy of the original Ego." P. 308: "The whole man is a vehicle of the Moral Law." P. 342: "I am only an instrument, a mere tool of the Moral Law, not in any sense an end." P. 343: "The end laid before every one is to be the means of realising Reason: this is the ultimate purpose of his existence; for this alone he has his being, and if this end should not be attained, there is not the least occasion for him to live." P. 347: "I am an instrument of the Moral Law in the phaenomenal world." P. 360: "It is an ordinance of the Moral Law to nourish one's body, and study one's health; this of course should be done in no way, and for no other purpose, except to provide an *efficient instrument* for furthering the end decreed by Reason, *i.e.,* its realisation,"—(cf. p. 371.) P. 376: "Every human body is an instrument for furthering the end decreed by Reason, *i.e.,* its realisation; therefore the greatest possible fitness of each instrument must constitute for me an end: consequently I must take thought for every one."—This is Fichte's derivation of loving-kindness! P. 377: "I can and dare take thought for myself, solely because, and in so far as I am, *an instrument of the Moral Law.*" P. 388: "To defend a hunted man at the risk of one's own life, is an absolute duty; whenever the life of another human being is in danger, you have no right to think of the safety of your own." P. 420: "In the province of the Moral Law there is no way whatever of regarding my fellow-man except as an *instrument* of Reason."

strictly necessary result. Whoever remains unconvinced of this, is still, philosophically speaking, barbarous, and ignorant of the rudiments of exact knowledge. The perception of the strict necessity governing man's conduct forms the line of demarcation which separates philosophic heads from all others; arrived at this limit Fichte clearly showed that he belonged to the others. Moreover, following the footsteps of Kant (p. 303), he proceeds to make various statements which are in direct contradiction to the above mentioned passages; but this inconsistency, like many more in his writings, only proves that he, being one who was never serious in the search for truth, possessed no strong convictions to build on; as indeed for his purpose they were not in the least necessary. Nothing is more laughable than the fact that this man has received so much posthumous praise for strictly consequential reasoning; his pedantic style full of loud declamation about trifling matters being actually mistaken for such.

The most complete development of Fichte's system of **moral Fatalism** is found in his last work: *Die Wissenschaftslehre in ihrem Allgemeinen Umrisse Dargestellt,* Berlin, 1810. It has the advantage of being only forty-six pages (duodecimo) long, while it contains his whole philosophy in a nutshell. It is therefore to be recommended to all those who consider their time too precious to be wasted on his larger productions, which are framed with a length and tediousness worthy of Christian Wolff, and with the intention, in reality, of deluding, not of instructing the reader. In this little treatise we read on p. 32: "The intuitive perception of a phaenomenal world only came about, to the end that in such a world the Ego as the **absolute Ought** might be visible to itself." On p. 33 we actually find: "The **ought**," (*i.e.,* the moral necessity,) "of the **Ought's** visibility;" and on p. 36: "An **ought**," (*i.e.,* a moral necessity,) "of the perception that I **ought**." This, then, is what we have come to so soon after Kant! **His imperative Form**, with its unproved **Ought**, which it secured as a most convenient ποῦ στῶ (standpoint), is indeed an *exemplar vitiis imitabile!*

For the rest, all that I have said does not overthrow the service Fichte rendered. Kant's philosophy, this late masterpiece of human sagacity, in the very land where it arose, he obscured, nay, supplanted by empty, bombastic superlatives, by extravagances, and by the nonsense which is found, in his *Grundlage der gesammten Wissenschaftslehre,* appearing under the disguise of profound penetration. His merit was thus to show the world unmistakably what the capacity of the German philosophical public is; for he made it play the part of a child who is coaxed into giving up a precious gem in exchange for a Nürnberg toy. The fame he obtained in this fashion still lives on credit; and still Fichte is always mentioned in the same breath with Kant as being another such ('Ηρακλῆς καὶ πίθηκος!⁵⁷). Indeed his name is often placed above the latter's.⁵⁸ It was, of course, Fichte's example that encouraged his successors in the art of enveloping the German people in philosophic fog. These were animated by the same spirit, and crowned with the same prosperity. Every one knows their names; nor is this the place to consider them at length. Needless to say, their different opinions, down to the minutest details, are still set forth, and seriously discussed, by the Professors of Philosophy; as if one had really to do with philosophers! We must, then, thank Fichte for lucid documents now existing, which will have to be revised one day before the Tribunal of posterity, that Court of Appeal from the verdicts of the present, which—like the Last Judgment looked forward to by the Saints—at almost all periods, has been left to give to true merit its just award.

---

⁵⁷*I.e.,* Hercules and an ape. A Greek proverb denoting the juxtaposition of the sublime and the ridiculous. *V.* Greg. Cypr. *M.* 3, 66; Macar. 4, 53; Luc. *pisc.* 37; and *Schol. Bachm. An.* 2, 332.—(*Translator.*)

⁵⁸My proof for this is a passage from the latest philosophical literature. Herr Feuerbach, an Hegelian (*c'est tout dire!*) in his book, *Pierre Bayle: Ein Beitrag zur Geschichte der Philosophie,* 1838, p. 80, writes as follows: "But still more sublime than Kant's are Fichte's ideas as expressed in his Doctrine of Morals and elsewhere. Christianity has nothing in sublimity that could bear comparison with them."

PART III.

THE FOUNDING OF ETHICS

Chapter I.—Conditions of the Problem

THUS the foundation which Kant gave to Ethics, which for the last sixty years has been regarded as a sure basis, proves to be an inadmissible assumption, and merely theological Morals in disguise; it sinks therefore before our eyes into the deep gulf of philosophic error, which perhaps will never be filled up. That the previous attempts to lay a foundation are still less satisfactory, I take for granted, as I have already said. They consist, for the most part, of unproved assertions, drawn from the impalpable world of dreams, and at the same time—like Kant's system itself—full of an artificial subtlety dealing with the finest distinctions, and resting on the most abstract conceptions. We find difficult combinations; rules invented for the purpose; formulae balanced on a needle's point; and stilted maxims, from which it is no longer possible to look down and see life as it really is with all its turmoil. Such niceties are doubtless admirably adapted for the lecture-room, if only with a view to sharpening the wits; but they can never be the cause of the impulse to act justly and to do good, which is found in every man; as also they are powerless to counterbalance the deep-seated tendency to injustice and hardness of heart. Neither is it possible to fasten the reproaches of conscience upon them; to attribute the former to the breaking of such hair-splitting precepts only serves to make the same ridiculous. In a word, artificial associations of ideas like these cannot possibly—if we take the matter seriously—contain the true incentive to justice and loving-kindness. Rather must this be something that requires but little reflection, and still less abstraction and complicated synthesis; something that, independent of the training of the understanding, speaks to every one, even to the rudest,—a something resting simply on intuitive perception, and forcing its way home as a direct emanation from the reality of things. So long as Ethics cannot point to a foundation of this sort, she may go on with her discussions, and make a great display in the lecture-rooms; but real life will only pour contempt upon her. I must therefore give our moralists the paradoxical advice, first to look about them a little among their fellow-men.

Chapter II.—Sceptical View

BUT when we cast a retrospect over the attempts made, and made in vain, for more than two thousand years, to find a sure basis for Ethics, ought we not perhaps to think that after all there is no natural morality, independent of human institution? Shall we not conclude that all moral systems are nothing but artificial products, means invented for the better restraint of the selfish and wicked race of men; and further, that, as they have no internal credentials and no natural basis, they would fail in their purpose, if without the support of positive religion? The legal code and the police are not sufficient in all cases; there are offences, the discovery of which is too difficult; some, indeed, where punishment is a precarious matter; where, in short, we are left without public protection. Moreover, the civil law can at most enforce justice, not loving-kindness and beneficence; because, of course, these are qualities as regards which every one would like to play the passive, and no one the active, part. All this has given rise to the hypothesis that morality rests solely on religion, and that both have the same aim—that of being complementary to the necessary inadequacy of state machinery and legislation. Consequently, there cannot be (it is said) a natural morality, *i.e.,* one based simply on the nature of things, or of man, and the fruitless search of philosophers for its foundation is explained. This view is not without plausibility; and we find it as far back as the Pyrrhonians:

> οὔτε ἀγαθόν τί ἐστι φύσει, οὔτε κακόν,
> ἀλλὰ πρὸς ἀνθρώπων ταῦτα νόῳ κέκριται,
> κατὰ τὸν Τίμωνα.[1]
>
> —Sext. Emp. *adv. Math.,* XI., 140.

Also in modern times distinguished thinkers have given their adherence to it. A careful examination therefore it deserves; although the easier course would be to shelve it by giving an inquisitorial glance at the consciences of those in whom such a theory could arise.

We should fall into a great, a very childish blunder, if we believed all the just and legal actions of mankind to have a moral origin. This is far from being the case. As a rule, between the justice, which men practise, and genuine singleness of heart, there exists a relation analogous to that between polite expressions, and the true love of one's neighbour, which, unlike the former, does not ostensibly overcome Egoism, but really does so. That honesty of sentiment, everywhere so carefully exhibited, which

---

[1] *I.e.,* there is nothing either good or bad by nature, but these things are decided by human judgment, as Timon says. *V.* Sexti Empirici *Opera Quae Exstant: Adversus Mathematicos;* p. 462 A *ad fin.* Aurelianae: Petrus et Jacobus Chouët, 1621. *V.* also: Sexti Empirici *Opera,* edit. Jo. Albertus Fabricius: Lipsiae, 1718, Lib. XI., 140, p. 716.

requires to be regarded as above all suspicion; that deep indignation, which is stirred by the smallest sign of a doubt in this direction, and is ready to break out into furious anger;—To what are we to attribute these symptoms? None but the inexperienced and simple will take them for pure coin, for the working of a fine moral feeling, or conscience. In point of fact, the general correctness of conduct which is adopted in human intercourse, and insisted on as a rule no less immovable than the hills, depends principally on two external necessities; first, on legal ordinance, by virtue of which the rights of every man are protected by public authority; and secondly, on the recognised need of possessing civil honour, in other words, a good name, in order to advance in the world. This is why the steps taken by the individual are closely watched by public opinion, which is so inexorably severe that it never forgives even a single false move or slip, but remembers it against the guilty person as an indelible blot, all his life long. As far as this goes, public opinion is wise enough; for, starting from the fundamental principle: *Operari sequitur esse* (what one does is determined by what one is), it shows its conviction that the character is unchangeable, and that therefore what a man has once done, he will assuredly do again, if only the circumstances be precisely similar. Such are the two custodians that keep guard on the correct conduct of people, without which, to speak frankly, we should be in a sad case, especially with reference to property, this central point in human life, around which the chief part of its energy and activity revolves. For the purely ethical motives to integrity, assuming that they exist, cannot as a rule be applied, except very indirectly, to the question of ownership as guaranteed by the state. These motives, in fact, have a direct and essential bearing only on **natural** right; with **positive** right their connection is merely indirect, in so far as the latter is based on the former. Natural right, however, attaches to no other property than that which has been gained by one's own exertion; because, when this is seized, the owner is at the same time robbed of all the efforts he expended in acquiring it. The theory of preoccupancy I reject absolutely, but cannot here set forth its refutation.[2] Now of course all estate based on positive right ought ultimately and in the last instance (it matters not how many intermediate links are involved) to rest on the natural right of possession. But what a distance there is, in most cases, between the title-deeds, that belong to our civil life, and this natural right—their original source! Indeed their connection with the latter is generally either very difficult, or else impossible, to prove. What we hold is ours by inheritance, by marriage, by success in the lottery; or if in no way of this kind, still it is not gained by our own work, with the sweat of the brow, but rather by shrewdness and

---

[2]See *Die Welt als Wille und Vorstellung,* Vol. I., §62, p. 396 sqq., and Vol. II., chap. 47, p. 682.

bright ideas (*e.g.,* in the field of speculation), yes, and sometimes even by our very stupidity, which, through a conjunction of circumstances, is crowned and glorified by the *Deus eventus.* It is only in a very small minority of cases that property is the fruit of real labour and toil; and even then the work is usually mental, like that of lawyers, doctors, civilians, teachers, etc.; and this in the eyes of the rude appears to cost but little effort.

Now, when wealth is acquired in any such fashion, there is need of considerable education before the ethical right can be recognised and respected out of a purely moral impulse. Hence it comes about that not a few secretly regard the possessions of others as held merely by virtue of positive right. So, if they find means to wrest from another man his goods, by using, or perhaps by evading, the laws, they feel no scruples; for in their opinion he would lose what he holds, in the same way in which he had previously obtained it, and they consequently regard their own claims as equal to his. From their point of view, the right of the stronger in civil society is superseded by the right of the cleverer.

Incidentally we may notice that the **rich** man often shows an inflexible correctness of conduct. Why? Because with his whole heart he is attached to, and rigidly maintains, a rule, on the observance of which his entire wealth, and all its attendant advantages, depend. For this reason his profession of the principle: *Suum cuique* (to each his own), is thoroughly in earnest, and shows an unswerving consistency. No doubt there is an **objective** loyalty to sincerity and good faith, which avails to keep them sacred; but such loyalty is based simply on the fact that sincerity and good faith are the foundation of all free intercourse among men; of good order; and of secure ownership. Consequently they very often benefit **ourselves**, and with this end in view they must be preserved even at some cost: just as a good piece of land is worth a certain outlay. But integrity thus derived is, as a rule, only to be met with among wealthy people, or at least those who are engaged in a lucrative business. It is an especial characteristic of tradesmen; because they have the strongest conviction that for all the operations of commerce the one thing indispensable is mutual trust and credit; and this is why mercantile honour stands quite by itself. On the other hand, the **poor** man, who cannot make both ends meet, and who, by reason of the unequal division of property, sees himself condemned to want and hard work, while others before his eyes are lapped in luxury and idleness, will not easily perceive that the *raison d'être* of this inequality is a corresponding inequality of service and honest industry. And if he does **not** recognise this, how is he to be governed by the purely ethical motive to uprightness, which should keep him from stretching out his hand to grasp the superfluity of another? Generally, it is the order of government as established by law that restrains him. But should ever the rare occasion present itself when he discovers that he is beyond the reach of the police, and that he could by a single act throw off the galling burden of penury, which is aggravated by the sight of others' opulence; if he feels this, and realises that he could thus enter into the possession and enjoyment of all that he has so often coveted: what is there then to stay his hand? Religious dogmas? It is seldom that faith is so firm. A purely moral incentive to be just and upright? Perhaps in a few isolated cases. But in by far the greater number there is in reality nothing but the anxiety a man feels to keep his good name, his civil honour—a thing that touches closely even those in humble circumstances. He knows the imminent danger incurred of having to pay for dishonest conduct by being expelled from the great Masonic Lodge of honourable people who live correct lives. He knows that property all over the world is in their hands, and duly apportioned among themselves, and that they wield the power of making him an outcast for life from good society, in case he commit a single disgraceful action. He knows that whoever takes one false step in this direction is marked as a person that no one trusts, whose company every one shuns, and from whom all advancement is cut off; to whom, as being "a fellow that has stolen," the proverb is applied: "He who steals once is a thief all his life."

These, then, are the guards that watch over correct behaviour between man and man, and he who has lived, and kept his eyes open, will admit that the vast majority of honourable actions in human intercourse must be attributed to them; nay, he will go further, and say that there are not wanting people who hope to elude even **their** vigilance, and who regard justice and honesty merely as an external badge, as a flag, under the protection of which they can carry out their own freebooting propensities with better success. We need not therefore break out into holy wrath, and buckle on our armour, if a moralist is found to suggest that perhaps all integrity and uprightness may be at bottom only conventional. This is what Holbach, Helvetius, d'Alembert, and others of their time did; and, following out the theory, they endeavoured with great acumen to trace back all moral conduct to egoistic motives, however remote and indirect. That their position is literally true of most just actions, as having an ultimate foundation centred in the Self, I have shown above. That it is also true to a large extent of what is done in kindness and humanity, there can be no doubt; acts of this sort often arise from love of ostentation, still oftener from belief in a retribution to come, which may be dealt out in the second or even the third power;[3] or they can be explained by

---

[3] In other words: If a be a given offence, or virtuous act, and x the punishment, or reward, proportional to it; then the punishment, or reward, actually inflicted, instead of being x, may be x^2 or x^3.—(*Translator.*)

other egoistic motives. Nevertheless, it is equally certain that there occur actions of disinterested good-will and entirely voluntary justice. To prove the latter statement, I appeal only to the facts of experience, not to those of consciousness. There are isolated, yet indisputable cases on record, where not only the danger of legal prosecution, but also all chance of discovery, and even of suspicion has been excluded, and where, notwithstanding, the poor man has rendered to the rich his own. For example, things lost, and found, have been given back without any thought or hope of reward; a deposit made by a third person has been restored after his death to the rightful owner; a poor man, secretly intrusted with a treasure by a fugitive, has faithfully kept, and then returned, it. Instances of this sort can be found, beyond all doubt; only the surprise, the emotion, and the high respect awakened, when we hear of them, testify to the fact that they are unexpected and very exceptional. There are in truth really honest people: like four-leaved clover, their existence is not a fiction. But Hamlet uses no hyperbole when he says: "To be honest, as this world goes, is to be one man pick'd out of ten thousand." If it be objected that, after all, religious dogmas, involving rewards and penalties in another world, are at the root of conduct as above described; cases could probably be adduced where the actors possessed no religious faith whatever. And this is a thing by no means so infrequent as is generally maintained.

Those who combat the **sceptical view** appeal specially to the testimony of **conscience**. But conscience itself is impugned, and doubts are raised about its natural origin. Now, as a matter of fact, there is a *conscientia spuria* (false conscience), which is often confounded with the true. The regret and anxiety which many a man feels for what he has done is frequently, at bottom, nothing but fear of the possible consequences. Not a few people, if they break external, voluntary, and even absurd rules, suffer from painful searchings of heart, exactly similar to those inflicted by the real conscience. Thus, for instance, a bigoted Jew, if on Saturday he should smoke a pipe at home, becomes really oppressed with the sense of having disobeyed the command in Exodus xxxv. 3: "Ye shall kindle no fire throughout your habitations upon the Sabbath day." How often it happens that a nobleman or officer is the victim of self-reproach, because on some occasion or other he has not properly complied with that fools' codex, which is called knightly honour! Nay more: there are many of this class, who, if they see the impossibility of merely doing enough in some quarrel to satisfy the above-named code—to say nothing of keeping their pledged word of honour—are ready to shoot themselves. (Instances of both have come under my knowledge.) And this, while the selfsame man would with an easy mind break his promise every day, if only the shibboleth "Honour" be not involved. In short, every inconsequent, and thoughtless action, all conduct contrary to our prejudices, principles, or convictions, whatever these may be; indeed, every indiscretion, every mistake, every piece of stupidity rankles in us secretly, and leaves its sting behind. The average individual, who thinks his conscience such an imposing structure, would be surprised, could he see of what it actually consists: probably of about one-fifth, fear of men; one-fifth, superstition; one-fifth, prejudice; one-fifth, vanity; and one-fifth, habit. So that in reality he is no better than the Englishman, who said quite frankly: "I cannot afford to keep a conscience." Religious people of every creed, as a rule, understand by conscience nothing else than the dogmas and injunctions of their religion, and the self-examination based thereon; and it is in this sense that the expressions **coercion of conscience** and **liberty of conscience** are used. The same interpretation was always given by the theologians, schoolmen, and casuists of the middle ages and of later times. Whatever a man knew of the formulae and prescriptions of the Church, coupled with a resolution to believe and obey it, constituted his conscience. Thus we find the terms "a doubting conscience," "an opinionated conscience," "an erring conscience," and the like; and councils were held, and confessors employed, for the special purpose of setting such irregularities straight. How little the conception of conscience, just as other conceptions, is determined by its own object; how differently it is viewed by different people; how wavering and uncertain it appears in books; all this is briefly but clearly set forth in Stäudlin's *Geschichte der Lehre vom Gewissen.* These facts taken in conjunction are not calculated to establish the reality of the thing; they have rather given rise to the question whether there is in truth a genuine, inborn conscience. I have already had occasion in Part II., Chapter VIII., where the theory of Freedom is discussed, to touch on my view of conscience, and I shall return to it below.

All these sceptical objections added together do not in the least avail to prove that no true morality exists, however much they may moderate our expectations as to the moral tendency in man, and the natural basis of Ethics. Undoubtedly a great deal that is ascribed to the ethical sense can be proved to spring from other incentives; and when we contemplate the moral depravity of the world, it is sufficiently clear that the stimulus for good cannot be very powerful, especially as it often does not work even in cases where the opposing motives are weak, although then the individual difference of character makes itself fully felt.

It should be observed that this moral depravity is all the more difficult to discern, because its manifestations are checked and cloaked by public order, as enforced by law; by the necessity of having a good name; and even by ordinary polite manners. And this is not all. People commonly suppose that in the education of the young their moral interests are furthered by representing uprightness and virtue as principles generally followed by the world. Later on, it is often to their great harm that experience teaches them something else; for the discovery, that the instructors of their early years were the first to deceive them, is likely to have a more mischievous effect on their morality than if these persons had given them the first example of ingenuous truthfulness, by saying frankly: "The world is sunk in evil, and men are not what they ought to be; but be not misled thereby, and see that you do better." All this, as I have said, increases the difficulty of recognising the real immorality of mankind. The state—this masterpiece, which sums up the self-conscious, intelligent egoism of all—consigns the rights of each person to a power, which, being enormously superior to that of the individual, compels him to respect the rights of all others. This is the leash that restrains the limitless egoism of nearly every one, the malice of many, the cruelty of not a few. The illusion thus arising is so great that, when in special cases, where the executive power is ineffective, or is eluded, the insatiable covetousness, the base greed, the deep hypocrisy, or the spiteful tricks of men are apparent in all their ugliness, we recoil with horror, supposing that we have stumbled on some unheard-of monster: whereas, without the compulsion of law, and the necessity of keeping an honourable name, these sights would be of every day occurrence. In order to discover what, from a moral point of view, human beings are made of, we must study anarchist records, and the proceedings connected with criminals. The thousands that throng before our eyes, in peaceful intercourse each with the other, can only be regarded as so many tigers and wolves, whose teeth are secured by a strong muzzle. Let us now suppose this muzzle cast off, or, in other words, the power of the state abolished; the contemplation of the spectacle then to be awaited would make all thinking people shudder; and they would thus betray the small amount of trust they really have in the efficiency either of religion, or of conscience, or of the natural basis of Morals, whatever it be. But if these immoral, antinomian forces should be unshackled and let loose, it is precisely then that the true moral incentive, hidden before, would reveal its activity, and consequently be most easily recognised. And nothing would bring out so clearly as this the prodigious moral difference of character between man and man; it would be found to be as great as the intellectual, which is saying much.

The objection will perhaps be raised that Ethics is not concerned with what men actually do, but that it is the science which treats of what their conduct **ought** to be. Now this is exactly the position which I deny. In the critical part of the present treatise I have sufficiently demonstrated that the conception of **ought**, in other words, the **imperative form** of Ethics, is valid only in theological morals, outside of which it loses all sense and meaning. The end which I place before Ethical Science is to point out all the varied moral lines of human conduct; to explain them; and to trace them to their ultimate source. Consequently there remains no way of discovering the basis of Ethics except the empirical. We must search and see whether we can find any actions to which we are obliged to ascribe **genuine moral worth**: actions, that is, of voluntary justice, of pure loving-kindness, and of true nobleness. Such conduct, when found, is to be regarded as a given phaenomenon, which has to be properly accounted for; in other words, its real origin must be explored, and this will involve the investigation and explanation of the peculiar motives which lead men to actions so radically distinct from all others, that they form a class by themselves. These motives, together with a responsive susceptibility for them, will constitute the ultimate basis of morality, and the knowledge of them will be the foundation of Ethics. This is the humble path to which I direct the Science of Morals. It contains no construction *a priori,* no absolute legislation for all rational beings *in abstracto*; it lacks all official, academic sanction. Therefore, whoever thinks it not sufficiently fashionable, may return to the Categorical Imperative; to the Shibboleth of "Human Dignity"; to the empty phrases, the cobwebs, and the soap-bubbles of the Schools; to principles on which experience pours contempt at every step, and of which no one, outside the lecture-rooms knows anything, or has ever had the least notion. On the other hand, the foundation which is reached by following my path is upheld by experience; and it is experience which daily and hourly delivers its silent testimony in favour of my theory.

Chapter III.—Antimoral[4] Incentives

THE chief and fundamental incentive in man, as in animals, is **Egoism**, that is, the urgent impulse to exist, and exist under the best circumstances. The German word *Selbstsucht* (self-seeking) involves a false secondary idea of disease (*Sucht*).[5] The term *Eigennutz* (self-interest) de-

---

[4] I venture to use this word although irregularly formed, because "antiethical" would not here give an adequate meaning. *Sittlich* (in accordance with good manners) and *unsittlich* (contrary to good manners), which have lately come into vogue, are bad substitutes for *moralisch* (moral) and *unmoralisch* (immoral): first, because *moralisch* is a scientific conception, which, as such, requires to be denoted by a Greek and Latin term, for reasons which may be found in *Die Welt als Wille und Vorstellung,* vol. ii., chap. 12, p. 134 sqq.; and secondly, because *sittlich* is a weaker and tamer expression, difficult to distinguish from *sittsam* (modest) which in popular acceptation means *zimperlich* (simpering). No concessions must be made to this extravagant love of germanising!

[5] In *Sucht* (*siech* = sick) and *Selbst-sucht* (*suchen* = seek) there is an apparent confusion between the two bases SUK (*seuka*) to be ill, and SÔKYAN, to seek. *V.* Skeat's *Etymological Dictionary.*—(*Translator.*)

notes Egoism, so far as the latter is guided by reason, which enables it, by means of reflection, to prosecute its purposes systematically; so that animals may be called egoistic, but not self-interested (*eigennützig*). I shall therefore retain the word **Egoism** for the general idea. Now this Egoism is, both in animals and men, connected in the closest way with their very essence and being; indeed, it is one and the same thing. For this reason all human actions, as a rule, have their origin in Egoism, and to it, accordingly, we must always first turn, when we try to find the explanation of any given line of conduct; just as, when the endeavour is made to guide a man in any direction, the means to this end are universally calculated with reference to the same all-powerful motive. Egoism is, from its nature, limitless. The individual is filled with the unqualified desire of preserving his life, and of keeping it free from all pain, under which is included all want and privation. He wishes to have the greatest possible amount of pleasurable existence, and every gratification that he is capable of appreciating; indeed, he attempts, if possible, to evolve fresh capacities for enjoyment. Everything that opposes the strivings of his Egoism awakens his dislike, his anger, his hate: this is the mortal enemy, which he tries to annihilate. If it were possible, he would like to possess everything for his own pleasure; as this is impossible, he wishes at least to control everything. "All things for me, and nothing for others" is his maxim. Egoism is a huge giant overtopping the world. If each person were allowed to choose between his own destruction and that of the rest of mankind, I need not say what the decision would be in most cases. Thus it is that every human unit makes himself the centre of the world, which he views exclusively from that standpoint. Whatever occurs, even, for instance, the most sweeping changes in the destinies of nations, he brings into relation first and foremost with his own interests, which, however slightly and indirectly they may be affected, he is sure to think of before anything else. No sharper contrast can be imagined than that between the profound and exclusive attention which each person devotes to his own self, and the indifference with which, as a rule, all other people regard that self,—an indifference precisely like that with which he in turn looks upon them. To a certain extent it is actually comic to see how each individual out of innumerable multitudes considers himself, at least from the practical point of view, as the only **real** thing, and all others in some sort as mere phantoms. The ultimate reason of this lies in the fact that every one is **directly** conscious of himself, but of others only **indirectly**, through his mind's eye; and the direct impression asserts its right. In other words, it is in consequence of the subjectivity which is essential to our consciousness that each person is himself the whole world; for all that is objective exists only indirectly, as simply the mental picture of the subject; whence it comes about that everything is invariably expressed in terms of self-consciousness. The only world which the individual really grasps, and of which he has certain knowledge, he carries in himself, as a mirrored image fashioned by his brain; and he is, therefore, its centre. Consequently he is all in all to himself; and since he feels that he contains within his ego all that is real, nothing can be of greater importance to him than his own self.[6] Moreover this supremely important self, this microcosm, to which the macrocosm stands in relation as its mere modification or accident,—this, which is the individual's whole world, he knows perfectly well must be destroyed by death; which is therefore for him equivalent to the destruction of all things.

Such, then, are the elements out of which, on the basis of the Will to live, Egoism grows up, and like a broad trench it forms a perennial separation between man and man. If on any occasion some one actually jumps across, to help another, such an act is regarded as a sort of miracle, which calls forth amazement and wins approval. In Part II., Chapter VI., where Kant's principle of Morals is discussed, I had the opportunity of describing how Egoism behaves in everyday life, where it is always peering out of some corner or other, despite ordinary politeness, which, like the traditional fig-leaf, is used as a covering. In point of fact, politeness is the conventional and systematic disavowal of Egoism in the trifles of daily intercourse, and is, of course, a piece of recognised hypocrisy. Gentle manners are expected and commended, because that which they conceal—Egoism—is so odious, that no one wishes to see it, however much it is known to be there; just as people like to have repulsive objects hidden at least by a curtain. Now, unless external force (under which must be included every source of fear whether of human or superhuman powers), or else the real moral incentive is in effective operation, it is certain that Egoism always pursues its purposes with unqualified directness; hence without these checks, considering the countless number of egoistic individuals, the *bellum omnium contra omnes*[7] would be the order of the day, and prove the ruin of all. Thus is explained the early construction by reflecting reason of state government, which, arising, as it does, from a mutual fear of reciprocal violence, obviates the disastrous consequences of the general Egoism, as far as it is possible to do by **negative** procedure. Where, however, the two forces that oppose Egoism fail to be operative, the latter is not slow to reveal all its horrible dimensions, nor is the spectacle exactly attractive. In order to express the strength of this antimoral power in a few words, to portray it, so to say, at one stroke, some very emphatic hyperbole is wanted. It may be put thus: many a man would be

---

[6]It should be noticed that while from the *subjective* side a man's self assumes these gigantic proportions, *objectively* it shrinks to almost nothing—namely, to about the one-thousand-millionth part of the human race.

[7]The war of all against all. Hobbes uses this expression.—(*Translator.*)

quite capable of killing another, simply to rub his boots over with the victim's fat. I am only doubtful whether this, after all, is any exaggeration. **Egoism**, then, is the first and principal, though not the only, power that the **moral Motive** has to contend against; and it is surely sufficiently clear that the latter, in order to enter the lists against such an opponent, must be something more real than a hair-splitting sophism or an *a priori* soap-bubble. In war the first thing to be done is to know the enemy well; and in the shock of battle, now impending, **Egoism**, as the chief combatant on its own side, is best set against the virtue of **Justice**, which, in my opinion, is the first and original cardinal virtue.

The virtue of **loving-kindness**, on the other hand, is rather to be matched with **ill-will**, or **spitefulness**, the origin and successive stages of which we will now consider. Ill-will, in its lower degrees, is very frequent, indeed, almost a common thing; and it easily rises in the scale. Goethe is assuredly right when he says that in this world indifference and aversion are quite at home.—(*Wahlverwandtschaften,* Part I., chap. 3.) It is very fortunate for us that the cloak, which prudence and politeness throw over this vice, prevents us from seeing how general it is, and how the *bellum omnium contra omnes* is constantly waged, at least in thought. Yet ever and anon there is some appearance of it: for instance, in the relentless backbiting so frequently observed; while its clearest manifestation is found in all outbreaks of anger, which, for the most part, are quite disproportional to their cause, and which could hardly be so violent, had they not been compressed—like gunpowder—into the explosive compound formed of long cherished brooding hatred. Ill-will usually arises from the unavoidable collisions of Egoism which occur at every step. It is, moreover, objectively excited by the view of the weakness, the folly, the vices, failings, shortcomings, and imperfections of all kinds, which every one more or less, at least occasionally, affords to others. Indeed, the spectacle is such, that many a man, especially in moments of melancholy and depression, may be tempted to regard the world, from the aesthetic standpoint, as a cabinet of caricatures; from the intellectual, as a madhouse; and from the moral, as a nest of sharpers. If such a mental attitude be indulged, misanthropy is the result. Lastly, one of the chief sources of ill-will is **envy**; or rather, the latter is itself ill-will, kindled by the happiness, possessions, or advantages of others. No one is absolutely free from envy; and Herodotus (III. 80) said long ago: φθόνος ἀρχῆθεν ἐμφύεται ἀνθρώπῳ (envy is a natural growth in man from the beginning). But its degrees vary considerably. It is most poisonous and implacable when directed against personal qualities, because then the envious have nothing to hope for. And precisely in such cases its vilest form also appears, because men are made to hate what they ought to love and honour. Yet so "the world wags," even as Petrarca complained:

> *Di lor par più, che d'altri, invidia s'abbia,*
> *Che per se stessi son levati a volo,*
> *Uscendo fuor della commune gabbia.*
> (For envy fastens most of all on those,
> Who, rising on their own strong wings, escape
> The bars wherein the vulgar crowd is cag'd.)

The reader is referred to the Parerga, vol. ii., §114, for a more complete examination of envy.

In a certain sense the opposite of envy is the habit of gloating over the misfortunes of others. At any rate, while the former is human, the latter is diabolical. There is no sign more infallible of an entirely bad heart, and of profound moral worthlessness than open and candid enjoyment in seeing other people suffer. The man in whom this trait is observed ought to be for ever avoided: *Hic niger est, hunc tu, Romane, caveto.*[8] These two vices are in themselves merely theoretical; in practice they become malice and cruelty. It is true that Egoism may lead to wickedness and crime of every sort; but the resulting injury and pain to others are simply the means, not the end, and are therefore involved only as an accident. Whereas malice and cruelty make others' misery the end in itself, the realisation of which affords distinct pleasure. They therefore constitute a higher degree of moral turpitude. The maxim of Egoism, at its worst is: *Neminem juva, immo omnes, si forte conducit* (thus there is always a condition), *laede* (help no body, but rather injure all people, if it brings you any advantage). The guiding rule of malice is: *Omnes, quantum potes, laede* (injure all people as far as you can). As malicious joy is in fact theoretical cruelty, so, conversely, cruelty is nothing but malicious joy put into practice; and the latter is sure to show itself in the form of cruelty, directly an opportunity offers.

An examination of the special vices that spring from these two primary antimoral forces forms no part of the present treatise: its proper place would be found in a detailed system of Ethics. From **Egoism** we should probably derive greed, gluttony, lust, selfishness, avarice, covetousness, injustice, hardness of heart, pride, arrogance, etc.; while to **spitefulness** might be ascribed disaffection, envy, ill-will, malice, pleasure in seeing others suffer, prying curiosity, slander, insolence, petulance, hatred, anger, treachery, fraud, thirst for revenge, cruelty, etc. The first root is more bestial, the second more devilish; and according as either is the stronger; or according as the moral incentive, to be described below, predominates, so the salient points for the ethical classification of character are determined. No man is entirely free from some traces of all three.

---

[8]This man is black; of him shalt thou, O Roman, beware. *V.* Horace, *Sat.,* Lib. I. 4. 85.— (*Translator.*)

Here I bring to an end my review of these terrible powers of evil; it is an array reminding one of the Princes of Darkness in Milton's Pandemonium. But my plan, which in this respect of course differs from that of all other moralists, required me to consider at the outset this gloomy side of human nature, and, like Dante, to descend first to Tartarus.

It will now be fully apparent how difficult our problem is. We have to find a motive capable of making a man take up a line of conduct directly opposed to all those propensities which lie deeply ingrained in his nature; or, given such conduct as a fact of experience, we must search for a motive capable of supplying an adequate and non-artificial explanation of it. The difficulty, in fact, is so great that, in order to solve it, for the vast majority of mankind, it has been everywhere necessary to have recourse to machinery from another world. Gods have been pointed to, whose will and command the required mode of behaviour was said to be, and who were represented as emphasising this command by penalties and rewards either in this, or in another world, to which death would be the gate. Now let us assume that belief in a doctrine of this sort took general root (a thing which is certainly possible through strenuous inculcation at a very early age); and let us also assume that it brought about the intended effect,—though this is a much harder matter to admit, and not nearly so well confirmed by experience; we should then no doubt succeed in obtaining strict legality of action, even beyond the limits that justice and the police can reach; but every one feels that this would not in the least imply what we mean by morality of the heart. For obviously, every act arising from motives like those just mentioned is after all derived simply from pure Egoism. How can I talk of unselfishness when I am enticed by a promised guerdon, or deterred by a threatened punishment? A recompense in another world, thoroughly believed in, must be regarded as a bill of exchange, which is perfectly safe, though only payable at a very distant date. It is thus quite possible that the profuse assurances, which beggars so constantly make, that those, who relieve them, will receive a thousandfold more for their gifts in the next world, may lead many a miser to generous alms-giving; for such a one complacently views the matter as a good investment of money, being perfectly convinced that he will rise again as a Croesus. For the mass of mankind, it will perhaps be always necessary to continue the appeal to incentives of this nature, and we know that such is the teaching promulgated by the different religions, which are in fact the **metaphysics of the people**. Be it, however, observed in this connection that a man is sometimes just as much in error as to the true motives that govern his own acts, as he is with regard to those of others. Hence it is certain that many persons, while they can only account to themselves for their noblest actions by attributing them to motives of the kind above described, are, nevertheless, really guided in their conduct by far higher and purer incentives, though the latter may be much more difficult to discover. They are doing, no doubt, out of direct love of their neighbour, that which they can but explain as the command of their God. On the other hand, Philosophy, in dealing with this, as with all other problems, endeavours to extract the true and ultimate cause of the given phaenomena from the disclosures which the nature itself of man yields, and which, freed as they must be from all mythical interpretation, from all religious dogmas, and transcendent hypostases, she requires to see confirmed by external or internal experience. Now, as our present task is a philosophical one, we must entirely disregard all solutions conditioned by any religion; and I have here touched on them merely in order to throw a stronger light on the magnitude of the difficulty.

Chapter IV.—Criterion of Actions of Moral Worth

THERE is first the empirical question to be settled, whether actions of voluntary justice and unselfish loving-kindness, which are capable of rising to nobleness and magnanimity, actually occur in experience. Unfortunately, this inquiry cannot be decided altogether empirically, because it is invariably only the **act** that experience gives, the **incentives** not being apparent. Hence the possibility always remains that an egoistic motive may have had weight in determining a just or good deed. In a theoretical investigation like the present, I shall not avail myself of the inexcusable trick of shifting the matter on to the reader's conscience. But I believe there are few people who have any doubt about the matter, and who are not convinced from their own experience that just acts are often performed simply and solely to prevent a man suffering from injustice. Most of us, I do not hesitate to say, are persuaded that there are persons in whom the principle of giving others their due seems to be innate, who neither intentionally injure any one, nor unconditionally seek their own advantage, but in considering themselves show regard also for the rights of their neighbours; persons who, when they undertake matters involving reciprocal obligations, not only see that the other party does his duty, but also that he gets his own, because it is really against their will that any one, with whom they have to do, should be shabbily treated. These are the men of true probity, the few *aequi* (just) among the countless number of the *iniqui* (unjust). Such people exist. Similarly, it will be admitted, I think, that many help and give, perform services, and deny themselves, without having any further intention in their hearts than that of assisting another, whose distress they see. When Arnold von Winkelried exclaimed: "*Trüwen, lieben Eidgenossen, wullt's minem Wip und*

Kinde gedenken,"[9] and then clasped in his arms as many hostile spears as he could grasp; can any one believe that he had some selfish purpose? I cannot. To cases of voluntary justice, which cannot be denied without deliberate and wilful trifling with facts, I have already drawn attention in Chapter II. of this Part. Should any one, however, persist in refusing to believe that such actions ever happen, then, according to his view, Ethics would be a science without any real object, like Astrology and Alchemy, and it would be waste of time to discuss its basis any further. With him, therefore, I have nothing to do, and address myself to those who allow that we are dealing with something more than an imaginary creation.

It is, then, only to conduct of the above kind that genuine moral worth can be ascribed. Its special mark is that it rejects and excludes the whole class of motives by which otherwise all human action is prompted: I mean the **self-interested** motives, using the word in its widest sense. Consequently the moral value of an act is lowered by the disclosure of an accessory selfish incentive; while it is entirely destroyed, if that incentive stood alone. The absence of all egoistic motives is thus the **Criterion** of an action of moral value. It may, no doubt, be objected that also acts of pure malice and cruelty are not selfish.[10] But it is manifest that the latter cannot be meant, since they are, in kind, the exact opposite of those now being considered. If, however, the definition be insisted on in its strict sense, then we may expressly except such actions, because of their essential token—the compassing of others' suffering.

There is also another characteristic of conduct having real moral worth, which is entirely internal and therefore less obvious. I allude to the fact that it leaves behind a certain self-satisfaction which is called the approval of conscience: just as, on the other hand, injustice and unkindness, and still more malice and cruelty, involve a secret self-condemnation. Lastly, there is an external, secondary, and accidental sign that draws a clear line between the two classes. Acts of the former kind win the approval and respect of disinterested witnesses: those of the latter incur their disapproval and contempt.

Those actions that bear the stamp of moral value, so determined, and admitted to be realities, constitute the phaenomenon that lies before us, and which we have to explain. We must accordingly search out **what** it is that moves men to such conduct. If we succeed in our investigation, we shall necessarily bring to light the true moral incentive; and, as it is upon this that all ethical science must depend, our problem will then be solved.

---

[9]Comrades, true and loyal to our oath, care for my wife and child in remembrance of this.
[10]Acts of malice and cruelty are so many gratifications of the ego, and are therefore, in a certain sense, selfish. *V.* Introduction, pp. xvi. and xvii.—(*Translator.*)

Chapter V.—Statement and Proof of the Only True Moral Incentive

THE preceding considerations, which were unavoidably necessary in order to clear the ground, now enable me to indicate the true incentive which underlies all acts of real moral worth. The seriousness, and indisputable genuineness, with which we shall find it is distinguished, removes it far indeed from the hair-splittings, subtleties, sophisms, assertions formulated out of airy nothings, and *a priori* soap-bubbles, which all systems up to the present have tried to make at once the source of moral conduct and the basis of Ethics. This incentive I shall not put forward as an hypothesis to be accepted or rejected, as one pleases; I shall actually **prove** that it is the only possible one. But as this demonstration requires several fundamental truths to be borne in mind, the reader's attention is first called to certain propositions which we must presuppose, and which may properly be considered as axioms; except the last two, which result from the analysis contained in the preceding chapter, and in Part II., Chapter III.

(1) No action can take place without a sufficient motive; as little as a stone can move without a sufficient push or pull.

(2) Similarly, no action can be left undone, when, given the character of the doer, a sufficient motive is present; unless a stronger counter-motive necessarily prevents it.

(3) Whatever moves the Will,—this, and this alone, implies the sense of weal and woe, in the widest sense of the term; and conversely, weal and woe signify "that which is in conformity with, or which is contrary to, a Will." Hence every motive must have a connection with weal and woe.

(4) Consequently every action stands in relation to, and has as its ultimate object, a being susceptible of weal and woe.

(5) This being is either the doer himself; or another, whose position as regards the action is therefore **passive**; since it is done either to his harm, or to his benefit and advantage.

(6) Every action, which has to do, as its ultimate object, with the weal and woe of the agent himself, is **egoistic**.

(7) The foregoing propositions with regard to what is done apply equally to what is left undone, in all cases where motive and counter-motive play their parts.

(8) From the analysis in the foregoing chapter, it results that **Egoism** and the **moral worth** of an action absolutely exclude each other. If an act have an **egoistic** object as its motive, then no moral value can be attached to it; if an act is to have moral value, then no egoistic object, direct or indirect, near or remote, may be its motive.

(9) In consequence of my elimination in Part II., Chapter III., of alleged duties towards ourselves, the moral significance of our conduct can only lie in the effect produced upon others; its relation to the latter is alone that which lends it moral worth, or worthlessness, and constitutes it an act of justice, loving-kindness, etc., or the reverse.

From these propositions the following conclusion is obvious: The **weal and woe**, which (according to our third axiom) must, as its ultimate object, lie at the root of everything done, or left undone, is either that of the doer himself, or that of some other person, whose *rôle* with reference to the action is passive. Conduct in the first case is necessarily **egoistic**, as it is impelled by an interested motive. And this is not only true when men—as they nearly always do—plainly shape their acts for their own profit and advantage; it is equally true when from anything done we expect some benefit to ourselves, no matter how remote, whether in this or in another world. Nor is it less the fact when our honour, our good name, or the wish to win the respect of some one, the sympathy of the lookers on, etc., is the object we have in view; or when our intention is to uphold a rule of conduct, which, if generally followed, would occasionally be useful to ourselves, for instance, the principle of justice, of mutual succour and aid, and so forth. Similarly, the proceeding is at bottom egoistic, when a man considers it a prudent step to obey some absolute command issued by an unknown, but evidently supreme power; for in such a case nothing can be the motive but **fear** of the disastrous consequences of disobedience, however generally and indistinctly these may be conceived. Nor is it a whit the less Egoism that prompts us when we endeavour to emphasise, by something done or left undone, the high opinion (whether distinctly realised or not) which we have of ourselves, and of our value or dignity; for the diminution of self-satisfaction, which might otherwise occur, would involve the wounding of our pride. Lastly, it is still Egoism that is operative, when a man, following Wolf's principles, seeks by his conduct to work out his own perfection. In short, one may make the ultimate incentive to an action what one pleases; it will always turn out, no matter by how circuitous a path, that in the last resort what affects the actual weal and woe of the agent himself is the real motive; consequently what he does is **egoistic**, and therefore **without moral worth**. There is only a single case in which this fails to happen: namely, when the ultimate incentive for doing something, or leaving it undone, is precisely and exclusively centred in the weal and woe of some one else, who plays a passive part; that is to say, when the person on the active side, by what he does, or omits to do, simply and solely regards the weal and woe of another, and has absolutely no other object than to benefit him, by keeping harm from his door, or, it may be, even by affording help, assistance, and relief. It is this aim alone that gives to what is done, or left undone, the stamp of moral worth; which is thus seen to depend exclusively on the circumstance that the act is carried out, or omitted, purely for the benefit and advantage of another. If and when this is not so, then the question of weal and woe which incites to, or deters from, every action contemplated, can only relate to the agent himself; whence its performance, or non-performance is entirely egoistic, and without moral value.

But if what I do is to take place solely on account of some one else; then it follows that **his** weal and woe must directly constitute **my** motive; just as, ordinarily, **my own** weal and woe form it. This narrows the limits of our problem, which may now be stated as follows: How is it possible that another's weal and woe should influence my will directly, that is, exactly in the same way as otherwise my own move it? How can that which affects another for good or bad become my immediate motive, and actually sometimes assume such importance that it more or less supplants my own interests, which are, as a rule, the single source of the incentives that appeal to me? Obviously, only because that other person becomes the ultimate object of my will, precisely as usually I myself am that object; in other words, because I directly desire weal, and not woe, for him, just as habitually I do for myself. This, however, necessarily implies that I suffer with him, and feel his woe, exactly as in most cases I feel only mine, and therefore desire his weal as immediately as at other times I desire only my own. But, for this to be possible, I must in some way or other be **identified** with him; that is, the **difference** between myself and him, which is the precise *raison d'être* of my Egoism, must be **removed**, at least to a certain extent. Now, since I do not live in his skin, there remains only the knowledge, that is, the mental picture, I have of him, as the possible means whereby I can so far identify myself with him, that my action declares the difference to be practically effaced. The process here analysed is not a dream, a fancy floating in the air; it is perfectly real, and by no means infrequent. It is, what we see every day,—the phaenomenon of **Compassion**; in other words, the direct participation, independent of all ulterior considerations, in the sufferings of another, leading to sympathetic assistance in the effort to prevent or remove them; whereon in the last resort all satisfaction and all well-being and happiness depend. It is this Compassion alone which is the real basis of all **voluntary** justice and all **genuine** loving-kindness. Only so far as an action springs therefrom, has it moral value; and all conduct that proceeds from any other motive whatever has none. When once compassion is stirred within me, by another's pain, then his weal and woe go straight to my heart, exactly in the same way, if not always to the same degree, as otherwise I feel only my own. Consequently the difference between myself and him is no longer an absolute one.

No doubt this operation is astonishing, indeed hardly comprehensible. It is, in fact, the great mystery of Ethics, its original phaenomenon, and the boundary stone, past which only transcendental speculation may dare to take a step. Herein we see the wall of partition, which, according to the light of nature (as reason is called by old theologians), entirely separates being from being, broken down, and the non-ego to a certain extent identified with the ego. I wish for the moment to leave the metaphysical explanation of this enigma untouched, and first to inquire whether all acts of voluntary justice and true loving-kindness really arise from it. If so, our problem will be solved, for we shall have found the ultimate basis of morality, and shown that it lies in human nature itself. This foundation, however, in its turn cannot form a problem of Ethics, but rather, like every other ultimate fact as such, of Metaphysics. Only the solution, that the latter offers of the primary ethical phaenomenon, lies outside the limits of the question put by the Danish Royal Society, which is concerned solely with the basis; so that the transcendental explanation can be given merely as a voluntary and unessential appendix.

But before I turn to the derivation of the cardinal virtues from the original incentive, as here disclosed, I have still to bring to the notice of the reader two observations which the subject renders necessary.

(1) For the purpose of easier comprehension I have simplified the above presentation of compassion as the sole source of truly moral actions, by intentionally leaving out of consideration the incentive of **Malice**, which while it is equally useless to the self as compassion, makes the **pain** of others its ultimate purpose. We are now, however, in a position, by including it, to state the above proof more completely, and rigorously, as follows:—

There are only **three** fundamental springs of human conduct, and all possible motives arise from one or other of these. They are:

(*a*) Egoism; which desires the weal of the self, and is limitless.

(*b*) Malice; which desires the woe of others, and may develop to the utmost cruelty.

(*c*) Compassion; which desires the weal of others, and may rise to nobleness and magnanimity.

Every human act is referable to one of these springs; although two of them may work together. Now, as we have assumed that actions of moral worth are in point of fact realities; it follows that they also must proceed from one of these primal sources. But, by the eighth axiom, they cannot arise from the first, and still less from the second; since all conduct springing from the latter is morally worthless, while the offshoots of the former are in part neither good nor bad in themselves. Hence they must have their origin in the third incentive; and this will be established *a posteriori* in the sequel.

(2) Direct sympathy with another is limited to his sufferings, and is not immediately awakened by his well-being: the latter *per se* leaves us indifferent. J. J. Rousseau in his *Émile* (Bk. IV.) expresses the same view: "*Première maxime: il n'est pas dans le coeur humain, de se mettre à la place des gens, qui sont plus heureux que nous, mais seulement de ceux, qui sont plus à plaindre,*"[11] etc.

The reason of this is that pain or suffering, which includes all want, privation, need, indeed every wish, is **positive**, and works **directly** on the consciousness. Whereas the nature of satisfaction, of enjoyment, of happiness, and the like, consists solely in the fact that a hardship is done away with, a pain lulled: whence their effect is **negative**. We thus see why need or desire is the condition of every pleasure. Plato understood this well enough, and only excepted sweet odours, and intellectual enjoyment. (*De Rep.,* IX., p. 264 sq., edit. Bipont.)[12] And Voltaire says: "*Il n'est pas de vrais plaisirs, qu'avec de vrais besoins.*"[13] Pain, then, is **positive**, and makes itself known by itself: satisfaction or pleasure is **negative**—simply the removal of the former. This principle explains the fact that only the suffering, the want, the danger, the helplessness of another awakens our sympathy directly and as such. The lucky or contented man, **as such**, leaves us indifferent—in reality because his state is negative; he is without pain, indigence, or distress. We may of course take pleasure in the success, the well-being, the enjoyment of others; but if we do, it is a secondary pleasure, and caused by our having previously sorrowed over their sufferings and privations. Or else we share the joy and happiness of a man, not **as such**, but because, and in so far as, he is our child, father, friend, relation, servant, subject, etc. In a word, the good fortune, or pleasure of another, **purely as such**, does not arouse in us the same direct sympathy as is certainly elicited by his misfortune, privation, or misery, **purely as such**. If even on **our own behalf** it is only suffering (under which must be reckoned all wants, needs, wishes, and even ennui) that stirs our activity; and if contentment and prosperity fill us with indolence and lazy repose; why should it not be the same when others are concerned? For (as we have seen) our sympathy rests on an identification of ourselves with them. Indeed, the sight of success and enjoyment, **purely as such**, is very apt to raise the envy, to which every man is prone, and which has its place among the antimoral forces enumerated above.

In connection with the exposition of Compassion here given, as the coming into play of motives directly occasioned by another's calamity, I

---

[11]First maxim: it is not in our hearts to identify ourselves with those who are happier than we are, but only with those who are less happy.

[12]Stallbaum: p. 584, sq.—(*Translator.*)

[13]There are no real pleasures, without real needs.

take the opportunity of condemning the mistake of Cassina,[14] which has been so often repeated. His view is that compassion arises from a sudden hallucination, which makes us put ourselves in the place of the sufferer, and then imagine that we are undergoing **his** pain in **our own** person. This is not in the least the case. The conviction never leaves us for a moment that he is the sufferer, not we; and it is precisely in **his** person, not in ours, that we feel the distress which afflicts us. We suffer **with** him, and therefore **in** him; we feel his trouble as **his**, and are not under the delusion that it is ours; indeed, the happier we are, the greater the contrast between our own state and his, the more we are open to the promptings of Compassion. The explanation of the possibility of this extraordinary phaenomenon is, however, not so easy; nor is it to be reached by the path of pure psychology, as Cassina supposed. The key can be furnished by Metaphysics alone; and this I shall attempt to give in the last Part of the present treatise.

I now turn to consider the derivation of actions of real moral worth from the source which has been indicated. The general rule by which to test such conduct, and which, consequently, is the leading principle of Ethics, I have already enlarged upon in the foregoing Part, and enunciated as follows: *Neminem laede; immo omnes, quantum potes, juva.* (Do harm to no one; but rather help all people, as far as lies in your power.) As this formula contains two clauses, so the actions corresponding to it fall naturally into two classes.

Chapter VI.—The Virtue of Justice

IF we look more closely at this process called Compassion, which we have shown to be the primary ethical phaenomenon, we remark at once that there are two distinct degrees in which another's suffering may become directly my motive, that is, may urge me to do something, or to leave it undone. The first degree of Compassion is seen when, by counteracting egoistic and malicious motives, it keeps me from bringing pain on another, and from becoming myself the cause of trouble, which so far does not exist. The other higher degree is manifested, when it works positively, and incites me to active help. The distinction between the so-called duties of law and duties of virtue, better described as justice and loving-kindness, which was effected by Kant in such a forced and artificial manner, here results entirely of itself; whence the correctness of the principle is attested. It is the natural, unmistakable, and sharp separation between negative and positive, between doing no harm, and helping.

---

[14] *V.* his *Saggio Analitico sulla Compassione,* 1788; German translation by Pockels, 1790.

The terms in common use—namely, "the duties of law," and "the duties of virtue," (the latter being also called "duties of love," or "imperfect duties,") are in the first place faulty because they co-ordinate the *genus* with the *species*; for justice is one of the virtues. And next, they owe their origin to the mistake of giving a much too wide extension to the idea "Duty"; which I shall reduce to its proper limits below. In place, therefore, of these duties I put two virtues; the one, justice, and the other, loving-kindness; and I name them cardinal virtues, since from them all others not only in fact proceed, but also may be theoretically derived. Both have their root in natural Compassion. And this Compassion is an undeniable fact of human consciousness, is an essential part of it, and does not depend on assumptions, conceptions, religions, dogmas, myths, training, and education. On the contrary, it is original and immediate, and lies in human nature itself. It consequently remains unchanged under all circumstances, and reveals itself in every land, and at all times. This is why appeal is everywhere confidently made to it, as to something necessarily present in every man; and it is never an attribute of the "strange gods."[15] As he, who appears to be without compassion, is called inhuman; so "humanity" is often used as its synonyme.

The first degree, then, in which this natural and genuine moral incentive shows itself is only **negative**. Originally we are all disposed to injustice and violence, because our need, our desire, our anger and hate pass into the consciousness directly, and hence have the *Jus primi occupantis*. (The right of the first occupant.) Whereas the sufferings of others, caused by our injustice and violence, enter the consciousness **indirectly**, that is, by the secondary channel of a mental picture, and not till they are understood by experience. Thus Seneca (*Ep.* 50) says: *Ad neminem ante bona mens venit, quam mala.* (Good feelings never come before bad ones.) In its first degree, therefore, Compassion opposes and baffles the design to which I am urged by the antimoral forces dwelling within me, and which will bring trouble on a fellow-being. It calls out to me: "Stop!" and encircles the other as with a fence, so as to protect him from the injury which otherwise my egoism or malice would lead me to inflict on him. So arises out of this first degree of compassion the rule: *Neminem laede.* (Do harm to no one.) This is the fundamental principle of the virtue of justice, and here alone is to be found its origin, pure and simple,—an origin which is truly moral, and free from all extraneous admixture. Otherwise derived, justice would have to rest on Egoism,—a *reductio ad absurdum*. If my nature is susceptible of Compassion up to this

---

[15]Thus, when the first gleam of *Mitleid* stole into her heart, Brünnhilde could no longer remain a Walküre; and Wotan's end comes, when by the same solvent he is at length set free from the delusion of the *principium individuationis.*—(*Translator.*)

point, then it will avail to keep me back, whenever I should like to use others' pain as a means to obtain my ends; equally, whether this pain be immediate, or an after-consequence, whether it be effected directly, or indirectly, through intermediate links. I shall therefore lay hands on the property as little as on the person of another, and avoid causing him distress, no less mental than bodily. I shall thus not only abstain from doing him physical injury, but also, with equal care I shall guard against inflicting on him the suffering of mind, which mortification and calumny, anxiety and vexation so surely work. The same sense of Compassion will check me from gratifying my desires at the cost of women's happiness for life, or from seducing another man's wife, or from ruining youths morally and physically by tempting them to *paederastia*. Not that it is at all necessary in each single case that Compassion should be definitely excited; indeed it would often come too late; but rather the rule: *Neminem laede,* is formed by noble minds out of the knowledge, gained once for all, of the injury which every unjust act necessarily entails upon others, and which is aggravated by the feeling of having to endure wrong through a *force majeure.* Such natures are led by reflecting reason to carry out this principle with unswerving resolution. They respect the rights of every man, and abstain from all encroachment on them; they keep themselves free from self-reproach, by refusing to be the cause of others' trouble; they do not shift on to shoulders not their own, by force or by trickery, the burdens and sorrows of life, which circumstances bring to every one; they prefer to bear themselves the portions allotted to them, so as not to double those of their neighbours. For although generalising formulae, and abstract knowledge of whatever kind, are not in the least the cause, or the real basis of morality; these are nevertheless indispensable for a moral course of life. They are the cistern or reservoir, in which the habit of mind, that springs from the fount of all morality (a fount not at all moments flowing), may be stored up, thence to be drawn off, as occasion requires. There is thus an analogy between things moral and things physiological; among many instances of which we need only mention that of the gall-bladder, which is used for keeping the secretion of the liver. Without firmly held principles we should inevitably be at the mercy of the antimoral incentives, directly they are roused to activity by external influences; and **self-control** lies precisely in steadfast adherence and obedience to such principles, despite the motives which oppose them.

In general, the feminine half of humanity is inferior to the masculine in the virtue of justice, and its derivatives, uprightness, conscientiousness, etc.; the explanation is found in the fact that, owing to the weakness of its reasoning powers the former is much less capable than the latter of understanding and holding to general laws, and of taking them as a guiding thread. Hence injustice and falseness are women's besetting sins, and lies their proper element. On the other hand, they surpass men in the virtue of loving-kindness; because usually the stimulus to this is **intuitive**, and consequently appeals directly to the sense of Compassion, of which females are much more susceptible than males. For the former nothing but what is intuitive, present, and immediately real has a true existence; that which is knowable only by means of concepts, as for instance, the absent, the distant, the past, the future, they do not readily grasp. We thus find compensation here, as in so much else; justice is more the masculine, loving-kindness more the feminine virtue. The mere idea of seeing women sitting on the judges' bench raises a smile; but the sisters of mercy far excel the brothers of charity. Now animals, as they have no power of gaining knowledge by reason, that is, of forming abstract ideas, are entirely incapable of fixed resolutions, to say nothing of principles; they consequently totally lack **self-control**, and are helplessly given over to external impressions and internal impulses. This is why they have no conscious morality; although the different species show great contrasts of good and evil in their characters, and as regards the highest races these are traceable even in individuals.

From the foregoing considerations we see that in the single acts of the just man Compassion works only indirectly through his formulated principles, and not so much *actu* as *potentiâ*; much in the same way as in statics the greater length of one of the scale-beams, owing to its greater power of motion, balances the smaller weight attached to it with the larger on the other side, and works, while at rest, only *potentiâ,* not *actu*; yet with the same efficiency.

Nevertheless, Compassion is always ready to pass into active operation. Therefore, whenever, in special cases, the established rule shows signs of breaking down, the one incentive (for we exclude of course those based on Egoism), which is capable of infusing fresh life into it, is that drawn from the fountain-head itself—Compassion. This is true, not only where it is a question of personal violence, but also where property is concerned, for instance, when any one feels the desire to keep some valuable object which he has found. In such cases,—if we set aside all motives prompted by worldly wisdom, and by religion—nothing brings a man back so easily to the path of justice, as the realisation of the trouble, the grief, the lamentation of the loser. It is because this is felt to be true, that, when publicity is given to the loss of money, the assurance is so often added that the loser is a poor man, a servant, etc.

It is hoped that these considerations have made it clear that, however contrary appearances may be at first sight, yet undoubtedly justice, as a genuine and voluntary virtue has its origin in Compassion. But if any one should suppose such a soil too barren and meagre to bear this great cardinal virtue, let him reflect on what is said above, and remember how small is the amount of true, spontaneous, unselfish, unfeigned justice among men; how the real thing only occurs as a surprising exception, and how, to its counterfeit,—the justice that rests on mere worldly wisdom and is everywhere published abroad—it is related, both in quality and quantity, as gold is to copper. I should like to call the one δικαιοσύνη πάνδημος (common, ordinary justice), the other οὐρανία (heavenly justice).[16] For the latter is she, who, according to Hesiod,[17] leaves the earth in the iron age, to dwell with the celestial gods. To produce such a rare exotic as this the root we have indicated is surely vigorous enough.

It will now be seen that **injustice** or **wrong** always consists in **working harm** on another. Therefore the conception of wrong is **positive**, and antecedent to the conception of right, which is **negative**, and simply denotes the actions performable without injury to others; in other words, without wrong being done. That to this class belongs also whatever is effected with no other object than that of warding off from oneself meditated mischief is an easy inference. For no participation in another's interests, and no sympathy for him, can require me to let myself be harmed by him, that is, to undergo wrong. The theory that right is negative, in contradistinction to wrong as positive, we find supported by Hugo Grotius, the father of philosophical jurisprudence. The definition of justice which he gives at the beginning of his work, *De Jure Belli et Pacis* (Bk. I., chap. 1., §3), runs as follows:—*Jus hic nihil aliud, quam quod justum est, significat, idque negante magis sensu, quam aiente, ut jus sit, quod injustum non est.*[18] The negative character of justice is also established, little as it may appear, even by the familiar formula: "Give to each one his own." Now, there is no need to give a man his own, if he has it. The real meaning is therefore: "Take from none his own." Since the requirements of justice are only negative, they may be effected by coercion; for the *Neminem laede* can be practised by all alike. The coercive apparatus is the state, whose sole *raison d'être* is to protect its subjects, individually from each other, and collectively from external foes. It is true that a few German would-be philosophers of this venal age wish to distort the state into an institution for the spread of morality, education, and edifying instruction. But such a view contains, lurking in the background, the jesuitical aim of doing away with personal freedom and individual development, and of making men mere wheels in a huge Chinese governmental and religious machine. And this is the road that once led to

---

[16]There is here an allusion to the πάνδημος Ἔρως and Οὐρανία in Plato's *Symposium*. V. Chap. 8, sq. Edit. Schmelzer: Weidmann, Berlin, 1882.—(*Translator*.)

[17]V. Hesiod, *Opera et Dies,* 174–201.—(*Translator*.)

[18]Justice here denotes nothing else than that which is just, and this, rather in a negative than in a positive sense; so that what is not unjust is to be regarded as justice.

Inquisitions, to Autos-da-fé, and religious wars. Frederick the Great showed that he at least never wished to tread it, when he said: "In my land every one shall care for his own salvation, as he himself thinks best." Nevertheless, we still see everywhere (with the more apparent than real exception of North America) that the state undertakes to provide for the metaphysical needs of its members. The governments appear to have adopted as their guiding principle the tenet of Quintus Curtius: *Nulla res efficacius multitudinem regit, quam superstitio: alioquin impotens, saeva, mutabilis; ubi vana religione capta est, melius vatibus, quam ducibus suis paret.*[19]

We have seen that "wrong" and "right" are convertible synonymes of "to do harm" and "to refrain from doing it," and that under "right" is included the warding off of injury from oneself. It will be obvious that these conceptions are independent of, and antecedent to, all positive legislation. There is, therefore, a pure ethical right, or natural right, and a pure doctrine of right, detached from all positive statutes. The first principles of this doctrine have no doubt an empirical origin, so far as they arise from the idea of harm done, but *per se* they rest on the pure understanding, which *a priori* furnishes ready to hand the axiom: *causa causae est causa effectus*. (The cause of a cause is the cause of the effect.) Taken in this connection the words mean: if any one desires to injure me, it is not I, but he, that is the cause of whatever I am obliged to do in self-defence; and I can consequently oppose all encroachments on his part, without wronging him. Here we have, so to say, a law of moral repercussion. Thus it comes about that the union of the empirical idea of injury done with the axiom supplied by the pure understanding, gives rise to the fundamental conceptions of wrong and right, which every one grasps *a priori*, and learns by actual trial to immediately adopt. The empiric, who denies this, and refuses to accept anything but the verdict of experience, may be referred to the testimony of the savage races, who all distinguish between wrong and right quite correctly, often indeed with nice precision; as is strikingly manifested when they are engaged in bartering and other transactions with Europeans, or visit their ships. They are bold and self-assured, when they are in the right; but uneasy, when they know they are wrong. In disputes a just settlement satisfies them, whereas unjust procedure drives them to war. The Doctrine of Right is a branch of Ethics, whose function is to determine those actions which may not be performed, unless one wishes to injure others, that is, to be guilty of wrongdoing; and here the **active** part played is kept in view. But legislation

---

[19]There is no more efficient instrument in ruling the masses than superstition. Without this they have no self-control; they are brutish; they are changeable; but once they are caught by some vain form of religion, they lend a more willing ear to its soothsayers than to their own leaders.

applies this chapter of moral science conversely, that is, with reference to the **passive** side of the question, and declares that the same actions need not be endured, since no one ought to have wrong inflicted on him. To frustrate such conduct the state constructs the complete edifice of the law, as positive Right. Its intention is that no one shall **suffer** wrong; the intention of the Doctrine of Moral Right is that no one shall **do** wrong.[20]

If by unjust action I molest some one, whether in his person, his freedom, his property, or his honour, the wrong as regards **quality** remains the same. But with respect to **quantity** it may vary very much. This difference in the amount of wrong effected appears not to have been as yet investigated by moralists, although it is everywhere recognised in real life, because the censure passed is always proportional to the harm inflicted. So also with just actions, the right done is constant in quality, but not in quantity. To explain this better: he, who when dying of starvation steals a loaf, commits a wrong; but how small is this wrong in comparison with the act of an opulent proprietor, who, in whatever way, despoils a poor man of his last penny! Again: the rich person who pays his hired labourer, acts justly; but how insignificant is this piece of justice when contrasted with that of a penniless toiler, who voluntarily returns to its wealthy owner a purse of gold which he has found! The measure, however, of this striking difference in the quantity of justice, and injustice (the **quality** being always constant), is not direct and absolute, as on a graduated scale; it is indirect and relative, like the ratio of sines and tangents. I give therefore the following definition: the amount of injustice in my conduct varies as the amount of evil, which I thereby bring on another, divided by the amount of advantage, which I myself gain; and the amount of justice in my conduct varies as the amount of advantage, which injury done to another brings me, divided by the amount of harm which he thereby suffers.

We have further to notice a **double** form of injustice which is specifically different from the simple kind, be it never so great. This variety may be detected by the fact that the amount of indignation shown by disinterested witnesses, which is always proportional to the amount of wrong inflicted, never reaches the **maximum** except when it is present. We then see how the deed is loathed, as something revolting and heinous, as an ἄγος (*i.e.,* abomination), before which, as it were, the gods veil their faces. **Double** injustice occurs when some one, after definitely undertaking the obligation of protecting his friend, master, client, etc., in a special way, not only is guilty of non-fulfilment of that duty (which of

---

[20]The Doctrine of Right in detail may be found in *Die Welt als Wille und Vorstellung,* vol. i., §62.

itself would be injurious to the other, and therefore a wrong); but when, in addition, he turns round, and attacks the man, and strikes at the very spot which he promised to guard. Instances are: the appointed watch, or guide, who becomes an assassin; the trusted caretaker, who becomes a thief; the guardian, who robs his ward of her property; the lawyer, who prevaricates; the judge, who is corruptible; the adviser, who deliberately gives some fatal counsel. All such conduct is known by the name of **treachery**, and is viewed with abhorrence by the whole world. Hence Dante puts traitors in the lowest circle of Hell, where Satan himself is found (*Inferno*: xi, 61–66).

As we have here had occasion to mention the word "obligation," this is the place to determine the conception of **Duty**, which is so often spoken of both in Ethics and in real life, but with too wide an extension of meaning. We have seen that wrong always signifies injury done to another, whether it be in his person, his freedom, his property, or his honour. The consequence appears to be that every wrong must imply a positive aggression, and so a definite act. Only there **are** actions, the simple **omission** of which constitutes a wrong; and these are Duties. This is the true philosophic definition of the conception "Duty,"—a term which loses its characteristic note, and hence becomes valueless, if it is used (as hitherto it has been in Moral Science) to designate all praiseworthy conduct. It is forgotten that "Duty"[21] necessarily means a **debt** which is owing, being thus an action, by the simple omission of which another suffers harm, that is, a wrong comes about. Clearly in this case the injury only takes place through the person, who neglects the duty, having distinctly pledged or bound himself to it. Consequently all duties depend on an obligation which has been entered into. This, as a rule, takes the form of a definite, if sometimes tacit, agreement between two parties: as for instance, between prince and people, government and its servants, master and man, lawyer and client, physician and patient; in a word, between any and every one who undertakes to perform some task, and his employer in the widest sense of the word. Hence every duty involves a right; since no one undertakes an obligation without a motive, which means, in this case, without seeing some advantage for himself. There is only **one** obligation that I know of which is not subject to an agreement, but arises directly and solely through an act; this is because one of the persons with whom it has to do was not in existence when it was contracted. I refer to the duty of parents towards their children. Whoever brings a child into the world, has incumbent on him the duty of supporting his offspring, until the latter is able to maintain himself; and should this time never come, owing to incapacity from blind-

---

[21]Duty = τò δέον = le devoir = Pflicht [cf. *plight*, O. H. G. *plegan*].—(*Translator.*)

ness, deformity, cretinism, and the like, neither does the duty ever come
to an end. It is clear that merely by failing to provide for the needs of
his son, that is, by a simple omission, the father would injure him, indeed jeopardise his life. Children's duty towards their parents is not so
direct and imperative. It rests on the fact that, as every duty involves a
right, parents also must have some just claim on their issue. This is the
foundation of the duty of filial obedience, which, however, in course of
time ceases simultaneously with the right out of which it sprang. It is
replaced by gratitude for that which was done by father and mother
over and above their strict duty. Nevertheless, although ingratitude is a
hateful, often indeed a revolting vice, gratitude cannot be called a **duty**;
because its omission inflicts no injury on the other side, and is therefore
no **wrong**. Otherwise we should have to suppose that in his heart of
hearts the benefactor aims at making a good bargain. It should be noticed that reparation made for harm done may also be regarded as a duty
arising directly through an action. This, however, is something purely
negative, as it is nothing but an attempt to remove and blot out the consequences of an unjust deed, as a thing that ought never to have taken
place. Be it also observed that equity[22] is the foe of justice, and often
comes into harsh collision with it; so that the former ought only to be
admitted within certain limits. The German is a friend of equity, while
the Englishman holds to justice.

The law of motivation is just as strict as that of physical causality,
and hence involves the same irresistible necessity. Consequently wrong
may be compassed not only by violence, but also by cunning. If by violence I am able to kill or rob another, or compel him to obey me, I
can equally use cunning to accomplish the same ends; that is, I can
place false motives before his intellect, by reason of which he must do
what otherwise he would not. These false motives are effected by **lies**.
In reality lies are unjustifiable solely in so far as they are instruments
of cunning, in other words, of compulsion, by means of motivation.[23]
And this is precisely their function, as a rule. For, in the first place, I
cannot tell a falsehood without a motive, and this motive will certainly

---

[22]The word here translated "equity" (*Billigkeit*: Lat. *aequitas*) means the sense of fairness, or
of natural justice which determines what is fitting and due in all human relations, as opposed to justice (*Gerechtigkeit*) taken as positive written law.—(*Translator*.)

[23]Motivation is defined in Part II., Chapter VIII., as "the law of Causality acting through
the medium of the intellect." It is thus the law of the determination of conduct by motives.—(*Translator*.)

be, with the rarest exceptions, an unjust one; namely, the intention of holding others, over whom I have no power, under my will, that is, of coercing them through the agency of motivation. Also in mere exaggerations and untruthful bombast there is the same purpose at work; for, by employing such language, a man tries to place himself higher in the sight of others than is his due. The binding force of a promise or a compact is contained in the fact that, if it be not observed, it is a deliberate lie, pronounced in the most solemn manner,—a lie, whose intention (that of putting others under moral compulsion) is, in this case, all the clearer, because its motive, the desired performance of something on the other side, is expressly declared. The contemptible part of the fraud is that hypocrisy is used to disarm the victim before he is attacked. The highest point of villainy is reached in **treachery**, which, as we have seen, is a **double** injustice, and is always regarded with loathing.

It is, then, obvious that, just as I am not wrong, that is, right in resisting violence by violence, so where violence is not feasible, or it appears more convenient, I am at liberty to resort to cunning; accordingly, whenever I am entitled to use force, I may, if I please, employ falsehood; for instance, against robbers and miscreants of every sort, whom in this way I entice into a trap. Hence a promise which is extorted by violence is not binding. But, as a matter of fact, the right to avail myself of lies extends further. It occurs whenever an unjustifiable question is asked, which has to do with my private, or business affairs, and is hence prompted by curiosity; for to answer it, or even to put it off by the suspicion-awakening words, "I can't tell you," would expose me to danger. Here an untruth is the indispensable weapon against unwarranted inquisitiveness, whose motive is hardly ever a well-meaning one. For, just as I have the right to oppose the apparent bad will of another, and to anticipate with physical resistance, to the danger of my would-be aggressor, the physical violence presumably thence resulting; so that, for instance, as a precaution, I can protect my garden wall with sharp spikes, let loose savage dogs in my court at night, and even, if circumstances require it, set man-traps and spring-guns, for the evil consequences of which the burglar has only himself to thank:—if I have the right to do this, then I am equally authorised in keeping secret, at any price, that which, if known, would lay me bare to the attack of others. And I have good reason for acting thus, because, in moral, no less than in physical, relations, I am driven to assume that the bad will of others is very possible, and must therefore take all necessary preventive measures beforehand. Whence Ariosto says:—

> *Quantunque il simular sia le più volte*
> *Ripreso, e dia di mala mente indici,*
> *Si trova pure in molte cose e molte*
> *Avere fatti evidenti benefici,*
> *E danni e biasmi e morti avere tolte:*
> *Che non conversiam' sempre con gli amici,*
> *In questa assai più oscura che serena*
> *Vita mortal, tutta d'invidia piena.*[24]
>
> —*Orl. Fur.,* IV., 1.

I may, then, without any injustice match cunning with cunning, and anticipate all crafty encroachments on me, even if they be only probable; and I need neither render an account to him who unwarrantably pries into my personal circumstances, nor by replying: "I cannot answer this," show him the spot where I have a secret, which perilous to me, and perhaps advantageous to him, in any case puts me in his power, if divulged: *Scire volunt secreta domus, atque inde timeri.* (They wish to know family secrets, and thus become feared.) On the contrary, I am justified in putting him off with a lie, involving danger to himself, in case he is thereby led into a mistake that works him harm. Indeed, a falsehood is the only means of opposing inquisitive and suspicious curiosity; to meet which it is the one weapon of necessary self-defence. "Ask me no questions, and I'll tell you no lies" is here the right maxim. For among the English, who regard the reproach of being a liar as the deepest insult, and who on that account are really more truthful than other nations, all unjustifiable questions, having to do with another's affairs, are looked upon as a piece of ill-breeding, which is denoted by the expression, "to ask questions." Certainly every sensible person, even when he is of the strictest rectitude, follows the principle above set forth. Suppose, for instance, such a one is returning from a remote spot, where he has raised a sum of money; and suppose an unknown traveller joins him, and after the customary "whither" and "whence" gradually proceeds to inquire what may have taken him to that place; the former will undoubtedly give a false answer in order to avoid the danger of robbery. Again: if a man be found in the house of another, whose daughter he is wooing;

---

[24]However much we're wont to blame a lie,
  As index of a mind estranged from right,
  Yet times unnumber'd it hath shap'd results
  Of good most evident; disgrace and loss,
  It chang'd; e'en death it cheated. For with friends,
  Alas! not always in this mortal life,
  Where envy fills all hearts, and gloom prevails
  Much more than light, are we in converse join'd.

  —(*Translator.*)

and he is asked the cause of his unexpected presence; unless he has entirely lost his head, he will not give the true reason, but unhesitatingly invent a pretext. And the cases are numberless in which every reasonable being tells an untruth, without the least scruple of conscience. It is this view of the matter alone that removes the crying contradiction between the morality which is taught, and that which is daily practised, even by the best and most upright of men. At the same time, the restriction of a falsehood to the single purpose of self-defence must be rigidly observed; for otherwise this doctrine would admit of terrible abuse, a lie being in itself a very dangerous instrument. But just as, even in time of public peace, the law allows every one to carry weapons and to use them, when required for self-defence, so Ethics permits lies to be employed for the same purpose, and—be it observed—for this one purpose only. Every mendacious word is a wrong, excepting only when the occasion arises of defending oneself against violence or cunning. Hence justice requires truthfulness towards all men. But the entirely unconditional and unreserved condemnation of lies, as properly involved in their nature, is sufficiently refuted by well known facts. Thus, there are cases where a falsehood is a **duty**, especially for doctors; and there are **magnanimous** lies, as, for instance, that of the Marquis Posa in *Don Carlos*,[25] or that in the *Gerusalemme Liberata,* II., 22;[26] they occur, indeed, whenever a man wills to take on himself the guilt of another; and lastly, Jesus Christ himself is reported (*John* vii. 8; cf. ver. 10) on one occasion to have intentionally told an untruth. The reader will remember that Campanella, in his *Poesie Filosofiche* (Della Bellezza: Madr. 9), does not hesitate to say: "*Bello è il mentir, se a fare gran ben' si trova.*"[27] On the other hand, the current teaching as regards necessary falsehoods is a wretched patch on the dress of a poverty-stricken morality. Kant is responsible for the theory found in many text-books, which derives the unjustifiableness of lies from man's faculty of speech; but the arguments are so tame, childish and absurd that one might well be tempted, if only to pour contempt on them, to join sides with the devil, and say with Talleyrand: *l'homme a reçu la parole pour pouvoir cacher sa pensèe.*[28] The unqualified and boundless horror shown by Kant for falsehoods, whenever he has the opportunity, is due either to affectation, or to prejudice. In the chapter of his "*Tugendlehre,*" dealing with lies, he loads them with every kind of

---

[25] *Vide,* Schiller's *Don Carlos:* Act V., Sc. 3.—(*Translator.*)

[26] "*Magnanima menzogna, or quando è il vero*
    Sì bello che si possa a te preporre?"
    Cf. also the Horatian *splendide mendax. Carm.* III., 11, 35.—(*Translator.*)

[27] 'Tis well to lie, an there result much good therefrom. *Vide, Opere* di Tommaso Campanella, da Alessandro d'Ancona, Torino, 1854.—(*Translator.*)

[28] Man has received the gift of language, so as to be able to conceal his thoughts.

defamatory epithet, but does not adduce a single adequate reason for their condemnation; which would have been more to the point. Declamation is easier than demonstration, and to moralise less difficult than to be sincere. Kant would have done better to open the vials of his wrath on that vice which takes pleasure in seeing others suffer; it is the latter, and not a falsehood, which is truly fiendish. For malignant joy is the exact opposite of Compassion, and nothing else but powerless cruelty, which, unable itself to bring about the misery it so gladly beholds others enduring, is thankful to Τύχη for having done so instead. According to the code of knightly honour, the reproach of being a liar is of extreme gravity, and only to be washed out with the accuser's blood. Now this obtains, not because the lie is **wrong** in itself, since, were such the reason, to accuse a man of an injury done by violence would certainly be regarded as equally outrageous,—which is not the case, as every one knows; but it is due to that principle of chivalry, which in reality bases right on might; so that whoever, when trying to work mischief, has recourse to falsehood, proves that he lacks either power, or the requisite courage. Every untruth bears witness of his fear; and this is why a fatal verdict is passed on him.

Chapter VII.—The Virtue of Loving-Kindness

THUS justice is the primary and essentially cardinal virtue. Ancient philosophers recognised it as such, but made it co-ordinate with three others unsuitably chosen.[29] Loving-kindness (*caritas,* ἀγάπη) was not as yet ranked as a virtue. Plato himself, who rises highest in moral science, reaches only so far as voluntary, disinterested justice. It is true that loving-kindness has existed at all times in practice and in fact; but it was reserved for Christianity,—whose greatest service is seen in this—to theoretically formulate, and expressly advance it not only as a virtue, but as the queen of all; and to extend it even to enemies. We are thinking of course only of Europe. For in Asia, a thousand years before, the boundless love of one's neighbour had been prescribed and taught, as well as practised: the

---

[29]Plato taught that Justice (δικαιοσύνη) includes in itself the three other virtues of Wisdom (σοφία), Fortitude (ἀνδρεία), and Temperance (σωφροσύνη). With Aristotle, too, Justice is the chief of virtues; while the Stoic doctrine is that Virtue is manifested in four leading co-ordinate forms: Wisdom, Justice, Fortitude, and Temperance.— (*Translator.*)

Vedas[30] are full of it; while in the Dharma-Śāstra,[31] Itihāsa,[32] and Purāṇa[33] it constantly recurs, to say nothing of the preaching of Śakya-muni, the Buddha. And to be quite accurate we must admit that there are traces to be found among the Greeks and Romans of a recommendation to follow loving-kindness; for instance, in Cicero, *De Finibus,* V., 23;[34] and also in Pythagoras, according to Iamblichus, *De vita Pythagorae,* chap. 33.[35] My task is now to give a philosophical derivation of this virtue from the principle I have laid down.

It has been demonstrated in Chapter V. of this Part, that the sense of Compassion, however much its origin is shrouded in mystery, is the one and sole cause whereby the suffering I see in another, of itself, and as such, becomes directly my motive; and we have seen that the first stage of this process is **negative.** The second degree is sharply distinguished from the first, through the **positive** character of the actions resulting therefrom; for at this point Compassion does more than keep me back from injuring my neighbour; it impels me to help him. And according as, on the one hand, my sense of direct participation is keen and deep, and, on the other hand, the distress is great and urgent, so shall I be constrained by this motive, which (be it noted) is purely and wholly moral, to make a greater or less sacrifice in order to meet the need or the calamity which I observe; and this sacrifice may involve the expenditure of my bodily or mental powers, the loss of my property, freedom, or even life. So that in this direct **suffering with** another, which rests on no arguments and requires none, is found the one simple origin of loving-kindness, *caritas,* ἀγάπη· in other words, that virtue whose rule is: *Omnes, quantum potes, juva* (help all people, as far as lies in your power); and from which all those actions proceed which are prescribed by Ethics under the name of duties of virtue, otherwise called duties of love, or imperfect duties. It is solely by direct and, as it were, instinctive participation in the sufferings which we see, in other words, by Compassion, that conduct so

---

[30]There are four Vedas: the *Rig-Veda, Yajur-Veda, Sāma-Veda,* and *Atharva-Veda.*—(*Translator.*)

[31]*Dharma-Śāstra* ("a law book"): the body or code of Hindu law.—(*Translator.*)

[32]*Itihāsa* (iti-ha-āsa, "so indeed it is"): talk, legend, traditional accounts of former events, heroic history; *e.g.,* the Mahā-bhārata.—(*Translator.*)

[33]*Purāṇa* (ancient, legendary): the name given to certain well-known sacred works, eighteen in number, comprising the whole body of modern Hindu mythology. *V.* Monier Williams' *Sanskrit Dictionary.*—(*Translator.*)

[34]*Ipsa* CARITAS *generis humani, quae nata a primo satu, quod a procreatoribus nati diliguntur, et tota domus conjugio et stirpe conjungitur, serpit sensim foras, cognationibus primum, tum affinitatibus, deinde amicitiis, post vicinitatibus tum civibus et iis, qui publice socii atque amici sunt, deinde* TOTIUS COMPLEXU GENTIS HUMANAE.

[35]This chapter describes the Pythagorean φιλία πάντων πρὸς ἅπαντας, which comes very near to loving-kindness. It contains also certain καλὰ τῆς φιλίας τεκμήπια.—(*Translator.*)

defined is occasioned; at least when it can be said to have moral worth, that is, be declared free from all egoistic motives, and when on that account it awakens in us that inward contentment which is called a good, satisfied, approving conscience, and elicits from the spectator (not without making him cast a humiliating glance at himself), that remarkable commendation, respect, and admiration which are too well-known to be denied.

But if a beneficent action have any other motive whatever, then it must be egoistic, if not actually malicious. For as the fundamental springs of all human conduct (*v.* Chapter V. of this Part), are three, namely, Egoism, Malice, Compassion; so the various motives which are capable of affecting men may be grouped under three general heads: (1) one's own weal; (2) others' woe; (3) others' weal. Now if the motive of a kind act does not belong to the third class, it must of course be found in the first or second. To the second it is occasionally to be ascribed; for instance, if I do good to some one, in order to vex another, to whom I am hostile; or to make the latter's sufferings more acute; or, it may be, to put to shame a third person, who refrained from helping; or lastly, to inflict a mortification on the man whom I benefit. But it much more usually springs from the first class. And this is the case whenever, in doing some good, I have in view my own weal, no matter how remote or indirect it may be; that is, whenever I am influenced by the thought of reward whether in this, or in another, world, or by the hope of winning high esteem, and of gaining a reputation for nobleness of character; or again, when I reflect that the person, whom I now aid, may one day be able to assist me in return, or otherwise be of some service and benefit; or when, lastly, I am guided by the consideration that I must keep the rules of magnanimity and beneficence, because I too may on some occasion profit thereby. In a word, my motive is egoistic as soon as it is anything other than the purely **objective** desire of simply knowing, without any ulterior purpose, that my neighbour is helped, delivered from his distress and need, or freed from his suffering. If such an aim—shorn, as it is, of all subjectivity—be really mine, then, and then only, have I given proof of that loving-kindness, *caritas,* ἀγάπη, which it is the great and distinguishing merit of Christianity to have preached. It should be observed, in this connection, that the injunctions which the Gospel adds to its commandment of love, *e.g.,* μὴ γνώτω ἡ ἀριστερά σου, τί ποιεῖ ἡ δεξιά σου (let not thy left hand know what thy right hand doeth), and the like, are, in point of fact, based on a consciousness of the conclusion I have here reached,—namely, that another's distress, of itself alone, without any further consideration, must be my motive, if what I do is to be of moral value. And in the same place (*Matth.* vi. 2) we find it stated with perfect truth that ostentatious almsgivers ἀπέχουσιν τὸν μισθὸν αὐτῶν.

(Get in full—exhaust their reward.) Although, in this respect too, the Vedas shed on us the light of a higher teaching. They repeatedly declare that he, who desires any sort of recompense for his work, is still wandering in the path of darkness, and not yet ripe for deliverance. If any one should ask me what he gets from a charitable act, my answer in all sincerity would be: "This, that the lot of the poor man you relieve is just so much the lighter; otherwise absolutely nothing. If you are not satisfied, and feel that such is not a sufficient end, then your wish was not to give alms, but to make a purchase; and you have effected a bad bargain. But if the one thing you are concerned with is that he should feel the pressure of poverty less; then you have gained your object; you have diminished his suffering, and you see exactly how far your gift is requited."

Now, how is it possible that trouble which is not mine, and by which I am untouched, should become as direct a motive to me as if it were my own, and incite me to action? As already explained, only through the fact that, although it comes before me merely as something outside myself, by means of the external medium of sight or hearing; I am, nevertheless, sensible of it **with** the sufferer; I feel it as my own, not indeed **in myself**, but **in him**. And so what Calderon said comes to pass:

> *que entre el ver*
> *Padecer y el padecer*
> *Ninguna distancia habia.*
> (*No Siempre lo Peor es Cierto.* Jorn. II., Esc. 9.)[36]

This, however, presupposes that to a certain extent I have become identified with the other, and consequently that the barrier between the ego and the non-ego is, for the moment, broken down. It is then, and then only, that I make his interests, his need, his distress, his suffering directly my own; it is then that the empirical picture I have of him vanishes, and I no longer see the stranger, who is entirely unlike myself, and to whom I am indifferent; but I share his pain **in him**, despite the certainty that his skin does not enclose my nerves. Only in this way is it possible for **his** woe, **his** distress to become a motive **for me**; otherwise I should be influenced solely by my own. This process is, I repeat, **mysterious**. For it is one which Reason can give no direct account of, and its causes lie outside the field of experience. And yet it is of daily occurrence. Every one has often felt its working within himself; even to the

---

[36]For between the view
Of pain, and pain itself, I never knew
A distance lie.
It is not Always the Worst that is Certain: Act II., Sc. 9.—(*Translator.*)

most hard-hearted and selfish it is not unknown. Each day that passes
brings it before our eyes, in single acts, on a small scale; whenever a man,
by direct impulse, without much reflection, helps a fellow-creature and
comes to his aid, sometimes even exposing himself to the most imminent
peril for the sake of one he has never seen before, and this, without once
thinking of anything but the fact that he witnesses another's great distress
and danger. It was manifested on a large scale, when after long consideration, and many a stormy debate, the noble-hearted British nation gave
twenty millions of pounds to ransom the negroes in its colonies, with the
approbation and joy of a whole world. If any one refuses to recognise in
Compassion the cause of this deed, magnificent as it is in its grand proportions, and prefers to ascribe it to Christianity; let him remember that
in the whole of the New Testament not one word is said against slavery,
though at that time it was practically universal; and further, that as late as
A.D. 1860, in North America, when the question was being discussed, a
man was found who thought to strengthen his case by appealing to the
fact that Abraham and Jacob kept slaves!

What will be in each separate case the practical effect of this mysterious inner process may be left to Ethics to analyse, in chapters and paragraphs entitled "Duties of Virtue," "Duties of Love," "Imperfect
Duties," or whatever other name be used. The root, the basis of all these
is the one here indicated; for out of it arises the primary precept: *Omnes,
quantum potes, juva*; from which in turn everything else required can very
easily be deduced; just as out of the *Neminem laede*—the first half of my
principle—all duties of justice are derivable. Ethics is in truth the easiest
of all sciences. And this is only to be expected, since it is incumbent on
each person to construct it for himself, and himself form the rule for
every case, as it occurs, out of the fundamental law which lies deep in his
heart; for few have leisure and patience enough to learn a ready-made
system of Morals. From justice and loving-kindness spring all the other
virtues; for which reason these two may properly be called cardinal, and
the disclosure of their origin lays the corner-stone of Moral Science.
The entire ethical content of the Old Testament is justice; loving-
kindness being that of the New. The latter is the καινὴ ἐντολὴ (the new
commandment [*John* xiii. 34]), which according to Paul (*Romans* xiii.
8–10) includes all Christian virtues.

Chapter VIII.—The Proof Now Given
Confirmed by Experience

THE truth I have here laid down, that Compassion is the sole non-egoistic stimulus, and therefore the only really moral one, is a strange, indeed almost incomprehensible paradox. I shall hope, therefore, to render it less extraordinary to the reader, if I show that it is confirmed by experience, and by the universal testimony of human sentiment.

(1) For this purpose I shall, in the first place, state an imaginary case, which in the present investigation may serve as an *experimentum crucis*[37] (a crucial test). But not to make the matter too easy, I shall take no instance of loving-kindness, but rather a breach of lawful right, and that of the worse kind. Let us suppose two young people, Caius and Titus, to be passionately in love, each with a different girl, and that both are completely thwarted by two other men who are preferred because of certain external circumstances. They have both resolved to put their rivals out of the way, and are perfectly secure from every chance of detection, even from all suspicion. But when they come to actually prepare for the murder, each of them, after an inward struggle, draws back. They are now to give us a truthful and clear account of the reasons why they abandoned their project. As for Caius, I leave it entirely to the reader to choose what motive he likes. It may be that religious grounds checked him; for instance, the thought of the Divine Will, of future retribution, of the judgment to come, etc. Or perhaps he may say: "I reflected that the principle I was going to apply in this case would not be adapted to provide a rule universally valid for all possible rational beings; because I should have treated my rival only as a means, and not at the same time as an end." Or, following Fichte, he may deliver himself as follows: "Every human life is a means towards realising the moral law; consequently, I cannot, without being indifferent to this realisation, destroy a being ordained to do his part in effecting it."—(*Sittenlehre,* p. 373.) (This scruple, be it observed in passing, he might well overcome by the hope of soon producing a new instrument of the moral law, when once in possession of his beloved.) Or, again, he may speak after the fashion of Wollastone: "I considered that such an action would be the expression of a false tenet." Or like Hutcheson: "The Moral Sense, whose perceptions, equally with those of every other sense, admit of no final explanation, forbade me to commit such a deed." Or like

---

[37]This term appears to have been first used by Newton and Boyle. The sense is undoubtedly derived from Bacon's phrase "*instantia crucis,*" which is one of his "Prerogative Instances." *Vide, Novum Organum*: Lib. II., xxxvi., where it is explained as follows: *Inter Praerogativas Instantiarum ponemus loco decimo quarto* INSTANTIAS CRUCIS; *translato vocabulo a Crucibus, quae erectae in Biviis, indicant et signant viarum separationes. Has etiam Instantias Decisorias et Judiciales, et in Casibus nonnullis Instantias Oraculi et Mandati, appellare consuevimus, etc.*—(*Translator.*)

Adam Smith: "I foresaw that my act would awaken no sympathy with me in the minds of the spectators." Or his language may be borrowed from Christian Wolf: "I recognised that I should thereby advance neither the work of making myself perfect, nor the same process in any one else." Or from Spinoza: "*Homini nihil utilius homine: ergo hominem interimere nolui.*" (To man nothing is more useful than man: therefore I was unwilling to destroy a man.) In short, he may say what one pleases. But Titus, whose explanation is supplied by myself, will speak as follows: "When I came to make arrangements for the work, and so, for the moment, had to occupy myself not with my own passion, but with my rival; then for the first time I saw clearly what was going to happen to him. But simultaneously I was seized with compassion and pity; sorrow for him laid hold upon me, and overmastered me: I could not strike the blow." Now I ask every honest and unprejudiced reader: Which of these two is the better man? To which would he prefer to entrust his own destiny? Which is restrained by the purer motive? Consequently, where does the basis of morality lie?

(2) There is nothing that revolts our moral sense so much as cruelty. Every other offence we can pardon, but not cruelty. The reason is found in the fact that cruelty is the exact opposite of Compassion. When we hear of intensely cruel conduct, as, for instance, the act, which has just been recorded in the papers, of a mother, who murdered her little son of five years, by pouring boiling oil into his throat, and her younger child, by burying it alive; or what was recently reported from Algiers: how a casual dispute between a Spaniard and an Algerine ended in a fight; and how the latter, having vanquished the other, tore out the whole of his lower jaw bone, and carried it off as a trophy, leaving his adversary still alive;—when we hear of cruelty like this, we are seized with horror, and exclaim: "How is it possible to do such a thing?" Now, let me ask what this question signifies. Does it mean: "How is it possible to fear so little the punishments of the future life?" It is difficult to admit this interpretation. Then perhaps it intends to say: "How is it possible to act according to a principle which is so absolutely unfitted to become a general law for all rational beings?" Certainly not. Or, once more: "How is it possible to neglect so utterly one's own perfection as well as that of another?" This is equally unimaginable. The sense of the question is assuredly nothing but this: "How is it possible to be so utterly bereft of compassion?" The conclusion is that when an action is characterised by an extraordinary absence of compassion, it bears the certain stamp of the deepest depravity and loathsomeness. Hence Compassion is the true moral incentive.

(3) The ethical basis, or the original moral stimulus, which I have disclosed, is the only one that can be justly said to have a real and extended sphere of effective influence. No one will surely venture to maintain as much of all the other moral principles that philosophers have set up; for

these are composed of abstract, sometimes even of hair-splitting propositions, with no foundation other than an artificial combination of ideas;
such that their application to actual conduct would often incline to the
comic. A good action, inspired solely by Kant's Moral Principle, would be
at bottom the work of philosophic pedantry; or else would lead the doer
into self-deception, through his reason interpreting conduct, which had
other, perhaps nobler, incentives, as the product of the Categorical
Imperative, and of the conception of Duty, which, as we have seen, rests on
nothing. But not only is it true that the **philosophic** moral principles,
purely theoretical as they are, have seldom any operative power; of those
established by **religion**, and expressly framed for practical purposes, it is
equally difficult to predicate any marked efficiency. The chief evidence of
this lies in the fact that in spite of the great religious differences in the
world, the amount of morality, or rather of immorality, shows no corresponding variation, but in essentials is pretty much the same everywhere.
Only it is important not to confound rudeness and refinement with morality and immorality. The religion of Hellas had an exceedingly small moral
tendency,—it hardly went further than respect for oaths. No dogma was
taught, and no system of Ethics publicly preached; nevertheless, all things
considered, it does not appear that the Greeks were morally inferior to the
men of the Christian era. The morality of Christianity is of a much higher
kind than that of any other religion which previously appeared in Europe.
But if any one should believe for this reason that European morals have
improved proportionally, and that now at any rate they surpass what obtains elsewhere, it would not be difficult to demonstrate that among the
Mohammedans, Guebres, Hindus, and Buddhists, there is at least as much
honesty, fidelity, toleration, gentleness, beneficence, nobleness, and self-denial as among Christian peoples. Indeed, the scale will be found rather to
turn unfavourably for Christendom, when we put into the balance the
long list of inhuman cruelties which have constantly been perpetrated
within its limits and often in its name. We need only recall for a moment
the numerous religious wars; the crusades that nothing can justify; the ex-
tirpation of a large part of the American aborigines, and the peopling of
that continent by negroes, brought over from Africa, without the shadow
of a right, torn from their families, their country, their hemisphere, and, as
slaves, condemned for life to forced labour; the tireless persecution of
heretics; the unspeakable atrocities of the Inquisition, that cried aloud to
heaven; the Massacre of St. Bartholomew; the execution of 18,000 persons
in the Netherlands by the Duke of Alva; and these are but a few facts
among many.[38] Speaking generally, however, if we compare with the per-

---

[38]According to Buxton (*The African Slave-trade,* 1839), their number is even now yearly increased by about 150,000 freshly imported; and to these more than 200,000 must be
added, who perish miserably at the time of their capture, or on the voyage.

formances of its followers the excellent morality which Christianity, and, more or less, every creed preaches, and then try to imagine how far theory would become practice, if crime were not impeded by the secular arm of the state; nay more, what would probably happen, if, for only one day all laws should be suspended; we shall be obliged to confess that the effect of the various religions on Morals is in fact very small. This is of course due to weakness of faith. Theoretically, and so long as it is only a question of piety in the abstract, every one supposes his belief to be firm enough. Only the searching touch-stone of all our convictions is—what we do. When the moment for acting arrives, and our faith has to be tested by great self-denial and heavy sacrifices, then its feebleness becomes evident. If a man is seriously planning some evil, he has already broken the bounds of true and pure morality. Thenceforward the chief restraint that checks him is invariably the dread of justice and the police. Should he be so hopeful of escaping detection as to cast such fears aside, the next barrier that meets him is regard for his honour. If this second rampart be crossed, there is very little likelihood, after both these powerful hindrances are withdrawn, that any religious dogma will appeal to him strongly enough to keep him back from the deed. For if he be not frightened by near and immediate dangers, he will hardly be curbed by terrors which are distant, and rest merely on belief. Moreover, there is a positive objection that may be brought against all good conduct proceeding solely from religious conviction; it is not purged of self-interest, but done out of regard for reward and punishment, and hence can have no purely moral value. This view we find very clearly expressed in a letter of the celebrated Grand-Duke of Weimar, Karl August. He writes: "Baron Weyhers was himself of opinion that he, who is good through religion, and not by natural inclination, must be a bad fellow at heart. *In vino veritas.*"[39]—(*Letters to J. H. Merck*; No. 229.) But now let us turn to the moral incentive which I have disclosed. Who ventures for a moment to deny that it displays a marked and truly wonderful influence at all times, among all peoples, in all circumstances of life; even when constitutional law is suspended, and the horrors of revolutions and wars fill the air; in small things and in great, every day and every hour? Who will refuse to admit that it is constantly preventing much wrong, and calling into existence many a good action, often quite unexpectedly, and where there is no hope of reward? Is there any one who will gainsay the fact that, where it and it alone has been operative, we all with deep respect and emotion unreservedly recognise the presence of genuine moral worth?

(4) Boundless compassion for all living beings is the surest and most certain guarantee of pure moral conduct, and needs no casuistry.

---

[39] *I.e.,* under the influence of wine one speaks the truth. Cf. Pliny, *Nat. Hist.,* xiv., chap. 22, §28, 141, edit. Teubner; *vulgoque* VERITAS *jam attributa* VINO *est.* Gk. οἶνος καὶ ἀλήθεια. *V. Paroemiographi,* edit. Gaisford.—(*Translator.*)

Whoever is filled with it will assuredly injure no one, do harm to no one, encroach on no man's rights; he will rather have regard for every one, forgive every one, help every one as far as he can, and all his actions will bear the stamp of justice and loving-kindness. On the other hand, if we try to say: "This man is virtuous, but he is a stranger to Compassion"; or: "he is an unjust and malicious man, yet very compassionate"; the contradiction at once leaps to light. In former times the English plays used to finish with a petition for the King. The old Indian dramas close with these words: "May all living beings be delivered from pain." Tastes differ; but in my opinion there is no more beautiful prayer than this.

(5) Also from separate matters of detail it may be inferred that the original stimulus of true morality is Compassion. For instance, to make a man lose a hundred thalers, by legal tricks involving no danger, is equally unjust, whether he be rich or poor; but in the latter case the rapping of conscience is much louder, the censure of disinterested witnesses more emphatic. Aristotle was well aware of this, and said: δεινότερον δέ ἐστι τὸν ἀτυχοῦντα, ἢ τον εὐτυχοῦντα, ἀδικεῖν. (It is worse to injure a man in adversity than one who is prosperous.)—(*Probl.* xxix. 2.) If the man have wealth, self-reproach is proportionally faint, and grows still fainter, if it be the treasury that has been overreached; for state coffers can form no object of Compassion. It thus appears that the grounds for self-accusation as well as for the spectators' blame are not furnished directly by the infringement of the law, but chiefly by the suffering thereby brought upon others. The violation of right, by itself and as such, which is involved in cheating the exchequer, (to take the above instance,) will be disapproved by the conscience alike of actor and witness; but only because, and in so far as, the rule of respecting **every** right, which forms the *sine qua non* of all honourable conduct, is in consequence broken. The stricture passed will, in fact, be indirect and limited. If, however, it be a confidential *employé* in the service that commits the fraud, the case assumes quite another aspect; it then has all the specific attributes of, and belongs to, that class of actions described above, whose characteristic is a **double injustice**. The analysis here given explains why the worst charge which can ever be brought against rapacious extortioners and legal sharpers is, that they appropriate for themselves the goods of widows and orphans. The reason appears in the fact that the latter, more than others, owing to their helplessness, might be expected to excite Compassion in the most callous heart. Hence we conclude that the entire absence of this sense is sufficient to lower a man to the last degree of villainy.

(6) Compassion is the root no less of justice than of loving-kindness; but it is more clearly evidenced in the latter than in the former. We never receive proofs of genuine loving-kindness on the part of others, so long as we are in all respects prosperous. The happy man may, no doubt, often

hear the words of good-will on his relations' and friends' lips; but the expression of that pure, disinterested, objective participation in the condition and lot of others, which loving-kindness begets, is reserved for him who is stricken with some sorrow or suffering, whatever it be. For the fortunate as such we do not feel sympathy; unless they have some other claim on us, they remain alien to our hearts: *habeant sibi sua*. (They may keep their own affairs, pleasures, etc., to themselves.) Nay, if a man has many advantages over others, he will easily become an object of envy, which is ready, should he once fall from his height of prosperity, to turn into malignant joy. Nevertheless this menace is, for the most part, not fulfilled; the Sophoclean γελῶσι δ' ἐχθροί (his enemies laugh) does not generally become an actual fact. As soon as the day of ruin comes to one of fortune's spoiled children, there usually takes place a great transformation in the minds of his acquaintances, which for us in this connection is very instructive. In the first place this change clearly reveals the real nature of the interest that the friends of his happiness took in him: *diffugiunt cadis cum faece siccatis amici*. (When the casks are drained to the dregs, one's friends run away.)[40] On the other hand, the exultation of those who envied his prosperity, the mocking laugh of malicious satisfaction, which he feared more than adversity itself, and the contemplation of which he could not face, are things usually spared him. Jealousy is appeased, and disappears with its cause; while Compassion which takes its place is the parent of loving-kindness. Those who were envious of, and hostile to, a man in the full tide of success, after his downfall, have not seldom become his friends, ready to protect, comfort, and help. Who has not, at least in a small way, himself experienced something of the sort? Where is the man, who, when overtaken by some calamity, of whatever nature, has not noticed with surprise how the persons that previously had displayed the greatest coldness, nay, ill-will towards him, then came forward with unfeigned sympathy? For misfortune is the condition of Compassion, and Compassion the source of loving-kindness. When our wrath is kindled against a person, nothing quenches it so quickly, even when it is righteous, as the words: "He is an unfortunate man." And the reason is obvious: Compassion is to anger as water to fire. Therefore, whoever would fain have nothing to repent of, let him listen to my advice. When he is inflamed with rage, and meditates doing some one a grievous injury, he should bring the thing vividly before his mind, as a *fait accompli*; he should clearly picture to himself this other fellow-being tormented with mental or bodily pain, or struggling with need and misery; so that he is forced to exclaim: "This is my work!" Such thoughts as these, if anything, will avail to moderate his wrath. For Compassion is the

---

[40]Hor., *Carm.*, I., 35, 26.—(*Translator.*)

true antidote of anger; and by practising on oneself this artifice of the imagination, one awakes beforehand, while there is yet time,

> *la pitié, dont la voix,*
> *Alors qu'on est vengé, fait entendre ses lois.*[41]
> —(Voltaire, *Sémiramis,* V. 6.)

And in general, the hatred we may cherish for others is overcome by nothing so easily as by our taking a point of view whence they can appeal to our Compassion. The reason indeed why parents, as a rule, specially love the sickly one of their children is because the sight of it perpetually stirs their Compassion.

(7) There is another proof that the moral incentive disclosed by me is the true one. I mean the fact that animals also are included under its protecting aegis. In the other European systems of Ethics no place is found for them,—strange and inexcusable as this may appear. It is asserted that beasts have no rights; the illusion is harboured that our conduct, so far as they are concerned, has no moral significance, or, as it is put in the language of these codes, that "there are no duties to be fulfilled towards animals." Such a view is one of revolting coarseness, a barbarism of the West, whose source is Judaism. In philosophy, however, it rests on the assumption, despite all evidence to the contrary, of the radical difference between man and beast,—a doctrine which, as is well known, was proclaimed with more trenchant emphasis by Descartes than by any one else: it was indeed the necessary consequence of his mistakes. When Leibnitz and Wolff, following out the Cartesian view, built up out of abstract ideas their Rational Psychology, and constructed a deathless *anima rationalis* (rational soul); then the natural claims of the animal kingdom visibly rose up against this exclusive privilege, this human patent of immortality, and Nature, as always in such circumstances, entered her silent protest. Our philosophers, owing to the qualms of their intellectual conscience, were soon forced to seek aid for their Rational Psychology from the empirical method; they accordingly tried to reveal the existence of a vast chasm, an immeasurable gulf between animals and men, in order to represent them, in the teeth of opposing testimony, as existences essentially different. These efforts did not escape the ridicule of Boileau; for we find him saying:

> *Les animaux ont-ils des universités?*
> *Voit-on fleurir chez eux des quatre facultés?*[42]

---

[41]Compassion, who with no uncertain tone,
The work of vengeance done, her laws makes known.
[42]Have beasts, forsooth, their universities,
Endowed, like ours, with all four faculties?

Such a supposition would end in animals being pronounced incapable of distinguishing themselves from the external world, and of having any self-consciousness, any ego! As answer to such absurd tenets, it would only be necessary to point to the boundless Egoism innate in every animal, even the smallest and humblest; this amply proves how perfectly they are conscious of their self, as opposed to the world, which lies outside it. If any one of the Cartesian persuasion, with views like these in his head, should find himself in the claws of a tiger, he would be taught in the most forcible manner what a sharp distinction such a beast draws between his ego and the non-ego. Corresponding to these philosophical fallacies we notice a peculiar sophism in the speech of many peoples, especially the Germans. For the commonest matters connected with the processes of life,—for food, drink, conception, the bringing forth of young; for death, and the dead body; such languages have special words applicable only to animals, not to men. In this way the necessity of using the same terms for both is avoided, and the perfect identity of the thing concealed under verbal differences. Now, since the ancient tongues show no trace of such a dual mode of expression, but frankly denote the same things by the same words; it follows that this miserable artifice is beyond all doubt the work of European priestcraft, which, in its profanity, knows no limit to its disavowal of, and blasphemy against, the Eternal Reality that lives in every animal. Thus was laid the foundation of that harshness and cruelty towards beasts which is customary in Europe, and on which a native of the Asiatic uplands could not look without righteous horror. In English this infamous invention is not to be found; assuredly because the Saxons, when they conquered England, were not yet Christians. Nevertheless the English language shows something analogous in the strange fact that it makes all animals of the neuter gender, the pronoun "it" being employed for them, just as if they were lifeless things. This idiom has a very objectionable sound, especially in the case of dogs, monkeys, and other Primates, and is unmistakably a priestly trick, designed to reduce beasts to the level of inanimate objects. The ancient Egyptians, who dedicated all their days to religion, were accustomed to place in the same vault with a human mummy that of an ibis, a crocodile, etc.; in Europe it is a crime, an abomination to bury a faithful dog beside the resting-place of his master, though it is there perhaps that he, with a fidelity and attachment unknown to the sons of men, awaited his own end. To a recognition of the identity, in all essentials, of the phaenomena which we call "man" and "beast," nothing leads more surely than the study of zoology and anatomy. What shall we say then, when in these days (1839) a canting dissector has been found, who presumes to insist on an absolute and radical difference between human beings and animals, and who goes so far as to attack and calumniate honest zoologists that keep aloof from all priestly guile, eye-service, and hypocrisy, and dare to follow the leading of nature and of truth?

Those persons must indeed be totally blind, or else completely chloroformed by the *foetor Judaicus* (Jewish stench), who do not discern that the truly essential and fundamental part in man and beast is identically the same thing. That which distinguishes the one from the other does not lie in the primary and original principle, in the inner nature, in the kernel of the two phaenomena (this kernel being in both alike the Will of the individual); it is found in what is secondary, in the intellect, in the degree of perceptive capacity. It is true that the latter is incomparably higher in man, by reason of his added faculty of abstract knowledge, called Reason; nevertheless this superiority is traceable solely to a greater cerebral development, in other words, to the corporeal difference, which is quantitative, not qualitative, of a single part, the brain. In all other respects the similarity between men and animals, both psychical and bodily, is sufficiently striking. So that we must remind our judaised friends in the West, who despise animals, and idolise Reason, that if they were suckled by their mothers, so also was the dog by his. Even Kant fell into this common mistake of his age, and of his country, and I have already administered the censure[43] which it is impossible to withhold. The fact that Christian morality takes no thought for beasts is a defect in the system which is better admitted than perpetuated. One's astonishment is, however, all the greater, because, with this exception, it shows the closest agreement with the Ethics of Brahmanism and Buddhism, being only less strongly expressed, and not carried to the last consequences imposed by logic. On the whole, there seems little room for doubting that, in common with the idea of a god become man, or Avatar,[44] it has an Asiatic origin, and probably came to Judaea by way of Egypt; so that Christianity would be a secondary reflection of the primordial light that shone in India, which, falling first on Egypt, was unhappily refracted from its ruins upon Jewish soil. An apt symbol of the insensibility of Christian Ethics to animals, while in other points its similarity to the Indian is so great, may be found in the circumstance that John the Baptist comes before us in all respects like a Hindu Sannyāsin,[45] except that he is clothed in skins: a thing which would be, as is well known, an abomination in the eyes of every follower of Brahmanism or Buddhism. The Royal Society of Calcutta only received their copy of the Vedas on their distinctly promising that they would not have it bound in leather, after European fashion.

---

[43] *V.* Part II., Chapter VI.

[44] Avatāra (ava-tṛī to descend), descent of a deity from heaven; *e.g.,* the ten incarnations of Vishṇu. *V.* Monier Williams' *Sanskṛit Dictionary.*—(*Translator.*)

[45] Sannyāsin (one who lays down, or resigns), an ascetic; a religious mendicant, or Brāhman of the fourth order. *V.* Monier Williams' *Sanskṛit Dictionary.*—(*Translator.*)

In silken binding, therefore, it is now to be seen on the shelves of their library. Again: the Gospel story of Peter's draught of fishes, which the Saviour blesses so signally that the boats are overladen, and begin to sink (*Luke* v. 1–10), forms a characteristic contrast to what is related of Pythagoras. It is said that the latter, initiated as he was in all the wisdom of the Egyptians, bought the draught from the fishermen, while the net was still under water, in order to at once set at liberty the captive denizens of the sea. (Apuleius: *De Magia,* p. 36: edit. Bipont.)[46] Compassion for animals is intimately connected with goodness of character, and it may be confidently asserted that he, who is cruel to living creatures, cannot be a good man. Moreover, this compassion manifestly flows from the same source whence arise the virtues of justice and loving-kindness towards men. Thus, for instance, people of delicate sensitiveness, on realising that in a fit of ill-humour, or anger, or under the influence of wine, they punished their dog, their horse, their ape undeservedly, or unnecessarily, or excessively, are seized with the same remorse, feel the same dissatisfaction with themselves, as when they are conscious of having done some wrong to one of their fellows. The only difference—a purely nominal one—is that in the latter case this remorse, this dissatisfaction is called the voice of conscience rising in rebuke. I remember having read of an Englishman, who, when hunting in India, had killed a monkey, that he could not forget the dying look which the creature cast on him; so that he never fired at these animals again. Another sportsman, William Harris by name, a true Nimrod, has much the same story to tell. During the years 1836–7 he travelled far into the heart of Africa, merely to indulge his passion for the chase. A passage in his book, published at Bombay in 1838, describes how he shot his first elephant, a female. Next morning on going to look for his game, he found that all the elephants had fled from the neighbourhood, except a young one which had spent the night beside its dead mother. Seeing the huntsmen, it forgot all fear, and came to meet them, with the clearest and most lively signs of disconsolate grief, and put its tiny trunk about them, as if to beg for help. "Then," says Harris, "I was filled with real remorse for what I had done, and felt as if I had committed a murder."

The English nation, with its fine sensibility, is, in fact, distinguished above all others for extraordinary compassion towards animals, which appears at every opportunity, and is so strong that, despite the "cold superstition" which otherwise degrades them, these Anglo-Saxons have been

---

[46] *V.* Apuleius: *Apologia sive De Magia Liber* (Lipsiae, Teubner, 1900: page 41, chap. xxxi): *Pythagoram . . . memoriae prodiderunt, cum animaduertisset proxime Metapontum in litore Italiae suae, quam subsiciuam Graeciam fecerat, a quibusdam piscatoribus euerriculum trahi, fortunam iactus eius emisse et pretio dato iussisse, ilico piscis eos qui capti tenebantur solui retibus et reddi profundo.—(Translator.)*

led through its operation to fill up by legislation the *lacuna* that their religion leaves in morality. For this gap is precisely the reason why in Europe and America there is need of societies for the protection of animals, which are entirely dependent on the law for their efficiency. In Asia the religions themselves suffice, consequently no one there ever thinks of such associations. Meanwhile Europeans are awakening more and more to a sense that beasts have rights, in proportion as the strange notion is being gradually overcome and outgrown, that the animal kingdom came into existence solely for the benefit and pleasure of man. This view,[47] with the corollary that non-human living creatures are to be regarded merely as things, is at the root of the rough and altogether reckless treatment of them, which obtains in the West. To the honour, then, of the English be it said that they are the first people who have, in downright earnest, extended the protecting arm of the law to animals: in England the miscreant, that commits an outrage on beasts, has to pay for it, equally whether they are his own or not. Nor is this all. There exists in London the Society for the Prevention of Cruelty to Animals, a corporate body voluntarily formed, which, without state assistance, and at great cost, is of no small service in lessening the tale of tortures inflicted on animals. Its emissaries are ubiquitous, and keep secret watch in order to inform against the tormentors of dumb, sensitive creatures; and such persons have therefore good reason to stand in fear of them.[48] At all the

---

[47]In Vol. II. of my *Parerga*, §177, I have shown that its origin can be traced to the Old Testament.

[48]How seriously the matter is being taken up may be seen from the following case which is quite recent. I quote from the *Birmingham Journal* of December, 1839. "Arrest of a company of eighty-four abettors of dog-fights.—It had come to the knowledge of the Society of Animals' Friends that the Square in Fox Street, Birmingham, was yesterday to be the scene of a dog-fight. Measures were accordingly taken to secure the assistance of the police, and a strong detachment of constables was sent to the spot. At the right moment all the persons present were arrested. These precious conspirators were then handcuffed together in pairs, and the whole party was made fast by a long rope passing between each couple. In this fashion they were marched off to the Police Station, where mayor and magistrate were sitting in readiness for them. The two ringleaders were condemned to pay, each, a fine of £1, and 8s. 6d. costs; in default, to undergo 14 days' hard labour." The coxcombs whose habit is never to miss noble sport of this sort, must have looked somewhat crestfallen in the midst of the procession. But the *Times* of April 6, 1855, p. 6, supplies a still more striking instance from the present day; and here we find the paper itself assuming judicial functions, and imposing the right punishment. It recounts the case of a very wealthy Scotch baronet's daughter. The matter had been brought before the law, and the evidence showed that the girl had used a cudgel and knife on her horse with the greatest cruelty; for which she was ordered to pay a fine of £5. But for one in her position such a sum means nothing, and she would practically have got off scot-free, had not the *Times* intervened to inflict on her a proper correction, such as she would really feel. It twice mentions the young lady's name in full, printing it in large type, and concludes as follows: "We cannot help saying that a few months'

steep bridges in London this Society stations a pair of horses, which
without any charge is attached to heavy freight-waggons. Is not this admirable? Does it not elicit our approval, as unfailingly as any beneficent
action towards men? Also the Philanthropic Society of London has done
its part. In 1837 it offered a prize of £30 for the best exposition of the
moral reasons which exist to keep men from torturing animals. The line
of argument, however, had to be taken almost exclusively from
Christianity, whereby the difficulty of the task was, of course, increased;
but two years later, in 1839, Mr. Macnamara was the successful competitor. At Philadelphia there is an Animals' Friends' Society, having the
same aims; and it is to the President of the latter that a book called
*Philozoia; or, Moral Reflections on the Actual Condition of Animals, and the
Means of Improving the Same* (Brussels, 1839), has been dedicated by its author, T. Forster. It is original and well written. Mr. Forster earnestly com-
mends to his readers the humane treatment of animals. As an Englishman
he naturally tries to strengthen his position by the support of the Bible;
but he is on slippery ground, and meets with such poor success that he
ends by catching at the following ingenious position: Jesus Christ (he
says) was born in a stable among oxen and asses; which was meant to indicate symbolically that we ought to regard the beasts as our brothers, and
treat them accordingly. All that I have here adduced sufficiently proves
that the moral chord, of which we are speaking, is now at length beginning to vibrate also in the West. For the rest, we may observe that compassion for sentient beings is not to carry us to the length of abstaining
from flesh, like the Brahmans. This is because, by a natural law, capacity
for pain keeps pace with the intelligence; consequently men, by going
without animal food, especially in the North, would suffer more than
beasts do through a quick death, which is always unforeseen; although
the latter ought to be made still easier by means of chloroform. Indeed
without meat nourishment mankind would be quite unable to withstand

---

imprisonment with the addition of an occasional whipping administered in private, but
by the most muscular woman in Hampshire, would have been a much more suitable
penalty for Miss M. N. A wretched being of this sort has forfeited all the consideration
and the privileges that attach to her sex; we cannot regard her any longer as a woman."
These newspaper paragraphs I would especially recommend to the notice of the associations now formed in Germany against cruelty to animals; for they show what lines
should be adopted, in order to reach some solid result. At the same time I desire to express my cordial appreciation of the praiseworthy zeal shown by Herrn Hofrath Perner,
of Munich, who has entirely devoted himself to this branch of well-doing, and succeeded in arousing interest in it all over the country. [It should be observed that the first
portion of this note belongs to the earliest edition of the work, published September,
1840; the latter part was written for the second edition, which appeared in August, 1860.
This explains why Schopenhauer says that the first instance, dated 1839, is "quite recent,"
and that the second, dated 1855, is taken "from the present day."—(*Translator.*)

the rigours of the Northern climate. The same reasoning explains, too, why we are right in making animals work for us; it is only when they are subjected to an excessive amount of toil that cruelty begins.

(8) It is perhaps not impossible to investigate and explain metaphysically the ultimate cause of that Compassion in which alone all non-egoistic conduct can have its source; but let us for the moment put aside such inquiries, and consider the phaenomenon in question, from the empirical point of view, simply as a natural arrangement. Now if Nature's intention was to soften as much as possible the numberless sufferings of every sort, to which our life is exposed, and which no one altogether escapes; if she wished to provide some counterbalance for the burning Egoism, which fills all beings, and often develops into malice; it will at once strike every one as obvious that she could not have chosen any method more effectual than that of planting in the human heart the wonderful disposition, which inclines one man to share the pain of another, and from which proceeds the voice that bids us, in tones strong and unmistakable, take thought for our neighbour; calling, at one time, "Protect!" at another, "Help!" Assuredly, from the mutual succour thus arising, there was more to be hoped for, towards the attainment of universal well-being, than from a stern Command of duty, couched in general, abstract terms,—the product of certain reasoning processes, and of artificial combinations of conceptions. From such an Imperative, indeed, all the less result could be expected because to the rough human unit general propositions and abstract truths are unintelligible, the concrete only having some meaning for him. And it should be remembered that mankind in its entirety, a very small part alone excepted, has always been rude, and must remain so, since the large amount of bodily toil, which for the race as a whole is inevitable, leaves no time for mental culture. Whereas, in order to awaken that sense, which has been proved to be the sole source of disinterested action, and consequently the true basis of Morals, there is no need of abstract knowledge, but only of intuitive perception, of the simple comprehension of a concrete case. To this Compassion is at once responsive, without the mediation of other thoughts.

(9) The following circumstance will be found in complete accord with the last paragraph. The foundation, which I have given to Ethics, leaves me without a forerunner among the School Philosophers; indeed, my position is paradoxical, as far as their teaching goes, and many of them, for instance, the Stoics (Seneca, *De Clementia,* II., 5), Spinoza (*Ethica,* IV., prop. 50), and Kant (*Kritik der Praktischen Vernunft,* p. 213; R. p. 257) only notice the motive of Compassion to utterly reject and contemn it. On the other hand, my basis is supported by the authority of the greatest moralist of modern times; for such, undoubtedly, J. J. Rousseau is,—that profound reader of the human heart, who drew his wisdom not from books, but from life, and intended his doctrine not for the profes-

sorial chair, but for humanity; he, the foe of all prejudice, the foster-child of nature, whom alone she endowed with the gift of being able to moralise without tediousness, because he hit the truth and stirred the heart. I shall therefore venture here to cite some passages from his works in support of my theory, observing that, so far, I have been as sparing as possible with regard to quotations.

In the *Discours sur l'Origine de l'Inégalité*, p. 91 (edit. Bipont.), he says: *Il y a un autre principe, que Hobbes n'a point aperçu, et qui ayant été donné à l'homme pour adoucir, en certaines circonstances, la férocité de son amour-propre, tempère l'ardeur qu'il a pour son bien-être par une RÉPUGNANCE INNÉE À VOIR SOUFFRIR SON SEMBLABLE. Je ne crois pas avoir aucune contradiction à craindre en accordant à l'homme la SEULE VERTU NATURELLE qu'ait été forcé de recon-naître le détracteur le plus outré des vertus humaines. Je parle DE LA PITIÉ, etc.*[49]

P. 92: *Mandeville a bien senti qu'avec toute leur morale les hommes n'eussent jamais été que des monstres, si la nature ne leur eut donné LA PITIÉ à l'appui de la raison: mais il n'a pas vu, que DE CETTE SEULE QUALITÉ DECOULENT TOUTES LES VERTUS SOCIALES, qu'il veut disputer aux hommes. En effet, qu'est-ce que la générosité, la clémence, l'humanité, sinon LA PITIÉ, appliquée aux faibles, aux coupables, ou à l'espèce humaine en général? La bienveillance et l'ami-tié même sont, à le bien prendre, des productions d'une pitié constante, fixée sur un objet particulier; car désirer que quelqu'un ne souffre point, qu'est-ce autre chose, que désirer qu'il soit heureux? . . . La commisération sera d'autant plus én-ergique, que L'ANIMAL SPECTATEUR S'IDENTIFIERA plus intimement avec L'AN-IMAL SOUFFRANT.*[50]

P. 94: *Il est donc bien certain, que la pitié est un sentiment naturel, qui, mod-érant dans chaque individu l'amour de soi-même, concourt à la conservation mutuelle de toute l'espèce. C'est elle, qui dans l'état de nature, tient lieu de lois, de moeurs, et de vertus, avec cet avantage, que nul ne sera tenté de désobéir à sa douce voix: c'est elle, qui détournera tout sauvage robuste d'enlever à un faible*

---

[49]There is another principle which Hobbes did not perceive at all. It was implanted in man in order to soften, in certain circumstances, the fierceness of his self-love, and it moder-ates the ardour, which he feels for his own well-being, by producing a certain *innate aver-sion to the sight of a fellow-creature's suffering.* In attributing to man *the only natural virtue*, which even the most advanced scepticism has been forced to recognise, I stand, assuredly, in no fear of any contradiction. I allude to *compassion*, etc.

[50]Mandeville was right in thinking that with all their systems of morality, men would never have been anything but monsters, if nature had not given them *compassion* to sup-port their reason; but he failed to see that *from this one quality spring all the social virtues*, which he was unwilling to credit mankind with. In reality, what is generosity, clemency, humanity, if not *compassion*, applied to the weak, to the guilty, or to the human race, as a whole? Even benevolence and friendship, if we look at the matter rightly, are seen to re-sult from a constant compassion, directed upon a particular object; for to desire that some one should not suffer is nothing else than to desire that he should be happy. . . . The more closely *the living spectator identifies himself with the living sufferer,* the more active does pity become.

enfant, ou à un vieillard infirme, sa subsistence acquise avec peine, si lui même espère pouvoir trouver la sienne ailleurs: c'est elle qui, au lieu de cette maxime sublime de justice raisonnée: "Fais à autrui comme tu veux qu'on te fasse"; inspire à tous les hommes cette autre maxime de bonté naturelle, bien moins parfaite, mais plus utile peut-être que la précédente: "Fais ton bien avec le moindre mal d'autrui qu'il est possible." C'est, en un mot, DANS CE SENTIMENT NATUREL PLUTÔT, QUE DANS LES ARGUMENTS SUBTILS, qu'il faut chercher la cause de la répugnance qu'éprouverait tout homme à mal faire, même indépendamment des maximes de l'éducation.[51]

Let this be compared with what he says in *Émile*, Bk. IV., pp. 115–120 (edit. Bipont.) where the following passage occurs among others:—

En effet, comment nous laissons-nous émouvoir à la pitié, si ce n'est en nous transportant hors de nous et en nous IDENTIFIANT AVEC L'ANIMAL SOUFFRANT: EN QUITTANT, pour ainsi dire, NOTRE ÊTRE, POUR PRENDRE LE SIEN? Nous ne souffrons qu'autant que nous jugeons qu'il souffre: CE N'EST PAS DANS NOUS, C'EST DANS LUI, que nous souffrons . . . offrir au jeune homme des objets, sur lesquels puisse agir la force expansive de son coeur, qui le dilatent, qui l'étendent sur les autres êtres, qui le fassent partout SE RETROUVER HORS DE LUI; écarter avec soin ceux, qui le resserrent, le concentrent, et tendent le ressort DU MOI HUMAIN, etc.[52]

Inside the pale of the Schools, as above remarked, there is not a single authority in favour of my position; but outside, I have other testimony to cite, in addition to Rousseau's. The Chinese admit five cardinal virtues (Tschang), of which the chief is Compassion (Sin). The other four are:

---

[51]It is, then, quite certain that compassion is a natural feeling, which checking, as it does, the love of self in each individual, helps by a reciprocal process to preserve the whole race. This it is, which in the state of nature, takes the place of laws, customs, and virtues, with the added advantage that no one will be tempted to disobey its gentle voice; this it is, which will restrain every able-bodied savage, provided he hope to find his own livelihood elsewhere, from robbing a weak child, or depriving an infirm old man of the subsistence won by hard toil; this it is, which inspires all men, not indeed with that sublime maxim of reasoned justice: "Do to others as you would they should do unto you"; but with another rule of natural goodness, no doubt less perfect, but perhaps more useful, namely: "Do what is good for yourself with the least possible harm to others." In a word, it is *in this natural feeling rather than in subtle arguments* that we must look for the reason of the repugnance with which every one is accustomed to view bad conduct, quite independently of the principles laid down by education.

[52]In fact, how is it that we let ourselves be moved to pity, if not by getting out of our own consciousness, and *becoming identified with the living sufferer; by leaving,* so to say, *our own being, and entering into his?* We do not suffer, except as we suppose he suffers; *it is not in us, it is in him,* that we suffer . . . offer a young man objects, on which the expansive force of his heart can act; objects such as may enlarge his nature, and incline it to go out to *other beings,* in whom he may everywhere *find himself again.* Keep carefully away those things which narrow his view, and make him self-centred, and which tighten the strings of the *human ego.* [*Tendent le ressort* (stretch the spring) *du moi humain: i.e.,* stimulate the egoistic tendency.—(*Translator.*)]

justice, courtesy, wisdom, and sincerity.[53] Similarly, among the Hindus, we find that on the tablets placed to the memory of dead chieftains, compassion for men and animals takes the first place in the record of their virtues. At Athens there was an altar to Compassion in the Agora, as we know from Pausanias, I. 17:

> Ἀθηναίοις
> δὲ ἐν τῇ ἀγορᾷ ἐστι Ἐλέου βωμός, ᾧ, μάλιστα θεῶν
> ἐς ἀνθρώπινον βίον καὶ μεταβολὰς πραγμάτων ὅτι ὠ-
> φέλιμος, μόνοι τιμὰς Ἑλλήνων νέμουσιν Ἀθηναῖοι.[54]

Lucian also mentions this altar in the Timon, §99.[55] A phrase of Phocion, preserved by Stobaeus, describes Compassion as the most sacred thing in human life:

> οὔτε ἐξ ἱεροῦ βωμόν, οὔτε ἐκ τῆς ἀνθρωπίνης φύσεως
> ἀφαιρετέον τὸν ἔλεον.[56]

In the *Sapientia Indorum,* the Greek translation of the Pańca-tantra, we read (Section 3, p. 220):

> Λέγεται γάρ, ὡς πρώτη τῶν ἀρετῶν ἡ ἐλεημοσύνη.[57]

It is clear, then, that the real source of morality has been distinctly recognised at all times and in all countries; Europe alone excepted, owing to the *foetor Judaicus* (Jewish stench), which here pervades everything, and is the reason why the Western races require for the object of their obedi-

---

[53]*Journal Asiatique,* Vol. ix., p. 62. Cf. Meng-Tseu (otherwise called Mencius), edited by Stanislas Julien, 1824, Bk. 1, §45; also Meng-Tseu in the *Livres Sacrés de l'Orient,* by Panthier p. 281.

V. *Dictionnaire Français—Latin—Chinois,* par Paul Perny (Didot Frères, Paris, 1869); where the five cardinal virtues (五常) are transliterated: oú chầṅg. V. also: *A Syllabic Dictionary of the Chinese Language*; by S. Wells Williams, LL.B. (Shanghai: 1874); where Sin (Sín), *i.e.,* humanity, love of one's neighbour, is written Sin'.—(*Translator.*)

[54]The Athenians have an altar in their Agora to Compassion; for this deity, they believe, is of all the gods the most helpful in human life, and its vicissitudes. They are the only Greeks who have instituted this cultus.—(*Translator.*)

[55]V. Lucian, *Timon,* chap. 42 (*Ausgewählte Schriften des Lucian,* edit. Julius Sommerbrodt; Weidmann, Berlin, 1872, p. 75): φίλος δὲ ἢ ξένος ἢ ἑταῖρος ἢ Ἐλέου βωμὸς ὕθλος πολύς. V. also Apollodorus (edit. J. Bekker); 2, 8, 1. 3, 7, 1. Dem. (edit. Reisk.), 57. Scholiast on Soph. *Oed. Col.,* 258.—(*Translator.*)

[56]A temple must not be despoiled of its altar, nor human nature of compassion. V. Joannis Stobaei *Anthologium,* edit. Curtius Wachsmuth et Otto Hense; Weidmann, Berlin, 1894; Vol. III., p. 20, Nr. 52.—(*Translator.*)

[57]The chief of virtues is said to be Compassion. The *Pańca-tantra* is a well-known collection of moral stories and fables in five (*pańćan*) books or chapters (*tantra*), from which the author of the *Hitopadeśa* drew a large portion of his materials. V. Monier Williams' *Sanskrit Dictionary.*—(*Translator.*)

ence a command of duty, a moral law, an imperative, in short, an order and decree. They remain wedded to this habit of thought, and refuse to open their eyes to the fact that such a view is, after all, based upon nothing but Egoism. Of course, now and then, isolated individuals of fine perception have felt the truth, and given it utterance: such a one was Rousseau; and such, Lessing. In a letter written by the latter in 1756 we read: "The best man, and the one most likely to excel in all social virtues, in all forms of magnanimity, is he who is most compassionate."

Chapter IX.—On the Ethical Difference of Character

THERE still remains a question to be resolved, before the basis which I have given to Ethics can be presented in all its completeness. It is this. On what does the great difference in the moral behaviour of men rest? If Compassion be the original incentive of all true, that is, disinterested justice and loving-kindness; how comes it that some are, while others are not, influenced thereby? Are we to suppose that Ethics, which discloses the moral stimulus, is also capable of setting it in motion? Can Ethics fashion the hard-hearted man anew, so that he becomes compassionate, and, as a consequence, just and humane? Certainly not. The difference of character is innate, and ineradicable. The wicked man is born with his wickedness as much as the serpent is with its poison-fangs and glands, nor can the former change his nature a whit more than the latter.[58] *Velle non discitur* (to use one's will is not a thing that can be taught) is a saying of Nero's tutor. In the *Meno,* Plato minutely investigates the nature of virtue, and inquires whether it can, or cannot, be taught. He quotes a passage from Theognis:

ἀλλὰ διδάσκων
Οὔποτε ποιήσεις τὸν κακὸν ἄνδρ' ἀγαθόν.
(But thou wilt ne'er,
By teaching make the bad man virtuous.)

and finally reaches this conclusion:

ἀρετὴ ἂν εἴη οὔτε
φύσει, οὔτε διδακτόν. ἀλλὰ θείᾳ μοίρᾳ παραγιγνομένη,
ἄνευ νοῦ, οἷς ἂν παραγίγνηται.[59]

---

[58]Cf. *Jeremiah* xiii. 23.—(*Translator.*)

[59]Virtue would appear not to come naturally (*i.e.,* through the physical order of things), nor can it be taught; but in whomsoever it dwells, there it is present, *apart from the intellect, under divine ordinance.* [*V.* Platonis *Opera,* edit. Didot, Paris, 1856; Vol. I. *Meno,* 96 and 99, *ad fin.*—(*Translator.*)]

Here the terms φύσει and θείᾳ μοίρᾳ form a distinction, in my opinion, much the same as that between "physical" and "metaphysical." Socrates, the father of Ethics, if we may trust Aristotle, declared that

οὐκ ἐφ' ἡμῖν γενέσθαι τὸ σπουδαίους εἶναι, ἢ φαύλους.[60]

(*Moralia Magna,* i. 9.) Moreover, Aristotle himself expresses the same view:

πᾶσι γὰρ δοκεῖ ἕκαστα τῶν ἠθῶν
ὑπάρχειν φύσει πως· καὶ γὰρ δίκαιοι, καὶ σωφρονικοὶ,
καὶ τἆλλα ἔχομεν εὐθὺς ἐκ γενετῆς.[61]

(*Eth. Nicom.* vi. 13.) We find also a similar conviction very decidedly expressed in the fragments attributed to the Pythagorean Archytas, and preserved by Stobaeus in the *Florilegium* (Chap. i. §77).[62] If not authentic, they are certainly very old. Orelli gives them in his *Opuscula Graecorum Sententiosa et Moralia.* There (Vol. II., p. 240) we read in the Dorian dialect as follows:—

Τὰς γὰρ λόγοις καὶ ἀποδείξεσιν ποτιχρωμένας ἀρετὰς
δέον ἐπιστάμας ποταγορεύεν, ἀρετὰν δέ, τὰν ἠθικὰν καὶ
βελτίσταν ἕξιν τῶ ἀλόγῳ μέρεος τᾶς ψυχᾶς, καθ'
ἂν καὶ ποιοί τινες ἦμεν λεγόμεθα κατὰ τὸ ἦθος, οἷον
ἐλευθέριοι, δίκαιοι καὶ σώφρονες.[63]

On examining the virtues and vices, as summarised by Aristotle in the *De Virtutibus et Vitiis,* it will be found that all of them, without exception, are not properly thinkable unless assumed to be inborn qualities, and that only as such can they be genuine. If, in consequence of reasoned reflection, we take them as voluntary, they are then seen to lose their reality, and pass into the region of empty forms; whence it immediately follows that their permanence and resistance under the storm and stress of circumstance could not be counted on. And the same is true of the virtue of loving-kindness, of which Aristotle, in common with all the ancients, knows nothing. Montaigne keeps, of course, his sceptical tone, but he

---

[60] *It is not in our power* to be either good or bad.

[61] For it appears that the different characters of all men are in some way implanted in them *by nature*; if we are just, and temperate, and otherwise virtuous, we are so *straightway from our birth.*

[62] *V.* Joannis Stobaei *Florilegium,* edit. Meineke, publ. Lipsiae, Teubner, 1855; Vol. I., p. 33, l. 14, sqq.—(*Translator.*)

[63] For the so-called virtues, that require reasoning and demonstration, ought to be called sciences. By the term "virtue" we mean rather a certain moral and excellent disposition of *the soul's unreasoning part.* This disposition determines the character which we show, and in accordance with which we are called generous, just, or temperate.

practically agrees with the venerable authorities above quoted, when he says: *Serait-il vrai, que pour être bon tout a fait, il nous le faille être par occulte, naturelle et universelle propriété, sans loi, sans raison, sans exemple?*[64]—(Liv. II., chap. 11.) Lichtenberg hits the mark exactly in his *Vermischte Schriften,* (*v. Moralische Bermerkungen*). He writes: "All virtue arising from premeditation is not worth much. What is wanted is feeling or habit." Lastly, it should be noted that Christianity itself, in its original teaching, recognises, and bears witness to this inherent, immutable difference between character and character. In the Sermon on the Mount we find the allegory of the fruit which is determined by the nature of the tree that bears it (*Luke* vi. 43, 44; cf. *Matthew* vii. 16–18); and then in the following verse (*Luke* vi. 45), we read:

ὁ ἀγαθὸς

ἄνθρωπος ἐκ τοῦ ἀγαθοῦ θησαυροῦ τῆς καρδίας αὐτοῦ προφέρει τὸ ἀγαθόν· καὶ ὁ πονηρὸς ἄνθρωπος ἐκ τοῦ πονηροῦ θησαυροῦ τῆς καρδίας αὐτοῦ προφέρει τὸ πονηρόν.[65]

(Cf. *Matthew* vii. 35.)

But it was Kant who first completely cleared up this important point through his profound doctrine of the **empirical** and **intelligible**[66] character. He showed that the empirical character, which manifests itself in time and in multiplicity of action, is a phaenomenon; while the reality behind it is the intelligible character, which, being the essential constitution of the Thing in itself underlying the phaenomenon, is independent of time, space, plurality, and change. In this way alone can be explained what is so astonishing, and yet so well known to all who have learnt life's lessons,—the fixed unchangeableness of human character. There are certain ethical writers, whose aim is the moral improvement of men, and who talk of progress made in the path of virtue; but their assurances are always met and victoriously confuted by the irrefragable facts of experience, which prove that virtue is nature's work and cannot be inculcated. The character is an original datum, immutable, and incapable of any amelioration through correction by the intellect. Now, were this not so; and further: if (as the above-mentioned dull-headed preachers maintain) an improvement of the character, and hence "a constant advance towards the good" were possible by means of moral instruction; then, unless we are prepared to suppose that all the various religious institutions, and all the efforts of the moralists fail in their purpose, we should certainly ex-

---

[64]Are we to believe it true that we can only be thoroughly good by virtue of a certain occult, natural, and universal faculty, without law, without reason, without precedent?

[65]The good man out of the good treasure of his heart bringeth forth that which is good; and the evil man out of the evil treasure of his heart bringeth forth that which is evil.

[66]*V.* Note on "intelligible," Part. II., Chapter I.—(*Translator.*)

pect to find that the older half of mankind, at least on an average, is distinctly better than the younger. This, however, is so far from being the case, that it is not to the old, who have, as we see, grown worse by experience, but to the young that we look for something good. It may happen that in his old age one man appears somewhat better, another worse, than he was in his youth. But the reason is not far to seek. It is simply because with length of days the intelligence by constant correction becomes riper, and hence the character stands out in purer and clearer shape; while early life is a prey to ignorance, mistakes, and chimeras, which now present false motives, and now veil the real. For a fuller explanation I would refer the reader to the principles laid down in Chapter III. of the preceding Essay, on "The Freedom of the Will."[67] It is true that among convicts the young have a large majority; but this is because, when a tendency to crime exists in the character, it soon finds a way of expressing itself in acts, and of reaching its goal—the galleys, or the gibbet; while he, whom all the inducements to wrong doing, which a long life offers, have failed to lead astray, is not likely to fall at the eleventh hour. Hence the respect paid to age is, in my opinion, due to the fact that the old are considered to have passed through a test of sixty or seventy years, and kept their integrity unsullied; for this of course is the *sine qua non* of the honour accorded them. These things are too well known for any one, in real life, to be misled by the promises of the moralists we have spoken of. He who has once been proved guilty of evil-doing, is never again trusted, just as the noble nature, of which a man has once given evidence, is always confidently believed in, whatever else may have changed. *Operari sequitur esse* (what one does follows from what one is) forms, as we have seen in Part II., Chapter VIII., a pregnant tenet of the Schoolmen. Everything in the world works according to the unchangeable constitution of which its being, its **essentia** is composed. And man is no exception. As the individual is, so will he, so must he, act: and the *liberum arbitrium indifferentiae* (free and indifferent choice) is an invention of philosophy in her childhood, long since exploded; although there are some old women, in doctor's academicals, who still like to drag it about with them.

The three fundamental springs of human action—Egoism, Malice, Compassion—are inherent in every one in different and strangely unequal proportions. Their combination in any given case determines the weight of the motives that present themselves, and shapes the resulting line of conduct. To an egoistic character egoistic motives alone appeal,

---

[67] *Die Freiheit des Willens* and the present treatise were published by Schopenhauer together, under the title of *Die Beiden Grundprobleme der Ethik. V.* Introduction, p. xv., note.— (*Translator.*)

and those, which suggest either compassion or malice, have no appreciable effect. Thus, a man of this type will sacrifice his interests as little to take vengeance on his foes, as to help his friends. Another, whose nature is highly susceptible to malicious motives, will not shrink from doing great harm to himself, so only he may injure his neighbour. For there are characters which take such delight in working mischief on others, that they forget their own loss, which is perhaps, equal to what they inflict. One may say of such: *Dum alteri noceat sui negligens*[68] (disregarding himself so long as he injures the other). These are the people that plunge with passionate joy into the battle in which they expect to receive quite as many wounds as they deal; indeed, experience not seldom testifies that they are ready deliberately, first to kill the man who thwarts their purposes, and then themselves, in order to escape the penalty of the law. On the other hand, **goodness of heart** consists of a deeply felt, all-embracing Compassion for everything that has breath, and especially for man; because, in proportion as the intelligence develops, capacity for pain increases; and hence, the countless sufferings of human beings, in mind and body, have a much stronger claim to Compassion than those of animals, which are only physical, and in any case less acute. This goodness of heart, therefore, in the first place restrains a man from doing any sort of harm to others, and, next, it bids him give succour whenever and wherever he sees distress. And the path of Compassion may lead as far in one direction as Malice does in the other. Certain rare characters of fine sensibility take to heart the calamities of others more than their own, so that they make sacrifices, which, it may be, entail on themselves a greater amount of suffering than that removed from those they benefit. Nay, in cases where several, or, perhaps, a large number of persons, at one time, can be helped in this way, such men do not, if need be, flinch from absolute self-effacement. Arnold von Winkelried was one of these. So was Paulinus, Bishop of Nola, in the fifth century, when the Vandals crossed over from Africa and invaded Italy. Of him we read in Johann von Müller's *Weltgeschichte* (Bk. X., chap. 10) that "in order to ransom some of the prisoners, he had already disposed of all the church plate, his own and his friends' private property. Then, on seeing the anguish of a widow, whose only son was being carried off, he offered himself for servitude in the other's stead. For whoever was of suitable age, and had not fallen by the sword, was taken captive to Carthage."

There is, then, an enormous difference between character and character. Being original and innate, it measures the responsiveness of the individual to this or that motive, and those alone, to which he is specially sensitive, will appeal to him with anything like compelling force. As in

---

[68]Seneca, *De Ira,* I. 1.

chemistry, with unchangeable certainty, one substance reacts only upon acids, another only upon alkalies, so, with equal invariableness, different natures respond to different stimuli. The motives suggesting loving-kindness, which stir so deeply a good disposition, can, of themselves, effect nothing in a heart that listens only to the promptings of Egoism. If it be wished to induce the egoist to act with beneficence and humanity, this can be done but in one way: he must be made to believe that the assuaging of others' suffering will, somehow or other, surely turn out to his **own advantage**. What, indeed, are most moral systems but attempts of different kinds in this direction? But such procedure only misleads, does not better, the will. To make a real improvement, it would be necessary to transform the entire nature of the individual's susceptibility for motives. Thus, from one we should have to remove his indifference to the suffering of others as such; from another, the delight which he feels in causing pain; from a third, the natural tendency which makes him regard the smallest increase of his own well-being as so far outweighing all other motives, that the latter become as dust in the balance. Only it is far easier to change lead into gold than to accomplish such a task. For it means the turning round, so to say, of a man's heart in his body, the remoulding of his very being. In point of fact, all that can be done is to clear the **intellect**, correct the **judgment**, and so bring him to a better comprehension of the objective realities and actual relations of life. This effected, the only result gained is that his will reveals itself more logically, distinctly, and decidedly, with no false ring in its utterance. It should be noted that just as many a good act rests at bottom on false motives, on well-meant, yet illusory representations of an advantage to be obtained thereby in this, or another, world; so not a few misdeeds are due solely to an imperfect understanding of the conditions of human life. It is on this latter truth that the American penitentiary system is based. Here the aim is not, to improve the **heart**, but simply, to educate the **head** of the criminal, so that he may intellectually come to perceive that prosperity is more surely, indeed more easily, reached by work and honesty than by idleness and knavery.

By the proper presentment of motives **legality** may be secured, but not **morality**. It is possible to remodel what one does, but not what one **wills to do**; and it is to the will alone that real moral worth belongs. It is not possible to change the goal which the will strives after, but only the path expected to lead thither. Instruction may alter the selection of means, but not the choice of the ultimate object which the individual keeps before him in all he does; **this** is determined by his will in accordance with its original nature. It is true that the egoist may be brought to understand that, if he gives up certain small advantages, he will gain greater; and the malicious man may be taught that by injuring others he will injure himself still more. But Egoism itself, and Malice itself, will never be argued out of a person; as little as a cat can be talked out of her inclination for mice. Similarly with goodness of heart. If the judgment be trained, if the relations and conditions of life become understood, in a word, if the intellect be enlightened; the character dominated by loving-kindness will be led to express itself more consistently and completely than it otherwise could. This happens when we perceive the remoter consequences which our conduct has for others: the sufferings, perhaps, that overtake them indirectly, and only after lapse of time, through one act or another of ours, which we had no idea was so harmful. It occurs, too, when we come to discern the evil results of many a well-meant action, as, for instance, the screening of a criminal; and it is especially true when we realise that the *Neminem laede* (injure no one) has in all cases precedence over the *Omnes juva* (help all men). In this sense there is undoubtedly such a thing as a moral education, an ethical training capable of making men better. But it goes only as far as I have indicated, and its limits are quickly discovered. The head is filled with the light of knowledge; the heart remains unimproved. The fundamental and determining element, in things moral, no less than in things intellectual, and things physical, is that which is **inborn**. Art is always subordinate, and can only lend a helping hand. Each man is, what he is, as it were, "by the grace of God," *jure divino*, θείᾳ μοίρᾳ (by divine dispensation).

> *Du bist am Ende—WAS DU BIST.*
> *Setz' dir Perrücken auf von Millionen Locken,*
> *Setz' deinen Fuss auf ellenhohe Socken:*
> *DU BLEIBST DOCH IMMER WAS DU BIST.*[69]

But the reader, I am sure, has long been wishing to put the question: Where, then, does blame and merit come in? The answer is fully contained in Part II., Chapter VIII., to which I therefore beg to call particular attention. It is there that the explanation, which otherwise would now follow, found a natural place; because the matter is closely connected with Kant's doctrine of the co-existence of Freedom and Necessity. Our investigation led to the conclusion that, once the motives are brought into play, the *Operari* (what is done) is a thing of absolute necessity; consequently, Freedom, the existence of which is betokened solely by the sense of **responsibility**, cannot but belong to the *Esse* (what one is). No

---

[69]In spite of all, thou art still—*what thou art.*
   Though wigs with countless curls thy head-gear be,
   Though shoes an ell in height adorn thy feet:
   Unchang'd thou e'er remainest what thou art.

V. Goethe's *Faust,* Part I., Studirzimmer.—(*Translator.*)

doubt the reproaches of conscience have to do, in the first place, and ostensibly, with our acts, but through these they, in reality, reach down to what we are; for what we do is the only indisputable index of what we are, and reflects our character just as faithfully as symptoms betray the malady. Hence it is to this *Esse,* to what we **are**, that blame and merit must ultimately be attributed. Whatever we esteem and love, or else despise and hate, in others, is not a changeable, transient appearance, but something constant, stable, and persistent; it is that which they **are**. If we find reason to alter our first opinion about any one, we do not suppose that **he** is changed, but that **we** have been mistaken in him. In like manner, when we are pleased or displeased with our own conduct, we say that we are satisfied or dissatisfied with ourselves, meaning, in reality, with that which we **are**, and are unalterably, irreversibly; and the same is true with regard to our intellectual qualities, nay, it even applies to the physiognomy. How is it possible, then, for blame and merit to lie otherwise than in what we **are**? As we saw in Part II., Chapter VII., Conscience is that **register** of our acts, which is always growing longer, and therefore that acquaintance with ourselves which every day becomes more complete. Conscience concerns itself directly with all that we do; when, at one time, actuated by Egoism, or perhaps Malice, we turn a deaf ear to Compassion, which bids us at least refrain from harming others, if we will not afford them help and protection; or when again, at another time, we overcome the first two incentives, and listen to the voice of the third. Both cases measure **the distinction** we draw **between ourselves and others**. And on **this distinction** depends in the last resort the degree of our morality or immorality, that is, of our justice and loving-kindness, or the reverse. Little by little the number of those actions, whose testimony is significant on this point, accumulates in the storehouse of our memory; and thus the lineaments of our character are depicted with ever greater clearness, and a true knowledge of ourselves is nearer attainment. And out of such knowledge there springs a sense of satisfaction, or dissatisfaction with ourselves, with that which we **are**, according as we have been ruled by Egoism, by Malice, or else by Compassion; in other words, according as the difference we have made between ourselves and others is greater or smaller. And when we look outside ourselves, it is by the same standard that we judge those about us; and we become acquainted with their character—less perfectly indeed—yet by the same empirical method as we employ with reference to our own. In this case our feelings take the form of praise, approval, respect, or, on the other hand, of reproach, displeasure, contempt, and they are the objective translation, so to say, of the subjective satisfaction or dissatisfaction (the latter deepening perhaps into remorse), which arises in us when we sit in judgment on ourselves. Lastly, there is the evidence of language. We find certain constantly occurring forms of speech which bear eloquent testimony to the fact that the blame we cast upon others is in reality directed against their unchangeable character, touching but superficially what they do; that virtue and vice are practically, if tacitly, regarded as inherent unalterable qualities. The following are some of these expressions: *Jetzt sehe ich, wie du bist!* (Now I know your nature!) *In dir habe ich mich geirrt.* (I was mistaken in you.) "Now I see what you are!" *Voilà donc, comme tu es!* (This, then, is what you are!) *So bin ich nicht!* (I am not a person of that sort!) *Ich bin nicht der Mann, der fähig wäre, Sie zu hintergehen.* (I am not the man to impose upon you.) Also: *les âmes bien nées* (persons well-born, *i.e.,* noble-minded), the Spanish *bien nacido;* εὐγενής (properly "well-born"), εὐγένεια (properly "nobility of birth") used for "virtuous" and "virtue"; *generosioris animi amicus* (a friend of lofty mind. *Generosus*: lit. "of noble birth"), etc.

Reason is a necessary condition for conscience, but only because without the former a clear and connected recollection is impossible. From its very nature conscience does not speak till **after** the act; hence we talk of being arraigned before its **bar**. Strictly speaking, it is improper to say that conscience speaks **beforehand**; for it can only do so indirectly; that is, when the remembrance of particular cases in the past leads us, through reflection, to disapprove of some analogous course of action, while yet in embryo.

Such is the ethical fact as delivered by consciousness. It forms of itself a metaphysical problem, which does not directly belong to the present question, but which will be touched on in the last part.

Conscience, then, is nothing else than the acquaintance we make with our own changeless character through the instrumentality of our acts. A little consideration will show that this definition harmonises perfectly with, and hence receives additional confirmation from, what I have here specially emphasised: namely, the fact that **susceptibility** for the motives of Egoism, of Malice, and of Compassion, which is so widely dissimilar in different individuals, and on which the whole moral value of a man depends, cannot be interpreted by anything else, nor be gained, or removed, by instruction, as if it were something born in time, and therefore variable, and subject to chance. On the contrary, we have seen that it is innate and fixed, an ultimate datum, admitting of no further explanation. Thus an entire life, with the whole of its manifold activity, may be likened to a clock-dial, that marks every movement of the internal works, as they were made once for all; or it resembles a mirror, wherein alone, with the eye of his intellect, each person sees reflected the essential nature of his own Will, that is, the core of his being.

Whoever takes the trouble to thoroughly think out what has been put forward here, and in Part II., Chapter VIII., will discover in the founda-

tion given by me to Ethics a logical consecution, a rounded completeness, wanting to all other theories; to say nothing of the consonance of
my view with the facts of experience,—a consonance which he will
look for in vain elsewhere. For only the truth can uniformly and consistently agree with itself and with nature; while all false principles are
internally at variance with themselves, and externally contradict the testimony of experience, which at every step records its silent protest.

I am perfectly aware that the truths advanced in this Essay, and particularly here at the close, strike directly at many deeply rooted prejudices
and mistakes, and especially at those attaching to a certain rudimentary
system of morals, now much in vogue, and suitable for elementary
schools. But I cannot own to feeling any penitence or regret. For, in the
first place, I am addressing neither children, nor the *profanum vulgus,* but
an Academy of light and learning. Their inquiry is a purely theoretical
one, concerned with the ultimate fundamental verities of Ethics; and to
a most serious question a serious answer is undoubtedly expected. And
secondly, in my opinion, there can be no such thing as harmless mistakes,
still less privileged or useful ones. On the contrary, every error works in-
finitely more evil than good. If, however, it is wished to make existing
prepossessions the standard of truth, or the boundary beyond which its
investigation is not to go, then it would be more honest to abolish philosophical Faculties and Academies altogether. For where no reality exists,
there also no semblance of it should be.

PART IV.

ON THE METAPHYSICAL
EXPLANATION OF THE PRIMAL
ETHICAL PHAENOMENON

Chapter I.—How This Appendix Must Be Understood

IN the foregoing pages the moral incentive (Compassion) has been
established as a fact, and I have shown that from it alone can proceed unselfish justice and genuine loving-kindness, and that on these two cardinal virtues all the rest depend. Now, for the purpose of supplying Ethics
with a foundation, this is sufficient, in a certain sense; that is, in so far as
Moral Science necessarily requires to be supported by some actual and
demonstrable basis, whether existing in the external world, or in the consciousness. The only alternative is to tread in the footsteps that so many
of my predecessors have left, in other words, to choose arbitrarily some
proposition or other,—some bare and abstract formula—and make it the
source of all that morality prescribes; or, like Kant, to sublimate a mere
idea, that of **law**, into the key-stone of the ethical arch. But, dismissing
this method for the reasons discussed above, in the Second Part, the investigation proposed by the Royal Society appears to me now completed. For their question, as it stands, deals only with the foundation of
Ethics; as to a possible metaphysical explanation of this foundation nothing whatever is asked. Nevertheless at the point we have reached, I am
very sensible that the human spirit can find no abiding satisfaction, no
real repose. As in all branches of practical research, so also in Ethical
Science, when all is said, man is inevitably confronted with an ultimate
phaenomenon, which while it renders an account of everything that it
includes, and everything deducible from it, remains itself an unexplained
riddle. So that here, as elsewhere, the want is felt of a final interpretation
(which, obviously, cannot but be **metaphysical**) of the ultimate data, as
such, and through these,—if they be taken in their entirety—of the
world. And here, too, this want finds utterance in the question: How is
it that, what is present to our senses, and grasped by our intellect, is as it
is, and not otherwise? And how does the character of the phaenomenon,
as manifest to us, shape itself out of the essential nature of things? Indeed,
in Moral Science the need of a metaphysical basis is more urgent than in
any other, because all systems, philosophical no less than religious, are at
one in persistently attaching to **conduct** not only an ethical, but also a

metaphysical significance, which, passing beyond the mere appearance of things, transcends every possibility of experience, and therefore stands in the closest connection with human destiny and with the whole cosmic process. For if life (it is averred) have a meaning, then the supreme goal to which it points is undoubtedly ethical. Nor is this view a bare unsupported theory; it is sufficiently established by the undeniable fact that, as death draws nigh, the thoughts of each individual assume a moral trend, equally whether he be credulous of religious dogmas, or not; he is manifestly anxious to wind up the affairs of his life, now verging to its end, entirely from the **moral** standpoint. In this particular the testimony of the ancients is of special value, standing, as they do, outside the pale of Christian influence. I shall therefore here quote a remarkable passage preserved by Stobaeus, in his *Florilegium* (chap. 44, §.20). It has been attributed to the earliest Hellenic lawgiver, Zaleucus, though, according to Bentley and Heyne, its source is Pythagorean. The language is graphic and unmistakable.

> Δεῖ τίθεσθαι πρὸ ὀμμάτων τὸν καιρὸν
> τοῦτον, ἐν ᾧ γίγνεται τὸ τέλος ἑκάστῳ τῆς ἀπαλλαγῆς
> τοῦ ζῆν. Πᾶσι γὰρ ἐμπίπτει μεταμέλεια τοῖς μέλλουσι
> τελευτᾶν, μεμνημένοις ὧν ἠδικήκασι, καὶ ὁρμὴ τοῦ
> βούλεσθαι πάντα πεπράχθαι δικαίως αὐτοῖς.[1]

Furthermore, to come to an historical personage, we find Pericles, on his death-bed, unwilling to hear anything about his great achievements, and only anxious to know that he had never brought trouble on a citizen. (Plutarch, *Life of Pericles*.) Turning to modern times, if a very different case may be placed beside the preceding, I remember having noticed in a report of depositions made before an English jury the following occurrence. A rough negro lad, fifteen years old, had been mortally injured in some brawl on board a ship. As he was dying, he eagerly begged that all his companions might be fetched in haste: he wanted to ask if he had ever vexed or insulted any one of them, and after hearing that he had not, his mind appeared greatly relieved. It is indeed the uniform teaching of experience that those near death wish to be reconciled with every one before they pass away.

But there is evidence of another kind that Ethics can only be finally explained by Metaphysics. It is well known that, while the author of an intellectual performance,—even should it be a supreme masterpiece—is

---

[1] We ought to realise as if before our eyes that moment of time when the end comes to each one for deliverance from living. Because all who are about to die are seized with repentance, remembering, as they do, their unjust deeds, and being filled with the wish that they had always acted justly.—᾿Απαλλαγή = *Erlösung. V.* Joannes Stobeaus, *Florilegium*, edit. Meineke; publ. Lipsiae: Teubner, 1855. Vol. ii., p. 164, l. 7 sqq.—(*Translator.*)

quite willing to take whatever remuneration he can get, those, on the other hand, who have done something morally excellent, almost without exception, refuse compensation for it. The latter fact is specially observable where conduct rises to the heroic. For instance, when a man at the risk of his life has saved another, or perhaps many, from destruction, as a rule, he simply declines all reward, poor though he may be; because he instinctively feels that the metaphysical value of his act would be thereby impaired. At the end of Bürger's song, "The Brave Man," we find a poetical presentment of this psychological process. Nor does the reality, for the most part, differ at all from the ideal, as I have frequently noticed in English papers. Conduct of this kind occurs in every part of the world, and independently of all religious differences. In human beings there is an undeniable ethical tendency, rooted (however unconsciously) in Metaphysics, and without an explanation of life on these lines, no religion could gain standing-ground; for it is by virtue of their ethical side that they all alike keep their hold on the mind. Every religion makes its body of dogmas the basis of the moral incentive which each man feels, but which he does not, on that account, understand; and it unites the two so closely, that they appear to be inseparable. Indeed the priests take special pains to proclaim unbelief and immorality as one and the same thing. The reason is thus apparent, why believers regard unbelievers as identical with the vicious, and why expressions such as "godless," "atheistic," "unchristian," "heretic," etc., are used as synonymes for moral depravity. The religions have, in fact, a sufficiently easy task. **Faith** is the principle they start from. Hence they are in a position to simply insist on its application to their dogmas, and this, even to the point of employing threats. But philosophy has no such convenient instrument ready to hand. If the different systems be examined, it will be found that the situation is beset with difficulties, both as regards the foundation to be provided for Ethics, and in relation to the point of connection discoverable in any such foundation with the given metaphysical theory. And yet,— as I have emphasised in the introduction, with an appeal to the authority of Wolf and Kant—we are under the stringent necessity of obtaining from Metaphysics a support for Moral Science.

Now, of all the problems that the human intellect has to grapple with, that of Metaphysics is by far the hardest; so much so that it is regarded by many thinkers as absolutely insoluble. Apart from this, in the present case, I labour under the special disadvantage which the form of a detached monograph involves. In other words, I am not at liberty to start from some definite metaphysical system, of which I may be an adherent; because, if I did, either it would have to be expounded in detail, which would take too much space; or else there would be the necessity of supposing it granted and unquestioned,—an exceedingly precarious proceeding. The consequence is that I am as little able to use the synthetic method here as in the foregoing Part. Analysis alone is possible: that is, I must work backwards from the effects to their cause, and not *vice versâ*. This stern obligation, however, of having at the outset no previous hypothesis, no standpoint other than the commonly accepted one, made the discovery of the ethical basis so laborious that, as I look back upon the task, I seem to have accomplished some wondrous feat of dexterity, not unlike that of a man who executes with subtlest skill in mid air what otherwise is only done on a solid support. But now that we have come to the question whether there can be given a metaphysical explanation of the foundation obtained, the difficulty of proceeding without any assumption becomes so enormous, that but one course appears to me open, namely, to attempt nothing beyond a general sketch of the subject. I shall, therefore, indicate rather than elaborate the line of thought: I shall point out the way leading to the goal, but not follow it thither; in short, I shall present but a very small part of what, under other circumstances, could be adduced. In adopting this attitude for the reasons stated, I wish, before beginning, to emphatically remark, that in any case the actual problem put forward has now been solved; consequently, that what I here add is an *opus supererogationis,* an appendix to be given and taken entirely at will.

Chapter II.—The Metaphysical Groundwork

So far all our steps have been supported by the firm rock of experience. But at this point it fails us, and the solid earth sinks from under our feet, as we press forward in our search after a final theoretical satisfaction, there, where no experience can ever by any possibility penetrate; and happy shall we be, if perchance we gain one hint, one transient gleam, that may bring us a certain measure of content. What, however, shall not desert us is the honesty that has hitherto attended our procedure. We shall not make shift with dreams, and serve up fairy tales, after the fashion of the so-called post-Kantian philosophers; nor shall we, like them, seek, by a wordy exuberance, to impose upon the reader, and cast dust in his eyes. A little is all we promise; but that little will be presented in perfect sincerity.

The principle, which we discovered to be the final explanation of Ethics, now in turn itself requires explaining; so that our present problem has to deal with that natural Compassion, which in every man is innate and indestructible, and which has been shown to be the sole source of **non-egoistic** conduct, this kind alone being of real moral worth. Now many modern thinkers treat the conceptions of Good and Bad as

simple, that is, as neither needing, nor admitting any elucidation, and then they go on, for the most part, to talk very mysteriously and devoutly of an "Idea of the Good," out of which they make a pedestal for their moral system, or at least a cloak for their poverty.[2] Hence I am obliged in this connection to point out parenthetically, that these conceptions are anything but **simple**, much less *a priori*; that they in fact express a relation, and are derived from the commonest daily experience. Whatever is in conformity with the desires of any individual will, is, relatively to it, termed **good**; for instance, good food, good roads, a good omen; the contrary is called **bad**, and, in the case of living beings, **malicious**. And so one, who by virtue of his character, has no wish to oppose what others strive after, but rather, as far as he reasonably may, shows himself favourable and helpful to them; one, who, instead of injuring, assists his neighbours, and promotes their interests, when he can; is named by the latter, in respect to themselves, **a good man**; the term **good** being applied to him in the sense of the above definition, and from their own point of view, which is thus relative, empirical, and centred in the passive subject. Now, if we examine the nature of such a man, not only as it affects others, but as it is in itself, we are enabled by the foregoing exposition to perceive that the virtues of justice and loving-kindness, which he practises, are due to a direct participation in weal and woe external to himself; and we have learnt that the source of such participation is Compassion. If, further, we pause to consider what is the essential part in this type of character, we shall certainly find it to lie in the fact that such a person **draws less distinction between himself and others than is usually done**.

In the eyes of the malicious individual this difference is so great that he takes direct delight in the spectacle of suffering,—a delight, which he accordingly seeks without thought of any other benefit to himself, nay, sometimes, even to his own hurt. From the egoist's point of view the same difference is still large enough to make him bring much trouble on his neighbours, in order to obtain a small personal advantage. Hence for both of these, between the **ego**, which is limited to their own persons, and the **non-ego**, which includes all the rest of the world, there is fixed a great gulf, a mighty abyss: *Pereat mundus, dum ego salvus sim* (the world may perish, provided I be safe), is their maxim. For the good man, on the contrary, this distinction is by no means so pronounced; indeed, in the

---

[2]The conception of *the Good,* in its purity, is an *ultimate* one, "an *absolute Idea,* whose substance loses itself in infinity."—(Bouterweck: *Praktische Aphorismen,* p. 54).

It is obvious that this writer would like to transform the familiar, nay, trivial conception "*Good*" into a sort of Διϊπετής, to be set up as an idol in his temple. [Διϊπετής· lit., "fallen from Zeus"; and so "heaven-sent," "a thing of divine origin." Cf. Hom., *Il.* XVI., 174; *Od.* IV. 477. Eur., *Bacch.,* 1268.—(*Translator.*)]

case of magnanimous deeds, it appears to become a vanishing quantity, because then the weal of another is advanced at the cost of the benefactor, the self of another placed on an equality with his own. And when it is a question of saving a number of fellow-beings, total self-obliteration may be developed, the one giving his life for many.

The inquiry now presents itself, whether the latter way of looking at the relation subsisting between the ego and the non-ego, which forms the mainspring of a good man's conduct, is mistaken and due to an illusion; or whether the error does not rather attach to the opposite view, on which Egoism and Malice are based.

No doubt the theory lying at the root of Egoism is, **from the empirical standpoint**, perfectly justified. From the testimony of experience, the **distinction** between one's own person and that of another appears to be absolute. I do not occupy the same space as my neighbour, and this difference, which separates me from him physically, separates me also from his weal and woe. But in the first place, it should be observed that the knowledge we have of our own selves is by no means exhaustive and transparent to its depths. By means of the intuition, which the brain constructs out of the data supplied by the senses, that is to say, in an indirect manner, we recognise our body as an object in space; through an inward perception, we are aware of the continuous series of our desires, of our volitions, which arise through the agency of external motives; and finally, we come to discern the manifold movements, now stronger, now weaker, of our will itself, to which all feelings from within are ultimately traceable. And that is all: **for the perceiving faculty is not in its turn perceived**. On the contrary, the real substratum of our whole phaenomenal nature, our inmost essence **in itself**, that which wills and perceives, is not accessible to us. We see only the outward side of the ego; its inward part is veiled in darkness. Consequently, the knowledge we possess of ourselves is in no sort radical and complete, but rather very superficial. The larger and more important part of our being remains unknown, and forms a riddle to speculate about; or, as Kant puts it: "The ego knows itself only as a phaenomenon; of its real essence, whatever that may be, it has no knowledge." Now, as regards that side of the self which falls within our ken, we are, undoubtedly, sharply distinguished, each from the other; but it does not follow therefrom that the same is true of the remainder, which, shrouded in impenetrable obscurity, is yet, in fact, the very substance of which we consist. There remains at least the possibility that the latter is in all men uniform and identical.

What is the explanation of all plurality, of all numerical diversity of existence? Time and Space. Indeed it is only through the latter that the former is possible: because the concept "many" inevitably connotes the idea either of succession (time), or of relative position (space). Now, since

a homogeneous plurality is composed of **Individuals**, I call Space and
Time, as being the conditions of multiplicity, the *principium individuationis* (the principle of individuation); and I do not here pause to consider
whether this expression was exactly so employed by the Schoolmen.

If in the disclosures which Kant's wonderful acumen gave to the world
there is anything true beyond the shadow of a doubt, this is to be found
in the Transcendental Aesthetics, that is to say, in his doctrine of the ideality of Space and Time. On such solid foundations is the structure built
that no one has been able to raise even an apparent objection. It is Kant's
triumph, and belongs to the very small number of metaphysical theories
which may be regarded as really proved, and as actual conquests in that
field of research. It teaches us that Space and Time are the forms of our
own faculty of intuition, to which they consequently belong, and not to
the objects thereby perceived; and further, that they can in no way be a
condition of things in themselves, but rather attach only to their mode
of **appearing**, such as is alone possible for us who have a consciousness
of the external world determined by strictly physiological limits. Now, if
to the Thing in itself, that is, to the Reality underlying the kosmos, as we
perceive it, Time and Space are foreign; so also must multiplicity be.
Consequently that which is objectivated in the countless phaenomena of
this world of the senses cannot but be a unity, a single indivisible entity,
manifested in each and all of them. And conversely, the web of plurality,
woven in the loom of Time and Space, is not the Thing in itself, but
only its **appearance-form**. Externally to the thinking subject, this
appearance-form, as such, has no existence; it is merely an attribute of
our consciousness, bounded, as the latter is, by manifold conditions, indeed, depending on an organic function.

The view of things as above stated,—that all plurality is only apparent,
that in the endless series of individuals, passing simultaneously and successively into and out of life, generation after generation, age after age,
there is but one and the same entity really existing, which is present and
identical in all alike;—this theory, I say, was of course known long before
Kant; indeed, it may be carried back to the remotest antiquity. It is the
alpha and omega of the oldest book in the world, the sacred Vedas,
whose dogmatic part, or rather esoteric teaching, is found in the
Upanishads.[3] There, in almost every page this profound doctrine lies en-

---

[3] The genuineness of the Oupnek'hat has been disputed on the ground of certain marginal
glosses which were added by Mohammedan copyists, and then interpolated in the text.
It has, however, been fully established by the Sanskṛit scholar, F. H. H. Windischmann
(junior) in his *Sancara, sive de Theologumenis Vedanticorum,* 1833, p. xix; and also by
Bochinger in his book *De la Vie Contemplative chez les Indous,* 1831, p. 12. The reader
though ignorant of Sanskṛit, may yet convince himself that Anquetil Duperron's word
for word Latin translation of the Persion version of the Upanishads made by the martyr

shrined; with tireless repetition, in countless adaptations, by many varied parables and similes it is expounded and inculcated. That such was, moreover, the fount whence Pythagoras drew his wisdom, cannot be doubted, despite the scanty knowledge we possess of what he taught. That it formed practically the central point in the whole philosophy of the Eleatic School, is likewise a familiar fact. Later on, the New Platonists were steeped in the same, one of their chief tenets being: διὰ τὴν ἑνότητα ἁπάντων πάσας ψυχὰς μίαν εἶναι. (All souls are one, because all things form a unity.) In the ninth century we find it unexpectedly appearing in Europe. It kindles the spirit of no less a divine than Johannes Scotus Erigena, who endeavours to clothe it with the forms and terminology of the Christian religion. Among the Mohammedans we detect it again in the rapt mysticism of the Sûfi.[4] In the West Giordano Bruno cannot resist the impulse to utter it aloud; but his reward is a death of shame and torture. And at the same time we find the Christian Mystics losing themselves in it, against their own will and intention, whenever and wherever we read of them![5] Spinoza's name is identified with it. Lastly, in our own days, after Kant had annihilated the old dogmatism, and the world stood aghast at its smoking ruins, the same teaching was revived in Schelling's eclectic philosophy. The latter took all the systems of Plotinus, Spinoza, Kant, and Jacob Boehm, and mixing them together with the results of modern Natural Science, speedily served up a dish sufficient to satisfy for the moment the pressing needs of his contemporaries; and then proceeded to perform a series of varia-

---

of this creed, the Sultan Dârâ-Shukoh, is based on a thorough and exact knowledge of the language. He has only to compare it with recent translations of some of the Upanishads by Rammohun Roy, by Poley, and especially with that of Colebrooke, as also with Röer's, (the latest). These writers are obviously groping in obscurity, and driven to make shift with hazy conjectures, so that without doubt their work is much less accurate. More will be found on this subject in Vol. II. of the *Parerga*, chap. 16, §184. [*V. The Upanishads*, translated by Max Müller, in *The Sacred Books of the East*, Vols. I. and XV. Cf. also Max Müller, *The Science of Language*, Vol. I., p. 171. Now that an adequate translation of the original exists, the Oupnek'hat has only an historical interest. The value which Schopenhauer attached to the Upanishads is very clearly expressed also in the *Welt als Wille und Vorstellung*, Preface to the first Edition; and in the *Parerga*, II., chap. xvi., §184.— (*Translator.*)

[4]For the Sûfi, more correctly Ṣûfīy a sect which appeared already in the first century of the Hijrah, the reader is referred to: Tholuck's *Blüthensammlung aus der Morgenländischen Mystik* (Berlin, 1825); Tholuck's *Sûfismus, sive Theosophia Persarum Pantheistica* (Berlin, 1821); Kremer's *Geschichte der Herrschenden Ideen des Islâms* (Leipzig, 1868); Palmer's *Oriental Mysticism* (London, 1867); Gobineau's *Les Religions et les Philosophies dans l'Asie Centrale* (2nd edit. Paris, 1866); *A Dictionary of Islâm*, by T. P. Hughes (London, 1885), p. 608 sqq.—(*Translator.*)

[5]This is too well-known to need verification by references. The *Cantico del Sole* by St. Francis of Assisi sounds almost like a passage from the Upanishads or the Bhagavadgîtâ.— (*Translator.*)

tions on the original theme. The consequence is that in the learned cir-
cles of Germany this line of thought has come to be generally accepted;
indeed even among people of ordinary education, it is almost universally
diffused.[6] A solitary exception is formed by the University philosophers
of the present day. They have the hard task of fighting what is called
Pantheism. Being brought through the stress of battle into great embarrassment and difficulty, they anxiously catch now at the most pitiful
sophisms, now at phrases of choicest bombast, so only they may patch together some sort of respectable disguise, wherein to dress up the
favourite petticoat Philosophy, that has duly received official sanction. In
a word, the ''Εν καὶ πᾶν[7] has been in all ages the laughing-stock of
fools, for the wise a subject of perpetual meditation. Nevertheless, the
strict demonstration of this theory is only to be obtained from the
Kantian teaching, as I have just shown. Kant himself did not carry it out;
after the fashion of clever orators, he only gave the premises, leaving to
his hearers the pleasure of drawing the conclusion.

Now if plurality and difference belong only to the **appearance-form**;
if there is but one and the same Entity manifested in all living things: it
follows that, when we obliterate the distinction between the **ego** and the
non-ego, we are not the sport of an illusion. Rather are we so, when we
maintain the reality of individuation,—a thing the Hindus call Mâyâ,[8]
that is, a deceptive vision, a phantasma. The former theory we have
found to be the actual source of the phaenomenon of Compassion; indeed Compassion is nothing but its translation into definite expression.
This, therefore, is what I should regard as the metaphysical foundation of
Ethics, and should describe it as the sense which identifies the **ego** with
the **non-ego**, so that the individual directly recognises in **another** his
own self, his true and very being. From this standpoint the profoundest
teaching of theory pushed to its furthest limits may be shown in the end
to harmonise perfectly with the rules of justice and loving-kindness, as

---

[6]*On peut assez longtemps, chez notre espèce,*
  Fermer la porte à la Raison.
    Mais, dès qu elle entre avec adresse,
  Elle reste dans la maison,
    Et bientôt elle en est maîtresse.
                    —(Voltaire.)

(We men may, doubtless, all our lives
  To Reason bar the door.
But if to enter she contrives,
  The house she leaves no more,
And soon as mistress there presides.)

[7]Tὸ ἓν = the eternal Reality outside Time and Space Tὸ πᾶν = the phaenomenal universe.—(*Translator.*)

[8]Mâyâ is "the delusive reflection of the true eternal Entity."—(*Translator.*)

exercised; and conversely, it will be clear that practical philosophers, that is, the upright, the beneficent, the magnanimous, do but declare through their acts the same truth as the man of speculation wins by laborious research, by the loftiest flights of intellect. Meanwhile moral excellence stands higher than all theoretical sapience. The latter is at best nothing but a very unfinished and partial structure, and only by the circuitous path of reasoning attains the goal which the former reaches in one step. He who is morally noble, however deficient in mental penetration, reveals by his conduct the deepest insight, the truest wisdom; and puts to shame the most accomplished and learned genius, if the latter's acts betray that his heart is yet a stranger to this great principle,—the metaphysical unity of life.

"Individuation is real. The *principium individuationis,* with the consequent distinction of individuals, is the order of things in themselves. Each living unit is an entity radically different from all others. In my own self alone I have my true being; everything outside it belongs to the **non-ego**, and is foreign to me." This is the creed to the truth of which flesh and bone bear witness: which is at the root of all egoism, and which finds its objective expression in every loveless, unjust, or malicious act.

"Individuation is merely an appearance, born of Space and Time; the latter being nothing else than the forms under which the external world necessarily manifests itself to me, conditioned as they are by my brain's faculty of perception. Hence also the plurality and difference of individuals is but a **phaenomenon**, that is, exists only as my mental picture. My true inmost being subsists in every living thing, just as really, as directly as in my own consciousness it is evidenced only to myself." This is the higher knowledge: for which there is in Sanskrit the standing formula, **tat tvam asi**, "that art thou."[9] Out of the depths of human nature it wells up in the shape of Compassion, and is therefore the source of all genuine, that is, disinterested virtue, being, so to say, incarnate in every good deed. It is this which in the last resort is invoked, whenever we appeal to gentleness, to loving-kindness; whenever we pray for mercy instead of justice. For such appeal, such prayer is in reality the effort to remind a fellow-being of the ultimate truth that we are all one and the same entity. On the other hand, Egoism and its derivatives, envy, hatred, the spirit of persecution, hardness of heart, revenge, pleasure at the sight of suffering, and cruelty, all claim support from the other view of things, and seek their justification in it. The emotion and joy we experience when we hear of, still more, when we see, and most of all, when we ourselves do, a noble act, are at bottom traceable to the feeling of certainty such a deed

---

[9]This expression is used in the Brahmanical philosophy to denote the relation between the world-fiction as a whole and its individualised parts. *V.* A. E. Gough, *Philosophy of the Upanishads,* 1882.—(*Translator.*)

gives, that, beyond all plurality and distinction of individuals, which the *principium individuationis,* like a kaleidoscope, shows us in ever-shifting evanescent forms, there is an underlying unity, not only truly existing, but actually accessible to us; for lo! in tangible, objective form, it stands before our sight.

Of these two mental attitudes, according as the one or the other is adopted, so the φιλία (Love) or the νεῖκος (Hatred) of Empedocles appears between man and man. If any one, who is animated by νεῖκος, could forcibly break in upon his most detested foe, and compel him to lay bare the inmost recesses of his heart; to his surprise, he would find again in the latter his very self. For just as in dreams, all the persons that appear to us are but the masked images of ourselves; so in the dream of our waking life, it is our own being which looks on us from out our neighbours' eyes,—though this is not equally easy to discern. Nevertheless, **tat tvam asi**.

The preponderance of either mode of viewing life not only determines single acts; it shapes a man's whole nature and temperament. Hence the radical difference of mental habit between the **good** character and the **bad**. The latter feels everywhere that a thick wall of partition hedges him off from all others. For him the world is an **absolute non-ego**, and his relation to it an essentially hostile one; consequently, the key-note of his disposition is hatred, suspicion, envy, and pleasure in seeing distress. The good character, on the other hand, lives in an external world homogeneous with his own being; the rest of mankind is not in his eyes a **non-ego**; he thinks of it rather as "myself once more." He therefore stands on an essentially amicable footing with every one: he is conscious of being, in his inmost nature, akin to the whole human race,[10] takes direct interest in their weal and woe, and confidently assumes in their case the same interest in him. This is the source of his deep inward peace, and of that happy, calm, contented manner, which goes out on those around him, and is as the "presence of a good diffused." Whereas the bad character in time of trouble has no trust in the help of his fellow-creatures. If he invokes aid, he does so without confidence: obtained, he feels no real gratitude for it; because he can hardly discern therein anything but the effect of others' folly. For he is simply incapable of recognising his own self in some one else; and this, even after it has furnished the most incontestible signs of existence in that other person: on which fact the repulsive nature of all unthankfulness in reality depends. The moral isolation, which thus naturally and inevitably encompasses the bad man, is often the cause of his becoming the victim of despair. The good man, on the contrary, will appeal to his neighbours for

---

[10] *Homo sum: humani nil a me alienum puto.* Terence, *Heaut.,* I. 1, 25.—(*Translator.*)

assistance, with an assurance equal to the consciousness he has of being ready himself to help them. As I have said: to the one type, humanity is a **non-ego**; to the other, "myself once more." The magnanimous character, who forgives his enemy, and returns good for evil, rises to the sublime, and receives the highest meed of praise; because he recognises his real self even there where it is most conspicuously disowned.

Every purely beneficent act all help entirely and genuinely unselfish, being, as such, exclusively inspired by another's distress, is, in fact, if we probe the matter to the bottom, a dark enigma, a piece of mysticism put into practice; inasmuch as it springs out of, and finds its only true explanation in, the same higher knowledge that constitutes the essence of whatever is mystical.

For how, otherwise than metaphysically, are we to account for even the smallest offering of alms made with absolutely no other object than that of lessening the want which afflicts a fellow-creature? Such an act is only conceivable, only possible, in so far as the giver **knows** that it is his very self which stands before him, clad in the garments of suffering; in other words, so far as he recognises the essential part of his own being, under a form **not his own**.[11] It now becomes apparent, why in the foregoing part I have called Compassion the great mystery of Ethics.

He, who goes to meet death for his fatherland, has freed himself from the illusion which limits a man's existence to his own person. Such a one has broken the fetters of the *principium individuationis*. In his widened, enlightened nature he embraces all his countrymen, and in them lives on and on. Nay, he reaches forward to, and merges himself in the generations yet unborn, for whom he works; and he regards death as a wink of the eyelids, so momentary that it does not interrupt the sight.

We may here sum up the characteristics of the two human types above indicated. To the Egoist all other people are uniformly and intrinsically strangers. In point of fact, he considers nothing to be truly real, except his own person, and regards the rest of mankind practically as troops of phantoms, to whom he assigns merely a relative existence, so far as they may be instruments to serve, or barriers to obstruct, his purposes; the result being an immeasurable difference, a vast gulf between **his ego** on the one side, and the **non-ego** on the other. In a word, he lives exclusively centred in his own individuality, and on his death-day he sees all reality, indeed the whole world, coming to an end along with himself.[12] Whereas the Altruist discerns in all other persons, nay, in every living

---

[11]It is probable that many, perhaps, most cases of truly disinterested Compassion—when they really occur—are due not to any conscious *knowledge* of this sort, but to an unconscious impulse springing from the ultimate unity of all living things, and acting, so to say, automatically.—(*Translator.*)

[12]Cf. Richard Wagner: *Jesus von Nazareth*; pp. 79–90.—(*Translator.*)

thing, his own entity, and feels therefore that his being is commingled, is identical with the being of whatever is alive. By death he loses only a small part of himself. Putting off the narrow limitations of the individual, he passes into the larger life of all mankind, in whom he always recognised, and, recognising, loved, his very self; and the illusion of Time and Space, which separated his consciousness from that of others, vanishes. These two opposite modes of viewing the world are probably the chief, though not indeed the sole cause of the indifference we find between very good and exceptionally bad men, as to the manner in which they meet their last hour.

In all ages Truth, poor thing, has been put to shame for being paradoxical; and yet it is not her fault. She cannot assume the form of Error seated on his throne of world-wide sovereignty. So then, with a sigh, she looks up to her tutelary god, Time, who nods assurance to her of future victory and glory, but whose wings beat the air so slowly with their mighty strokes, that the individual perishes or ever the day of triumph be come. Hence I, too, am perfectly aware of the paradox which this metaphysical explanation of the ultimate ethical phaenomenon must present to Western minds, accustomed, as they are, to very different methods of providing Morals with a basis. Nevertheless, I cannot offer violence to the truth. All that is possible for me to do, out of consideration for European blindness, is to assert once more, and demonstrate by actual quotation, that the Metaphysics of Ethics, which I have here suggested, was thousands of years ago the fundamental principle of Indian wisdom. And to this wisdom I point back, as Copernicus did to the Pythagorean cosmic system, which was suppressed by Aristotle and Ptolemaeus. In the Bhagavadgîtâ (Lectio XIII.; 27, 28), according to A. W. von Schlegel's translation, we find the following passage: *Eundem in omnibus animantibus consistentem summum dominum, istis pereuntibus haud pereuntem qui cernit, is vere cernit. Eundem vero cernens ubique praesentem dominum, non violat semet ipsum sua ipsius culpa: exinde pergit ad summum iter.*[13]

---

[13]That man is endowed with true insight who sees that the same ruling power is inherent in all things, and that when these perish, it perishes not. For if he discerns the same ruling power everywhere present, he does not degrade himself by his own fault: thence he passes to the highest path.—For the *Bhagavadgîtâ* the reader is referred to Vol. VIII. of *The Sacred Books of the East* (Oxford: Clarendon Press), where (p. 105) this passage is translated as follows:—"He sees (truly) who sees the supreme lord abiding alike in all entities, and not destroyed though they are destroyed. For he who sees the lord abiding everywhere alike, does not destroy himself* by himself, and then reaches the highest goal."

*"Not to have true knowledge, is equivalent to self-destruction."

Cf. Fauche: Le Maha-Bharata: Paris, 1867; Vol. VII., p. 128:—

"Celui-là possède une vue nette des choses, qui voit ce principe souverain en tous les êtres d'une manière égale, et leur survivre, quand ils périssent. Il ne se fait aucun tort à

With these hints towards the elaboration of a metaphysical basis for Ethics I must close, although an important step still remains to be taken. The latter would presuppose a further advance in Moral Science itself; and this can hardly be made, because in the West the highest aim of Ethics is reached in the theory of justice and virtue. What lies beyond is unknown, or at any rate ignored. The omission, therefore, is unavoidable; and the reader need feel no surprise, if the above slight outline of the Metaphysics of Ethics does not bring into view—even remotely—the corner-stone of the whole metaphysical edifice, nor reveal the connection of all the parts composing the *Divina Commedia*. Such a presentment, moreover, is involved neither in the question set, nor in my own plan. A man cannot say everything in one day, and should not answer more than he is asked.

He who tries to promote human knowledge and insight is destined to always encounter the opposition of his age, which is like the dead weight of some mass that has to be dragged along: there on the ground it lies, a huge inert deformity, defying all efforts to quicken its shape with new life. But such a one must take comfort from the certainty that, although prejudices beset his path, yet the truth is with him. And Truth does but wait for her ally, Time, to join her; once he is at her side, she is perfectly sure of victory, which, if to-day delayed, will be won **to-morrow**.

---

soi-même par cette vue d'un principe qui subsiste également partout: puis, après cette vie, il entre dans la voie supérieure."

The obscurity of Schlegel's Latin in the second sentence is sufficiently removed by these more recent translations.—(*Translator.*)

JUDICIUM

Regiae Danicae Scientiarum Societatis

QUAESTIONEM anno 1837 *propositam, "utrum philosophiae moralis fons et fundamentum in idea moralitatis, quae immediate conscientia contineatur, et ceteris notionibus fundamentalibus, quae ex illa prodeant, explicandis quaerenda sint, an in alio cognoscendi principio," unus tantum scriptor explicare conatus est, cujus commentationem, germanico sermone compositam, et his verbis notatam: "*MORAL PREDIGEN IST LEICHT, MORAL BEGRÜNDEN IST SCHWER," *praemio dignam judicare nequivimus. Omisso enim eo, quod potissimum postulabatur, hoc expeti putavit, ut principium aliquod ethicae conderetur, itaque eam partem commentationis suae, in qua principii ethicae a se propositi et metaphysicae suae nexum exponit, appendicis loco habuit, in qua plus quam postulatum esset praestaret, quum tamen ipsum thema ejusmodi disputationem flagitaret, in qua vel praecipuo loco metaphysicae et ethicae nexus consideraretur. Quod autem scriptor in sympathia fundamentum ethicae constituere conatus est, neque ipsa disserendi forma nobis satisfecit, neque reapse, hoc fundamentum sufficere, evicit; quin ipse contra esse confiteri coactus est. Neque reticendum videtur, plures recentioris aetatis summos philosophos tam indecenter commemorari, ut justam et gravem offensionem habeat.*

Judgment of the Danish Royal Society of Sciences

In 1837 the following question was set as subject for a Prize Essay: "Is the fountain and basis of Morals to be sought for in an idea of morality which lies directly in the consciousness (or conscience), and in the analysis of the other leading ethical conceptions which arise from it? Or is it to be found in some other source of knowledge?" There was only one competitor; but his dissertation, written in German, and bearing the

145

motto: "*To preach Morality is easy, to found it is difficult,*"[1] we cannot ad-
judge worthy of the Prize. He has omitted to deal with the essential part
of the question, apparently thinking that he was asked to establish some
fundamental principle of Ethics. Consequently, that part of the treatise,
which explains how the moral basis he proposes is related to his system
of metaphysics, we find relegated to an appendix, as an "*opus supererogationis,*" although it was precisely the connection between Metaphysics
and Ethics that our question required to be put in the first and foremost
place. The writer attempts to show that compassion is the ultimate
source of morality; but neither does his mode of discussion appear satisfactory to us, nor has he, in point of fact, succeeded in proving that such
a foundation is adequate. Indeed he himself is obliged to admit that it is
not.[2] Lastly, the Society cannot pass over in silence the fact that he mentions several recent philosophers of the highest standing in an unseemly
manner, such as to justly occasion serious offence.

---

[1]The Academy has been good enough to insert the second "is" on its own account, by
way of proving the truth of Longinus' theory (*V. De Sublimitate*: chap. 39, *ad fin.*), that the
addition or subtraction of a single syllable is sufficient to destroy the whole force of a sentence. [*V.* Longinus: *De Sublimitate Libellus*; edit. Joannes Vahlen, Bonnae, 1887.—
(*Translator.*)
[2]I suppose this is the meaning of *contra esse confiteri.*—(*Translator.*)

A CATALOG OF SELECTED

DOVER BOOKS

IN ALL FIELDS OF INTEREST

A CATALOG OF SELECTED DOVER
BOOKS IN ALL FIELDS OF INTEREST

CONCERNING THE SPIRITUAL IN ART, Wassily Kandinsky. Pioneering work by father of abstract art. Thoughts on color theory, nature of art. Analysis of earlier masters. 12 illustrations. 80pp. of text. 5⅜ x 8½.   23411-8

ANIMALS: 1,419 Copyright-Free Illustrations of Mammals, Birds, Fish, Insects, etc., Jim Harter (ed.). Clear wood engravings present, in extremely lifelike poses, over 1,000 species of animals. One of the most extensive pictorial sourcebooks of its kind. Captions. Index. 284pp. 9 x 12.   23766-4

CELTIC ART: The Methods of Construction, George Bain. Simple geometric techniques for making Celtic interlacements, spirals, Kells-type initials, animals, humans, etc. Over 500 illustrations. 160pp. 9 x 12. (Available in U.S. only.)   22923-8

AN ATLAS OF ANATOMY FOR ARTISTS, Fritz Schider. Most thorough reference work on art anatomy in the world. Hundreds of illustrations, including selections from works by Vesalius, Leonardo, Goya, Ingres, Michelangelo, others. 593 illustrations. 192pp. 7⅛ x 10¼.   20241-0

CELTIC HAND STROKE-BY-STROKE (Irish Half-Uncial from "The Book of Kells"): An Arthur Baker Calligraphy Manual, Arthur Baker. Complete guide to creating each letter of the alphabet in distinctive Celtic manner. Covers hand position, strokes, pens, inks, paper, more. Illustrated. 48pp. 8¼ x 11.   24336-2

EASY ORIGAMI, John Montroll. Charming collection of 32 projects (hat, cup, pelican, piano, swan, many more) specially designed for the novice origami hobbyist. Clearly illustrated easy-to-follow instructions insure that even beginning papercrafters will achieve successful results. 48pp. 8¼ x 11.   27298-2

THE COMPLETE BOOK OF BIRDHOUSE CONSTRUCTION FOR WOOD-WORKERS, Scott D. Campbell. Detailed instructions, illustrations, tables. Also data on bird habitat and instinct patterns. Bibliography. 3 tables. 63 illustrations in 15 figures. 48pp. 5¼ x 8½.   24407-5

BLOOMINGDALE'S ILLUSTRATED 1886 CATALOG: Fashions, Dry Goods and Housewares, Bloomingdale Brothers. Famed merchants' extremely rare catalog depicting about 1,700 products: clothing, housewares, firearms, dry goods, jewelry, more. Invaluable for dating, identifying vintage items. Also, copyright-free graphics for artists, designers. Co-published with Henry Ford Museum & Greenfield Village. 160pp. 8¼ x 11.   25780-0

HISTORIC COSTUME IN PICTURES, Braun & Schneider. Over 1,450 costumed figures in clearly detailed engravings–from dawn of civilization to end of 19th century. Captions. Many folk costumes. 256pp. 8⅜ x 11¾.   23150-X

MY BONDAGE AND MY FREEDOM, Frederick Douglass. Born a slave, Douglass became outspoken force in antislavery movement. The best of Douglass' autobiographies. Graphic description of slave life. 464pp. 5⅜ x 8½.   22457-0

FOLLOWING THE EQUATOR: A Journey Around the World, Mark Twain. Fascinating humorous account of 1897 voyage to Hawaii, Australia, India, New Zealand, etc. Ironic, bemused reports on peoples, customs, climate, flora and fauna, politics, much more. 197 illustrations. 720pp. 5⅜ x 8½.   26113-1

THE PEOPLE CALLED SHAKERS, Edward D. Andrews. Definitive study of Shakers: origins, beliefs, practices, dances, social organization, furniture and crafts, etc. 33 illustrations. 351pp. 5⅜ x 8½.   21081-2

THE MYTHS OF GREECE AND ROME, H. A. Guerber. A classic of mythology, generously illustrated, long prized for its simple, graphic, accurate retelling of the principal myths of Greece and Rome, and for its commentary on their origins and significance. With 64 illustrations by Michelangelo, Raphael, Titian, Rubens, Canova, Bernini and others. 480pp. 5⅜ x 8½.   27584-1

PSYCHOLOGY OF MUSIC, Carl E. Seashore. Classic work discusses music as a medium from psychological viewpoint. Clear treatment of physical acoustics, auditory apparatus, sound perception, development of musical skills, nature of musical feeling, host of other topics. 88 figures. 408pp. 5⅜ x 8½.   21851-1

THE PHILOSOPHY OF HISTORY, Georg W. Hegel. Great classic of Western thought develops concept that history is not chance but rational process, the evolution of freedom. 457pp. 5⅜ x 8½.   20112-0

THE BOOK OF TEA, Kakuzo Okakura. Minor classic of the Orient: entertaining, charming explanation, interpretation of traditional Japanese culture in terms of tea ceremony. 94pp. 5⅜ x 8½.   20070-1

LIFE IN ANCIENT EGYPT, Adolf Erman. Fullest, most thorough, detailed older account with much not in more recent books, domestic life, religion, magic, medicine, commerce, much more. Many illustrations reproduce tomb paintings, carvings, hieroglyphs, etc. 597pp. 5⅜ x 8½.   22632-8

SUNDIALS, Their Theory and Construction, Albert Waugh. Far and away the best, most thorough coverage of ideas, mathematics concerned, types, construction, adjusting anywhere. Simple, nontechnical treatment allows even children to build several of these dials. Over 100 illustrations. 230pp. 5⅜ x 8½.   22947-5

THEORETICAL HYDRODYNAMICS, L. M. Milne-Thomson. Classic exposition of the mathematical theory of fluid motion, applicable to both hydrodynamics and aerodynamics. Over 600 exercises. 768pp. 6⅛ x 9¼.   68970-0

SONGS OF EXPERIENCE: Facsimile Reproduction with 26 Plates in Full Color, William Blake. 26 full-color plates from a rare 1826 edition. Includes "The Tyger," "London," "Holy Thursday," and other poems. Printed text of poems. 48pp. 5¼ x 7.
    24636-1

OLD-TIME VIGNETTES IN FULL COLOR, Carol Belanger Grafton (ed.). Over 390 charming, often sentimental illustrations, selected from archives of Victorian graphics–pretty women posing, children playing, food, flowers, kittens and puppies, smiling cherubs, birds and butterflies, much more. All copyright-free. 48pp. 9¼ x 12¼.
    27269-9

CATALOG OF DOVER BOOKS

AUTOBIOGRAPHY: The Story of My Experiments with Truth, Mohandas K. Gandhi. Boyhood, legal studies, purification, the growth of the Satyagraha (nonviolent protest) movement. Critical, inspiring work of the man responsible for the freedom of India. 480pp. 5⅜ x 8½. (Available in U.S. only.) 24593-4

CELTIC MYTHS AND LEGENDS, T. W. Rolleston. Masterful retelling of Irish and Welsh stories and tales. Cuchulain, King Arthur, Deirdre, the Grail, many more. First paperback edition. 58 full-page illustrations. 512pp. 5⅜ x 8½. 26507-2

THE PRINCIPLES OF PSYCHOLOGY, William James. Famous long course complete, unabridged. Stream of thought, time perception, memory, experimental methods; great work decades ahead of its time. 94 figures. 1,391pp. 5⅜ x 8½. 2-vol. set.
Vol. I: 20381-6   Vol. II: 20382-4

THE WORLD AS WILL AND REPRESENTATION, Arthur Schopenhauer. Definitive English translation of Schopenhauer's life work, correcting more than 1,000 errors, omissions in earlier translations. Translated by E. F. J. Payne. Total of 1,269pp. 5⅜ x 8½. 2-vol. set.   Vol. 1: 21761-2   Vol. 2: 21762-0

MAGIC AND MYSTERY IN TIBET, Madame Alexandra David-Neel. Experiences among lamas, magicians, sages, sorcerers, Bonpa wizards. A true psychic discovery. 32 illustrations. 321pp. 5⅜ x 8½. (Available in U.S. only.) 22682-4

THE EGYPTIAN BOOK OF THE DEAD, E. A. Wallis Budge. Complete reproduction of Ani's papyrus, finest ever found. Full hieroglyphic text, interlinear transliteration, word-for-word translation, smooth translation. 533pp. 6½ x 9¼. 21866-X

MATHEMATICS FOR THE NONMATHEMATICIAN, Morris Kline. Detailed, college-level treatment of mathematics in cultural and historical context, with numerous exercises. Recommended Reading Lists. Tables. Numerous figures. 641pp. 5⅜ x 8½. 24823-2

PROBABILISTIC METHODS IN THE THEORY OF STRUCTURES, Isaac Elishakoff. Well-written introduction covers the elements of the theory of probability from two or more random variables, the reliability of such multivariable structures, the theory of random function, Monte Carlo methods of treating problems incapable of exact solution, and more. Examples. 502pp. 5⅜ x 8½. 40691-1

THE RIME OF THE ANCIENT MARINER, Gustave Doré, S. T. Coleridge. Doré's finest work; 34 plates capture moods, subtleties of poem. Flawless full-size reproductions printed on facing pages with authoritative text of poem. "Beautiful. Simply beautiful." —*Publisher's Weekly.* 77pp. 9¼ x 12. 22305-1

NORTH AMERICAN INDIAN DESIGNS FOR ARTISTS AND CRAFTSPEOPLE, Eva Wilson. Over 360 authentic copyright-free designs adapted from Navajo blankets, Hopi pottery, Sioux buffalo hides, more. Geometrics, symbolic figures, plant and animal motifs, etc. 128pp. 8⅜ x 11. (Not for sale in the United Kingdom.) 25341-4

SCULPTURE: Principles and Practice, Louis Slobodkin. Step-by-step approach to clay, plaster, metals, stone; classical and modern. 253 drawings, photos. 255pp. 8⅛ x 11. 22960-2

THE INFLUENCE OF SEA POWER UPON HISTORY, 1660–1783, A. T. Mahan. Influential classic of naval history and tactics still used as text in war colleges. First paperback edition. 4 maps. 24 battle plans. 640pp. 5⅜ x 8½. 25509-3

CATALOG OF DOVER BOOKS

THE STORY OF THE TITANIC AS TOLD BY ITS SURVIVORS, Jack Winocour (ed.). What it was really like. Panic, despair, shocking inefficiency, and a little heroism. More thrilling than any fictional account. 26 illustrations. 320pp. 5⅜ x 8½. 20610-6

FAIRY AND FOLK TALES OF THE IRISH PEASANTRY, William Butler Yeats (ed.). Treasury of 64 tales from the twilight world of Celtic myth and legend: "The Soul Cages," "The Kildare Pooka," "King O'Toole and his Goose," many more. Introduction and Notes by W. B. Yeats. 352pp. 5⅜ x 8½. 26941-8

BUDDHIST MAHAYANA TEXTS, E. B. Cowell and others (eds.). Superb, accurate translations of basic documents in Mahayana Buddhism, highly important in history of religions. The Buddha-karita of Asvaghosha, Larger Sukhavativyuha, more. 448pp. 5⅜ x 8½. 25552-2

ONE TWO THREE . . . INFINITY: Facts and Speculations of Science, George Gamow. Great physicist's fascinating, readable overview of contemporary science: number theory, relativity, fourth dimension, entropy, genes, atomic structure, much more. 128 illustrations. Index. 352pp. 5⅜ x 8½. 25664-2

EXPERIMENTATION AND MEASUREMENT, W. J. Youden. Introductory manual explains laws of measurement in simple terms and offers tips for achieving accuracy and minimizing errors. Mathematics of measurement, use of instruments, experimenting with machines. 1994 edition. Foreword. Preface. Introduction. Epilogue. Selected Readings. Glossary. Index. Tables and figures. 128pp. 5⅜ x 8½. 40451-X

DALÍ ON MODERN ART: The Cuckolds of Antiquated Modern Art, Salvador Dalí. Influential painter skewers modern art and its practitioners. Outrageous evaluations of Picasso, Cézanne, Turner, more. 15 renderings of paintings discussed. 44 calligraphic decorations by Dalí. 96pp. 5⅜ x 8½. (Available in U.S. only.) 29220-7

ANTIQUE PLAYING CARDS: A Pictorial History, Henry René D'Allemagne. Over 900 elaborate, decorative images from rare playing cards (14th–20th centuries): Bacchus, death, dancing dogs, hunting scenes, royal coats of arms, players cheating, much more. 96pp. 9¼ x 12¼. 29265-7

MAKING FURNITURE MASTERPIECES: 30 Projects with Measured Drawings, Franklin H. Gottshall. Step-by-step instructions, illustrations for constructing handsome, useful pieces, among them a Sheraton desk, Chippendale chair, Spanish desk, Queen Anne table and a William and Mary dressing mirror. 224pp. 8⅛ x 11¼. 29338-6

THE FOSSIL BOOK: A Record of Prehistoric Life, Patricia V. Rich et al. Profusely illustrated definitive guide covers everything from single-celled organisms and dinosaurs to birds and mammals and the interplay between climate and man. Over 1,500 illustrations. 760pp. 7½ x 10⅛. 29371-8

Paperbound unless otherwise indicated. Available at your book dealer, online at **www.doverpublications.com**, or by writing to Dept. GI, Dover Publications, Inc., 31 East 2nd Street, Mineola, NY 11501. For current price information or for free catalogues (please indicate field of interest), write to Dover Publications or log on to **www.doverpublications.com** and see every Dover book in print. Dover publishes more than 500 books each year on science, elementary and advanced mathematics, biology, music, art, literary history, social sciences, and other areas.